T0329369

CAMBRIDGE STUDIES IN ECONOMIC HISTORY
PUBLISHED WITH THE AID OF THE ELLEN McARTHUR FUND

GENERAL EDITOR
M. M. POSTAN
Professor of Economic History in the University of Cambridge

FREE TRADE AND PROTECTION IN THE NETHERLANDS
1816–30

FREE TRADE AND
PROTECTION IN THE
NETHERLANDS
1816-30

A STUDY OF
THE FIRST BENELUX

BY

H. R. C. WRIGHT

CAMBRIDGE
AT THE UNIVERSITY PRESS
1955

CAMBRIDGE UNIVERSITY PRESS
Cambridge, New York, Melbourne, Madrid, Cape Town,
Singapore, São Paulo, Delhi, Mexico City

Cambridge University Press
The Edinburgh Building, Cambridge CB2 8RU, UK

Published in the United States of America by Cambridge University Press, New York

www.cambridge.org
Information on this title: www.cambridge.org/9781107621800

First published 1955
First paperback edition 2013

A catalogue record for this publication is available from the British Library

ISBN 978-1-107-62180-0 Paperback

CONTENTS

LIST OF TABLES

PREFACE

Ultimately, the result of the collapse of the Dutch world market was the protective tariff system for the benefit of the Dutch textile and metal industries undertaken by King Willem I in 1816.... Ultimately, the results of the war were to lead to the economic re-orientation of the Netherlands under the competent guidance of Willem I.[1]

Thus Mr C. H. Wilson, after explaining why Dutch commerce could not recover from the fourth English war of 1780–4, looked forward into the nineteenth century. His book suggested to me the tariff policy of King William I as a topic for research. This led, however, not into a study of Dutch economic revival, for that occurred only in the second half of the century and under a policy of free trade, but of the union of the Dutch and Belgian Netherlands from 1815–30. It is true that many of the practical achievements of William I, though not in my opinion his tariff policy, ultimately contributed much to Dutch revival; but it has been necessary to limit the present study to short-term effects. It is a study, therefore, of an experiment that failed; for all William I's work, including that 'definitive tariff policy' which Mr Wilson considered to have been so effective,[2] was dominated until 1830 by the purpose of strengthening the union.

The kingdom entrusted to William I by the Allies after the defeat of Napoleon consisted of three elements: the Dutch provinces, whose economy, centred on the international staple market in Holland, had been disrupted by the Continental System; the Belgian provinces, where French rule, after breaking down local rigidities, had stimulated capitalist undertakings and then left them in the lurch; and the restored Dutch colonies, which under British rule had become dependent on British commerce. The aim of the king was so to integrate these fragments that each would be useful to the others, and the whole kingdom would be independent of the favours of foreign powers. By 1830 he had shaped a coherent policy to this end and had achieved much success, only to see his work ruined by failure on the political side.

William I's economic policy has been studied in some detail by Continental, though never by British, historians. Some have seen in it an anticipation of List's 'National System';[3] others merely a belated

[1] C. H. Wilson, *Anglo-Dutch Commerce and Finance in the Eighteenth Century* (Cambridge, 1941), pp. 200, 204.
[2] *Ibid.* p. 196.
[3] R. Häpke, 'Die Wirtschaftspolitik im Königreich der Niederlande, 1815–30' in *Vierteljahrschrift für Sozial- und Wirtschaftsgeschichte* (1923).

mercantilism.[1] The king himself was no theorist and had no 'system' in mind. He certainly did not foresee in 1815 that by 1830 the cumulative effect of decisions taken, each on its own merits, under pressure of circumstances would in fact be to create 'the economic system of William I'. This book, which is based on my Ph.D. thesis of 1948, owes much to the patient criticism and advice of Professor Postan, and Professor A. J. C. Rüter of Leiden University, my Directors of Studies. My thanks are also due to the Ministry of Education, whose grant enabled me to take up post-graduate research after the war.

I have used the term 'Belgium' whenever it has seemed convenient, without wishing to imply that a Belgian nation already existed at the particular date. I have also referred to King William I by that title on certain occasions when he had not yet assumed it.

H. R. C. W.

JOHANNESBURG
SOUTH AFRICA
1954

[1] I. J. Brugmans, 'De economische politiek van Koning Willem I', in *Bijdragen voor Vaderlandsche Geschiedenis en Oudheidkunde* (1930).

ABBREVIATIONS USED IN THE NOTES

A.R.A.	Algemeen Rijksarchief, The Hague.
Ged.	H. T. Colenbrander, *Gedenkstukken* (X deelen) (The Hague, 1905–22).
Knuttel	The *Knuttel* collection of pamphlets in the Koninklijke Bibliotheek at the Hague.
2de kamer	J. J. F. Noordziek (ed.), *Verslag der handelingen van de tweede kamer der Staten-General 1814–30* (The Hague, 1863).
Mem. en cor.	I. J. A. Gogel, *Memoriën en correspondentiën* (Amsterdam, 1844).
Post. Doc.	N. W. Posthumus, *Documenten betreffende de buitenlandsche handelspolitiek van Nederland in de 19de eeuw*, 6 vols. (The Hague, 1913–31).
Rec. Fin.	*Recueil des pièces relatives au nouveau système de finances du Royaume des Pays-Bas* (The Hague, 1822).
Verzam. gran.	*Verzameling van stukken betrekkelijk de onbeperkte vrijheid van den handel in granen* (The Hague, 1823).
B.K.I.	*Bijdragen van het Koninklijk Instituut voor de Taal-, Land- en Volkenkunde van Nederlandsch-Indië.*

Chapter I

DUTCH COMMERCE AND ITS DECLINE

(a) Holland's 'general market'

Geography assured Holland a share in the maritime trade of her hinterland, the area served by the Rhine and the Maas. For the rest, her prosperity in the seventeenth and eighteenth centuries was due to transient advantages. Of these, the most important was her suitability as a stapling place for trade by sea between northern and southern Europe. The limitations of navigational technique made such a stapling place necessary. Changes in course were inconvenient, because they increased the likelihood of delay by unfavourable winds, and, therefore, for some cargoes, the risk of deterioration. Short voyages were preferred, at the most favourable season in each case. Furthermore, international trade, like trade within each region, was still centripetal. Until there were enough goods for exchange between one region and another to justify direct trade, some intermediate centre of distribution had to be used. The ready access from Holland to many parts of Europe made her such a centre. Dutch enterprise brought in goods from across the oceans. Thus, all the types of merchandise in international trade could be obtained at Dutch ports; speculative buyers could be found for all supplies; and shipping was available for all errands. In Holland, therefore, took place much of the bargaining, sorting and inspecting necessary in an age when goods were not standardized. Bargains made in Holland tended to regulate prices elsewhere, although it seems unlikely that traders were compelled to use a single central market by inability to determine prices otherwise.[1] A single centre was certainly needed for the clearance of payments between various limited economic areas and colonial systems, some of which were insulated by mercantilist policy against other attractions of the Dutch market. The advantage of a large scale of operations, and of the accumulation in Holland of capital, information and skill, made it possible to compete down some existing direct trades, such as that plied by French ships between France and the Baltic in the sixteenth but not in the seventeenth century.[2] The capital accumulated by Dutch merchants enabled them to give credit, which attracted foreign merchants unable otherwise to finance adequate stocks of export or import goods.

[1] T. P. van der Kooy, *Hollands stapelmarkt en haar verval* (Rotterdam, 1931), p. 3.
[2] S. Elzinga, *Het voorspel van den oorlog van 1672* (Haarlem, 1926), p. 66.

The advantages of Holland and the need for a central market within Holland made Amsterdam the metropolis of international trade in the seventeenth and eighteenth centuries, while other Dutch cities specialized in humbler but closely related activities.

Rotterdam specialized in the river trade, the English trade and the ordinary import and export trade of the adjacent Dutch and Belgian territory. She was thus in the eighteenth century the main Dutch market for madder, flax and linseed, which were special products of the region; for white lead, snuff and smokers' tobacco, which her industries prepared from British raw materials; and for gin, which was distilled in her vicinity mainly for the English market. In addition, she was an alternative and auxiliary port to Amsterdam. When the wind was adverse at Amsterdam for sailings or arrivals, it was often favourable at Rotterdam; so it was convenient that all the facilities of Amsterdam as a central staple market should be available on a smaller scale at Rotterdam. Goods were exchanged between the two ports by inland waterways, and financial and commercial relations were close. Amsterdam was not a convenient port for any trade except that to the north-east, and sailings to other destinations were liable to such delay that it was sometimes necessary to send goods to Rotterdam for early dispatch. In the years immediately after the Napoleonic Wars, it was often found that such goods reached a Mediterranean port before they could otherwise have left Amsterdam.[1] Many of the Baltic and Scandinavian goods needed for Rotterdam's own trade came through the Amsterdam market. The small ships of the North German coasting trade could sail direct to Rotterdam by way of Amsterdam and Gouda.[2]

Another disadvantage of Amsterdam was that deep vessels could not reach her quays, but had to be loaded and unloaded by lighters. In the 1820's, when trade had become too competitive to tolerate these delays and costs, access to the sea was much improved, thanks largely to William I's initiative, by harbour works, canal construction and the services of steam tugs against adverse winds. The king was not discouraged by the fact that the increasing depth of ships tended to defeat his purposes, nor by the opposition of many prominent Amsterdammers, who disliked expenditure and held that commerce could be won back only by fidelity to tradition, not by innovation.[3]

If Rotterdam was a junior partner with the same functions as Amsterdam, with a Bourse, a public bank, a corporation of brokers and a few con-

---

[1] R. Beerenbroek, *De la liberté illimitée du commerce des grains dans les Pays-Bas* (Brussels, 1829) (*Knuttel* 25853).

[2] *Ged.* VI, 1360.

[3] A. Warin, *L'Influence du commerce sur la prospérité du royaume des Pays-Bas* (Brussels, 1827).

siderable houses of insurance and discount, the other towns serving the general market were subordinate and specialized. Zaandam was a centre of the Baltic timber trade and its associated industries. Some small towns such as Krommenie engaged specially in making sail, rope and other ships' stores. Many small ports of the north were grain depots on Amsterdam's account, served by coasters. Groningen, as the market town of a district that produced a surplus of grain, naturally shared in this. Small vessels which were built there carried local grain and peats across the Zuider Zee to Holland, and peats to Hamburg, for instance, returning with grain and linen on the account of either Amsterdam or Hamburg merchants.

Dordrecht's importance in the river trade was partly maintained by an ancient staple right, until its abolition in 1795. The boatmen of the gild that served the swifter and shallower stream above the town used different vessels from those below, and the town authorities argued that this proved a natural need for transhipment there. At the end of the eighteenth century, a boat left Rotterdam twice monthly on a direct service to Cologne, but many goods were still sent to Dordrecht for distribution up-river. The practice of transhipment at Dordrecht, like the closure of the Scheldt to maritime shipping, helped the Dutch to profit from Belgian trade. For instance, one Dordrecht industry prepared German smalt, partly for the glass-works of Liége. Another made cement from German tufa for hydro-engineering work in the polder country as a whole. Dordrecht was also the market for timber floated down the Rhine. This market was supplemented by imported Baltic wood. At the end of the eighteenth century, it fed thirty-six saw-mills, and ten shipyards, the largest of which employed 150 men. Dordrecht also specialized in the salt trade. Eighteen refineries on her outskirts, burning peat from Friesland, were the chief source of livelihood for the neighbouring township, Zwijndrecht.[1]

The international market in Holland necessarily dominated the internal economy of the United Provinces. Agriculture and industry had to be adapted. The only exceptions were backward agricultural districts, where production was for subsistence or for a mainly local market, and industries producing goods that did not yet enter international trade. Thus, the gilds of butchers, bakers, shoemakers, corn-millers, retail shopkeepers and so on were able to maintain their monopolies in most Dutch towns of the eighteenth century. Even after 1800, the shoemakers in Amsterdam were able to obtain the judicial confiscation of consignments of shoes made by rural Dutch craftsmen.[2] But although these local crafts and trades could

[1] *Ged.* v, 611–13; vi, 1342–7, 1384–9.
[2] *Ged.* vi, 912; C. Wiskerke, *De afschaffing der gilden in Nederland* (Amsterdam, 1938), pp. 118, 141.

isolate themselves from the competitive world around them, their prosperity, especially in the commercial towns, depended on the Dutch general market.

Industries producing goods that entered international trade had to adapt themselves, or perish. Flax was the only important raw material produced in the United Provinces with any special natural advantage, but the conversion of it into linen was too laborious for such an industry to thrive in Holland, where costs were higher than in Belgium or Germany. The flax of South Holland was marketed largely at Gouda, and was exported, after being heckled there under municipal regulations designed to maintain quality. In the eighteenth century, more and more flax had to be exported unheckled, owing to foreign competition and foreign tariffs.[1] Haarlem, the linen town of Holland, was the centre not of a native industry using Dutch raw materials, but of a commercial industry which served Amsterdam by bleaching, pressing and packing foreign linens. Textiles, including linens, were manufactured at Haarlem, but this was for the most part due to the presence of the bleach-fields, to the availability of all kinds of raw materials at Amsterdam, and especially to the opportunities which Dutch trade provided for successful specialization in certain goods of high quality for a limited international demand. Nothing could be done to protect the workers of Haarlem from foreign competition. Dutch merchants could not afford to sacrifice trade in foreign goods in the doubtful hope of preserving the home and colonial market for Dutch products which could no longer compete abroad. The capitalists of Haarlem could not refuse to arrange the finishing of foreign linen for re-export, the exclusion of which would have been of little advantage to the workers. The town government could do no good by attempts to exclude foreign linens or to deny them the Haarlem markings, though it made some gestures to that effect, in 1755 for example. At the end of the eighteenth century, the linen manufactures of Haarlem were dead, apart from a few specialities such as fine threads, tapes and inkles. These were so superior that some could still be exported, despite their high price; but the common varieties made in England and elsewhere were gaining ground at their expense.[2]

The fine cloths of Leiden were made of imported Spanish wool. Amsterdam was the chief European staple market for this wool, and from Amsterdam even England drew supplies from time to time. The Leiden industry, therefore, even in its greatest prosperity was in a sense com-

---

[1] *Ged.* v, 630.
[2] Lord J. Sheffield, *Observations on the Commerce of the American States* (London, 1784), p. 28; E. Baasch, *Holländische Wirtschaftsgeschichte* (Jena, 1927), p. 94.

mercial rather than native, for one of the advantages determining its location was propinquity to the Dutch general market. In the eighteenth century it became clear that Spanish wool could be sent for spinning and weaving to the agricultural, Catholic south, or outside Dutch territory to the vicinity of Verviers, Eupen or Aachen, or to France; and the cloth returned to Holland would be cheaper than that made at Leiden. Since the Dutch general market must have cloth that could compete abroad, nothing could be done to prevent the decline of Leiden. At first much of the cloth was sent there for finishing, but in the late eighteenth century this too was declining. Verviers, for instance, was finishing most of the cloth made in its district, though often the Leiden marks were still affixed. Leiden was left to produce a few specialities of high quality, and also certain articles that were unimportant in international trade, and for which therefore she could secure a market at home by effective protection or official encouragement, such as blankets, and *pover soldaat* and other coarse cloths for the uniforms of the Republic's mercenaries.[1]

(b) The 'First Hand'

The wealth of the merchants gave them social and political predominance. The small noble class of the maritime provinces kept itself socially distinct but was of little practical importance. Since the value of all real property there depended on commercial prosperity, its interests did not diverge from those of the merchants. The nobles of the inland provinces were less directly interested in the fortunes of the general market and maintained a traditional opposition to Holland on matters of taxation and provincial prestige, but since the revenues and strength of the United Provinces were mainly derived from Holland, they did not seriously challenge the predominance of the commercial interest, provided that their local powers were not disturbed.

The autonomous cities that controlled the maritime provinces were governed by an hereditary oligarchy of Regents, composed of whatever families had been left in power by the events of the sixteenth century. They were a governing class in the sense that they held a monopoly of office; but not a distinct economic class, for their income came from many sources, the spoils of office, urban and rural property, loans to Dutch or foreign governments, shares in public corporations such as the Bank of England and the Dutch East India Company, patronage in the Dutch East and West India Companies, trading and banking partnerships, insurance syndicates, shares in ships and sugar-refineries, or the ownership of flour-

[1] Lord Sheffield, *Observations*, p. 289; E. Luzac, *Hollands rijkdom* (Leiden, 1781), II, 327.

and oil-mills. Their interests were therefore closely linked but not identical with those of the merchant class in general. The spoils of office might be obtained in ways prejudicial to commerce.

The leading merchants mixed with the Regents on terms of social equality, subject to the respect due to office. The status of a merchant depended on his function as well as on his wealth. The chief criterion was participation in maritime trade. This was the function of the First Hand merchants, who imported and exported on their own account or as commission agents. Bankers and wealthy shipowners were always merchants as well. In eighteenth-century Amsterdam, the bankers were becoming more and more prominent, some specializing in the issue of foreign securities, but all retaining some First Hand business in commodities, as Hope's continued to do in the second half of the nineteenth century.[1]

These merchant princes, who controlled most of the financial and maritime resources of Holland, left much of the work of the staple market to smaller, independent men. Such were the Second Hand tradesmen. They specialized on particular groups of commodities, which they bought in the market, improved, sorted and stored for eventual sale either back to the First Hand to make up assorted cargoes for maritime trade, or to the Third Hand, which included the wholesalers of the Continental hinterland and the various Dutch districts, and Dutch traders dealing with the hinterland on their own account or as commission agents. Much of the work of the Second Hand was peculiar to Holland's function as a centre for sorting, inspecting and exchanging international commodities. In the eighteenth century, this work was becoming less necessary. Dutch capital was still needed to finance international trade, but this was of advantage only to the First Hand, which had the necessary overseas connexions. Thus the Second Hand tradesmen, who had been considered men of substance in the seventeenth century, became insignificant beside the wealthy financiers. No doubt much capital was withdrawn from Second Hand trade and invested otherwise. Second Hand transactions had always included quite small consignments, especially for the inland trade, and such dealings seemed humbler as the scale of international trade increased elsewhere. Thus, after the Napoleonic wars, the typical Second Hand merchant was considered to be a small man, but was respected because he was essential to the traditional operation of the general market.

Many commercial industries, such as salt refining, performed the Second Hand functions, with merely a greater manipulation of the imported materials. Their entrepreneurs did not form a distinct class.

---

[1] J. B. Manger, *Recherches sur les relations économiques entre la France et la Hollande 1785–95* (Paris, 1923), p. 47.

Most Schiedam distillers, for example, were small masters of narrow out-look; they bought their own grain, worked beside their few men, and sold their product mainly through a regulated municipal market, in order to preserve their independence from the Rotterdam merchants.[1] On the other hand, the master calico-printers, though they worked mainly on commission for merchants, were men of substance and often had members of the best merchant families as sleeping partners.

The Dutch commercial community, in fact, did not consist of neatly divided classes. First Hand merchants readily used surplus capital for Second Hand or industrial purposes, especially for those connected with the particular commodities they imported. The sugar, diamond, soap and silk industries provided examples of such investment. The successful industrial entrepreneur naturally sought direct foreign connexions, began to import and export on his own account, bought shares in ships, and perhaps transformed himself into a First Hand merchant. In the seventeenth century, it was possible for a master weaver, tanner or cooper to become a capitalist by putting out work to less successful master craftsmen, to extend his trade, and to found a new First Hand family,[2] which might even, if of the Dutch Reformed Church, marry into Regent families and win a place on the roster for office. In fact, religion was a more serious barrier than occupation at that final stage. In the eighteenth century, certainly, conditions changed. It became more difficult for industrial entrepreneurs or Second Hand traders to make a fortune, for big profits could be won only in First Hand and banking business that required great initial capital or credit. Municipal institutions, in common with gilds and all such oligarchic corporations, became more exclusive with each genera-tion. The changed atmosphere is shown in the apology of a Regent accused in the late eighteenth century of seeking preferment out of turn by currying favour with the Stadtholder:

As to my birth.... In a Republic that owes its whole welfare and even existence to commerce and shipping, it is fitting that worthy citizens who by energy and ability have acquired great fortunes, should be advanced either directly or by marriages to offices of dignity and to equal status with the greatest in the land. Many of the greatest families of to-day have been thus advanced, and if we went back a century, or a century and a half, would lose much of their present lustre. In our country, there can be no dishonour in this. A citizen who has come to great wealth from small beginnings, who with a winning hand has helped thousands to their liveli-hood, is a much more useful member of society than those who for centuries have come to office as though in hereditary succession through

[1] C. Wiskerke, *De afschaffing der gilden*, p. 70.
[2] J. Rogge, *Het handelshuis van Eeghen* (Amsterdam, 1948), pp. 26-8.

the influence of kinsmen. Thus, to reproach anyone for his birth, in our country, is ridiculous and shows a mean spirit. Whatever my own birth, I would not despise poor but honorable parents; especially not because they happened to own a brewery, since many of the greatest in our city have done so and still do....Nearly two centuries ago, my ancestors came to Holland from the Duchy of Lunenberg and bought a considerable property. One of them married a daughter of the Amsterdam family of Bikker, and settled here; and although, being Lutherans or Arminians, they did not become Regents until 1640, they were always respected, and united to the best families by marriage....For myself, I owe nothing to anyone except to my father, and to my uncle, Burgomaster Calkoen. It was by their influence that I became Magistrate...Director of Surinam... Burgomaster....[1]

Thus a social barrier grew out of a widening economic gulf, and the Second Hand was left on the wrong side. The First Hand, having more capital than it could easily employ, continued to extend its operations into the Second Hand, instead of selling its imported merchandise quickly, as it should have done, according to the traditional pattern of the general market, in order to release its capital for fresh ventures. Purely Second Hand firms were increasingly confined to small-scale business, and the competition of First Hand capital made it hard for the small man to advance himself. When he succeeded, he did not attempt to enter First Hand trade; at the beginning of the nineteenth century, an Amsterdam cooper who had made a fortune preferred to invest in urban houses and saw-mills.[2]

(c) The Dutch commercial decline

From about 1730, international trade had a centrifugal tendency adverse to Holland. As transport became cheaper, quicker and safer, and more goods were accordingly transported, the concentrated supply and demand in Holland had less power to pull trade away from its direct routes. Trade in cheaper and bulkier goods became possible, for which the costs of diversion were relatively greater. The increase in trade created new local accumulations of capital, information and skill, so that while the Dutch services became relatively more expensive, they were also less needed. Even Amsterdam's banking was menaced by the growing volume of transactions in the London market. The English as well as the Dutch, for instance, were offering the long credits needed for the Russian trade; and by 1768 payments between England and Russia were no longer

[1] J. Rendorp, *Memorien dienende tot opheldering van het gebeurde gedurende den laatsten Engelschen oorlog* (Amsterdam, 1792), I, 8–11.
[2] J. Rogge, *Het handelshuis van Eeghen*, p. 90.

arranged through Amsterdam, while English trade was becoming predominant in Russian ports.[1]

Up to 1780, the decline of Dutch commerce was relative, not absolute. Its volume did not diminish, but that of its competitors increased. New trade took the direct routes, but much of the old tolerated the inefficiency of traditional ways in order to avoid the trouble and cost of changes. Any decay in Holland's general market was compensated by the expansion of particular trades for which Holland lay on the direct route. The hinterland was enjoying an unaccustomed period of peace and prosperity. Even when Holland's competitors gained by the changed direction of trade, its expansion often brought increased financial business to Amsterdam. Thus, the next generation looked back on the period as one when, despite warning signs and exaggerated lamentations, Holland was still 'the foremost market and general banker, the only nation whose commerce embraced literally the generality of the four corners of the earth'.[2]

Although the volume of goods passing through Holland was probably still increasing, their manipulation there was diminishing. Conditions were becoming more favourable in many parts of Europe, and even in the hinterland, for industries using imported materials; and many governments adopted new measures of industrial protection. Thus, a Belgian industry for refining French and Spanish salt grew up, although its costs were higher than those of the Dutch refiners.[3] Other Dutch commercial industries, such as that for making hats from imported and native rabbit fur, were losing ground to their competitors even in the export markets that remained open. British complaints in 1777 that Dutch manufactures were being marketed to the prejudice of British by British slavers, were a tribute to the continued strength of the Dutch general market rather than to Dutch industry, for the goods probably contained little Dutch labour.[4] However, the soap still smuggled by the Dutch into the British West Indies may have been their own product.[5]

Until about 1750, Haarlem had had almost a European monopoly of the bleaching of fine linens. This was due partly to natural advantages and superior technique, and partly to the Dutch trade in foreign linens. The closure of the Scheldt made the Belgian industry dependent on Dutch

[1] *Le commerce de la Hollande, par l'auteur des 'Intérêts des nations de l'Europe'* (Amsterdam, 1768), II, 16–24.

[2] A. J. L. van den Bogaerde de Ter-Brugge, *Essai sur l'importance du commerce, de la navigation et de l'industrie dans le Royaume des Pays-Bas jusqu'en 1830* (The Hague, 1844–5), II, 45.

[3] H. van Houtte, *Histoire économique de la Belgique à la fin de l'Ancien Régime* (Ghent, 1920), pp. 271, 275.

[4] D. McPherson, *Annals of Commerce* (London, 1805), IV, 604.

[5] Lord Sheffield, *Observations*, p. 143.

export facilities. The Spanish authorities favoured these Dutch-Belgian exports for the lawful trade to their colonies, and the Dutch in the West Indies were well placed for smuggling. Bleaching took from four to six months and made a considerable capital necessary for the trade, so that Dutch credit facilities were attractive. In 1752, Scottish linens still mostly went to Holland for bleaching, and thence often to London as 'Scotch-Hollands'.[1] In the next thirty years, there was a rapid development of bleaching in Lancashire, Ireland, Scotland, Belgium and Silesia, and the range of fineness needing the costly services of Haarlem was reduced. East German linen more and more took the direct route from Hamburg to its oversea markets, instead of first coasting to Holland; and Belgian linen began to go to Spain through Ostend. Nevertheless, Dutch commerce and shipping remained strong enough for German linen sorted and packed, if not bleached, in Holland to enter many markets and to be smuggled into the British West Indies. The available statistics show little decline in the volume of linens handled at Amsterdam.[2]

The Dutch complained, argued, and discussed remedies for the decline of their commerce. They set up learned societies to study the matter. But they did not attempt any re-orientation which would replace their threatened general market by new forms of enterprise. They reduced their rates of profit when foreign connexions could thus be preserved. They seized any opportunity to revive the old economy. During the American Revolution, they energetically created a filial staple market at St Eustatius for the contraband trade. Some, however, saw that the trend was towards a Dutch market which retained only certain seemingly inalienable particular trades: that in Baltic grain, which, it was said, could reach southern Europe without heating only if handled with Dutch skill and transhipped in Holland; that in Dutch salt herring; the Levant trade, protected by Dutch relations with the Barbary powers; the trade of the Dutch colonies; and, above all, the trade of the Rhine and Maas. The growing importance of Hamburg was noted, but so far only as threatening Dutch maritime trade with northern Germany. French wine and Spanish salt, for example, were being sent direct to Hamburg in exchange for grain and linen, but were not as yet penetrating by that route areas served by the Dutch river trade. It was, however, recognized that the loss of the general market, if it happened, would weaken the remaining particular trades and that other threats might come.

---

[1] S. H. Higgins, *A History of Bleaching* (London, 1924), p. 17; D. Lindsay, *Reasons for Encouraging the Linen Manufactures of Scotland* (London, 1735), pp. 57–9.

[2] J. G. van Bel, *De linnenhandel van Amsterdam in de XVIIIe eeuw* (Amsterdam, 1940), pp. 122–4; Lord Sheffield, *Observations*, p. 37.

The riparians of the Rhine and its tributaries cannot choose any other route for their trade without injury to themselves.... Holland has here, to the exclusion of all others, a very advantageous commerce, which increasing wealth and luxury have made yet richer, and which will continue to grow as new objects come into trade.... Since tobacco, coffee, tea, sugar and cocoa came into such general use, this trade has much increased.... Even so, it is to be feared that this trade will fall off from time to time. The arrangements made to supply Brabant, Flanders and the Rhineland from Ostend and Dunkirk, and to send their produce from there to Spain and the Mediterranean give cause for anxiety.[1]

(d) The fourth English war

In the eighteenth century the undoubted decline of the textile industries in Holland brought much poverty and unemployment, and hurt many small capitalists and shopkeepers. The relative decline of Dutch commerce, and its concentration on financial rather than physical services, caused suffering and lamentation, and weakened the prestige of the Republic among the Powers. On the other hand, the Regents, First Hand merchants, and financiers prospered and their conspicuous expenditure increased. The income by which the Regents maintained their dignity had always been supplemented, partly by corrupt means, out of the taxes paid by the people. So long as the townspeople prospered, they were patient of expenditure that was to the honour of their cities, but when things were seen to be going badly, a dangerous discontent spread among the middle and lower classes. Apart from the protectionism of a few industrialists, this discontent was not anti-commercial, for none knew how commerce could be replaced as the main source of prosperity. Indeed, the decline of the export industries made the population more dependent than ever on the commercial community. The increasing luxury of the rich at home somewhat mitigated the loss of foreign markets for industrial goods, and contributed to agricultural prosperity. The facilities for foreign investment offered by the Amsterdam bankers, which attracted the savings of many, from the nobles of the eastern provinces to quite humble middle-class people in the western cities, were blamed for encouraging the export of capital that could be used to provide employment; but at least they ensured that it earned a revenue which was spent in the United Provinces and helped to pay for imports of grain to feed the urban population.[2]

Discontent became manifest whenever the Republic suffered humiliation

[1] E. Luzac, *Hollands rijkdom*, II, 121, 287–8.
[2] *Le commerce de la Hollande*, II, ch. xxi; *Geschiedenis van den Nederlandschen landbouw 1795–1940*, ed. Z. W. Sneller (Groningen, 1943), p. 27.

in diplomacy or arms. The urban poor had a permanent appetite for riot and plunder, but they could only indulge it when permitted by the disaffection of the town militias, the rank and file of which consisted of those middle classes rich enough to be required to buy military equipment, but not to buy themselves off the service. Only gradually, out of shame for the feebleness of the Republic, did there emerge, partly inspired by French philosophy, a national movement for radical reform and efficient government. In the troubles of 1747–8, the disaffected were content to call in the Prince of Orange to reform the higher mysteries of the Republic, and concentrated their own attack on their local Regents, and in particular on the excise farmers who got most of the blame for the Regents' system of corruption.

The movement of 1747–8 achieved little. The decline of commerce being unaccompanied by any corresponding growth of new economic forces or classes, no social revolution was possible, unless imposed from without. In Amsterdam, the Regents were forced to admit to their ranks men from the wider commercial classes, including some whose enterprises in trade or the ancillary industries were quite modest. Some Regents lost their offices, and some remunerative abuses were stopped. In 1752, however, the oligarchy was closed again, and the newcomers could only obtain promotion by making themselves pleasant to the old families.

Until the late eighteenth century, patriotism was purely local. The Republic was not thought of as a state; but as an alliance of local sovereignties, designed for collective defence, but also for the prevention of mutual interference. Within such a framework, the Princes of Orange could not fulfil the vague hopes of reform their name inspired, and William IV and William V wished to attempt nothing unconstitutional. Their failure, and their feeble foreign policy, led reformers to desire a central government, and thus national feeling came into being.

The main desire to strengthen the Republic, however, still arose from loyalty to commerce and to municipal independence. For Dutch commerce was not merely a means of livelihood; it was also a way of life, and the source of the greatness of the beloved cities. In the seventeenth century, the Dutch had as readily sacrificed themselves for their commerce as for their religion. Commerce brought power, and the purpose of the Republic was to use that power, not for prestige, but for tangible commercial advantage. There were many methods. The Algerian pirates, for instance, had to be dealt with, though their suppression was not desired; as an Englishmen wrote after the American Revolution, 'to the great maritime powers...the Barbary States are useful. The Americans cannot protect themselves from the latter: they cannot pretend to a navy'.[1] In Spain the diplomats struggled to win preferences for their countrymen by a favourable administration of the complicated and arbitrary customs system. The British had prevailed at the time of the Peace of Utrecht in getting preference for their woollens, but the Dutch were more skilful in maintaining a trade to the Spanish colonies through Spanish men of straw.[2] In 1791, it was considered that this arrangement gave advantage to the Dutch which would be lost in open competition and which had already been much injured by British smuggling: 'In order to maintain our trade, the best would be that no nations should have freedom to trade in the colonies except the Spaniards alone.'[3] Diplomatic and naval power was also required for the protection of Dutch trade with belligerents. Such trade, from time to time, created an illusion that the old glory of the general market was returning. British policy was the obstacle, for the French always desired the services of neutral shipping in war-time. Amsterdam wished for a strong Dutch fleet, to give convoy. The Princes of Orange, however, were aware that their position depended on the alliance with Britain and was threatened by France, and so they wished rather to strengthen the army. The inland provinces considered that naval expenditure should be borne solely by the maritime provinces, and that the customs revenue, which had been allotted to the Admiralties, would be quite adequate for the purpose if it were not systematically defrauded by the merchants. The result was that both the army and the navy were neglected.

The 'Patriot' movement of the 1780's combined all the anti-Orange and anti-English forces. The reformers turned against William V because he did not attack the Regents, yet many of the latter, though their privileges were respected, carried on a family feud against him out of respect for their ancestors. Other Regents and merchants were influenced by the profits of contraband trade or the desire for favours from the French government in regard to the issue of its securities. Many, also, were influenced by the knowledge that the expansion of the British economy had brought Holland more loss than gain, while French expansion had brought mainly gain. Baltic materials for the French warships and merchantmen were provided by the Dutch, and the increased supplies of

---

[1] Lord Sheffield, *Observations*, p. 252.

[2] N. W. Posthumus, *Geschiedenis van de Leidsche lakenindustrie* (The Hague, 1939), II, 1115; H. van Houtte, 'Contribution à l'histoire commerciale des États de l'empereur Joseph II', in *Vierteljahrschrift für Sozial- und Wirtschaftsgeschichte* (1910), p. 367.

[3] N. W. Posthumus, *Bronnen tot de geschiedenis van de Leidsche textielnijverheid* (The Hague, 1922), VI, 271; E. Luzac, *Hollands Rijkdom*, IV, 106.

colonial goods from the French West Indies served as returns that were useful for the Baltic trade. The French merchants found adequate use for their capital in their American trade and did not seek to compete with the Dutch for the more modest profits of the European coasting trade. They were accustomed to take advantage of Dutch credit by sending their surplus colonial goods to Holland on commission. The growth of industries in France also called for some additional services from Dutch shipping.[1] Thus the Patriots found much support among those First Hand and banking circles which had held aloof in 1747–8.

It was a fact of great political importance that in the second half of the eighteenth century most Amsterdam Regents were interested, actively or passively, personally or through family connexions, in the lucrative First Hand and financial business of the time, including the contraband trade. It has been suggested that this was a consequence of the events of 1747–8, which created a feeling that it was unwise to rely too much on the spoils of office. It seems probable, however, that the Regents had never ceased to share in commercial activity, though their duties and inclinations had caused them to leave most of the work to partners and had thus enabled their critics to accuse them of being mere rentiers, out of contact with the realities of the market. Their official positions enabled them to be useful to their partners in any dealings in municipal or provincial loans, and their prominence in business in the late eighteenth century may have been due to the increased importance of Stock Exchange dealings.[2]

The lower classes were less involved in the Patriot movement than they had been in the events of 1747–8. As Gogel, a middle-class revolutionary, wrote in 1794:

The greatest number of the nation—it is with pain that I have to use the word 'populace' in speaking of a part of the human race—is generally of the Orange party, or else follows the universal character of the populace by supporting the strongest. It is very fond of plunder, especially of liquor; tumultuous in a rising, but terrified at the sight of a few bayonnets and miserable hussars. Argumentative rather than enlightened, it has still a certain feeling for liberty, which might perhaps be cultivated successfully, but gradually.[3]

The merchants who pressed for convoys to protect the contraband trade overreached themselves, for they gave Britain a pretext to declare war in 1780 and thus killed their goose. This war has been regarded as the final

---

[1] *Le commerce de la Hollande*, II, ch. xii.
[2] S. E. Elias, *Geschiedenis van het Amsterdamsche Regentenpatriciaat* (The Hague, 1923), pp. 132–4.
[3] *Ged.* I, 378.

blow to that prosperity in Holland which had been typified until that moment by a continued rise in the price of patrician mansions in Amsterdam.[1] The direct consequences of the war were not, however, so disastrous. Dutch capitalists suffered considerable losses at the hands of British privateers and warships, although it was not the British policy, nor the desire of British merchants, 'to increase the calamities of war by establishing a predatory system', especially as much British capital had been employed in obtaining American tobacco through St Eustatius.[2] Much trade was diverted from Holland to Ostend, and some probably to the northern German ports, but it was still in the hands of Dutch merchants and carried in Dutch ships under simulated flags. No doubt this had some permanent effect in increasing the success of Austrian efforts to develop Ostend, for profits obtained during the war left the Belgian merchants with more capital for independent trade; but most of the trade returned to its old channels after the war. For instance, the war created a direct trade between Ostend and Scotland; this continued afterwards, but was reduced to negligible volume.[3] As a Brussels official foresaw in 1783,

Consumption in these provinces is insufficient to maintain a regular trade with each country in Europe whose products would be needed to make up complete cargoes for the Flemish ports, and this country has not enough goods for export to provide return cargoes; nor have our merchants enough correspondents in the greater part of Europe.

The low costs of Dutch shipping and the low Dutch rate of interest, he added were still too strong.[4] Eupen, Verviers and Aachen turned again after the war to Amsterdam for most of their Spanish wool, and even when they got it through Ostend the shipping and often the finance were still Dutch.[5]

The North American market, newly opened to free competition, offered a test of Dutch commercial vitality. Great hopes had been roused in 1780 that if the British colonial system were overthrown by the colonists, and British maritime power by the Armed Neutrality, Holland would recover much that had been lost to her rival and become the general central market

---

[1] S. E. Elias, *Het Amsterdamsche Regentenpatriciaat*, p. 235.

[2] D. McPherson, *Annals*, III, 682; N. Deerr, *The History of Sugar* (London, 1949), I, 212–13.

[3] Statistics in D. McPherson, *Annals*.

[4] Conseiller des Finances Delaplancq, quoted by H. van Houtte in *Vierteljahrschrift für Sozial- und Wirtschaftsgeschichte* (1910), pp. 356–66.

[5] H. van Houtte, *Histoire économique de la Belgique à la fin de l'Ancien Régime*, pp. 271, 275.

between Europe and America. Thus commercial fantasies had helped to create the new Dutch patriotism, which for the present had a ridiculous air because of the impotence of the Dutch to make good their warlike threats.

The Dutch merchants were rich enough to give the long credits needed in America, and after the war hopefully supplied goods on credit to American import merchants. The Dutch had not, however, the knowledge or the connexions necessary for wise risk-taking, and early losses forced them to be cautious. Many of these exports included an element of Dutch labour, though it is difficult to know how much, since the practice of giving goods the label that would sell them best was then universal and was approved by the best authorities as 'harmless deception'. Included were gin, Haarlem tapes and threads, lace, flower-bulbs, cordage, gun-powder, Leiden superfine broadcloth, casimirs, blankets, printed calico, clay tobacco pipes, white lead and painters' colours, drugs, dyestuffs, writing paper, sealing-wax, and even the products of some moribund Dutch industries, including silks, velvets, hats, beer and Delft ware; also merchandise of the Dutch East India Company, including tea, Javan arak, spices and calico; and products of the hinterland, including Belgian window glass, bed tick and lead, and Rhenish cutlery, ironmongery, mill-stones, wine and toys. More significantly, as proof of the vitality of Dutch general commerce, Dutch merchants sent to America from their own or other ports, Swedish steel, French wine, Spanish brandy and cork, Silesian linen, and Russian hemp, cordage, quills and duck.[1] One American historian has estimated the value of these Dutch imports from 1786–8 as over half that of British imports.[2] His computations do not accord with contemporary opinion.[3] The Austrian consul estimated the numbers of ships entering American ports from 1783 to 1788 as:[4]

From British ports	588
From Spanish and Portuguese ports	189
From French ports	157
From Dutch ports	81
From Russian and Scandinavian ports	42
From Trieste and Ostend	17
From Tuscan ports	2
Total from Europe	1076

[1] A. L. Kohlmeier, 'The Commerce between the United States and the Nether-lands 1783–9', in *Indiana University Studies*, nos. 66–8 (1925); J. Rogge, *Het handelshuis van Eeghen*, p. 95; D. McPherson, *Annals*, IV, 35.

[2] A. L. Kohlmeier, *loc. cit.*

[3] D. McPherson, *Annals*, IV, 9.

[4] H. van Houtte, in *Vierteljahrschrift für Sozial- und Wirtschaftsgeschichte* (1910), p. 388.

In any case, the Dutch effort failed. The official records show the average annual tonnage of arrivals from 1789 to 1792 as:[1]

	Tons (thousands)
From British ports	128
From Spanish and Portuguese ports	43
From French ports	27
From Dutch ports	14
From Hanseatic ports	6
From Russian and Scandinavian ports	5
	223

The nationality of arrivals from all foreign ports from 1789 to 1792 was:[2]

	U.S.A.	British	French	Dutch
Thousand tons (ann. av.)	318	182	12	4

	Spanish	Portuguese	Hanseatic	Danish
Thousand tons (ann. av.)	4	3	2	1

Almost all the Dutch ships came from Dutch, or Dutch West-Indian, ports. Their number must have been rather greater than the figures suggest, for the Dutch were known to be particularly skilful in getting their ships accepted as American for navigation dues, and in the other means of fraud and smuggling which conditions in America encouraged. Clearly, however, Dutch general commerce had but a small share in American trade, though Holland was still the most important export centre in northern Continental Europe.

Dutch capital, being unable to find much profit in the American import market in the face of experienced British merchants with British industrial superiority behind them, was invested instead in American public securities. These could be bought cheaply by Dutch bankers and sold at a good profit to Dutch investors who were uninformed about the state of American public credit.[3] Dutch firms accordingly sent representatives to America for financial purposes, although it was not thought worth while to create trading agencies. Some Dutch bankers tried to obtain trading privileges for their houses in return for financial services, but with little success. Indirectly, however, their efforts promoted trade, for those responsible for remitting interest payments to Holland often found it

---

[1] P. J. van Winter, *Het aandeel van den Amsterdamsche handel aan den opbouw van het Amerikaansche Gemeenebest* (The Hague, 1927), II, 41.
[2] J. McGregor, *Commercial Statistics* (London, 1847), III, 745.
[3] P. J. van Winter, *op. cit.*, I, 116, 137, 197.

WFT

convenient to send produce, until the outbreak of war in Europe made America's foreign exchanges more favourable.[1]

Holland had more success in attracting American exports than in providing imports. The average annual value of exports from 1789 to 1792 was recorded as:[2]

	($000)
To Great Britain	5400
To Spain and Portugal	2300
To the Dutch Netherlands	1200
To France	1200
To Hanseatic ports	400
To Russia and Scandinavia	150

Most of this trade, however, was controlled by British merchants, and Dutchmen found it more satisfactory to act in a subordinate capacity for London houses than to venture into direct dealings with America. American exporters preferred to consign their goods to London merchant bankers, who undertook to redirect the cargoes to European ports and to receive European payments.[3] In fact, London was the general market, in so far as the British customs system permitted. British merchants were rightly confident that 'American rice will still come here, in order to have a choice of the foreign markets, as they cannot know in America to what port in Holland or Germany it will be best to send it.'[4] American whale products, however, were not admitted to Britain even for re-export; and so they were largely distributed from Holland to southern as well as northern Europe, especially to Mediterranean ports which American ships could not safely approach until their government made an arrangement with the Barbary states in 1795.[5]

Thus Holland gained little by the independence of America. Rotterdam's close relations with London had already assured her a considerable share of American produce, and she had nothing to gain by British discomfiture. Amsterdam gained, but partly at the expense of Rotterdam, whose share of Dutch imports of American produce dropped from four-fifths to less than half in the 1780's.[6] Although Amsterdam could not, in free competition, challenge London's supremacy, she proved still able to claim second place. Her credit facilities and superior commercial apparatus gave her an advantage over Rotterdam and Hamburg in attracting the custom of American merchants who made use of their new freedom to form other

[1] P. J. van Winter, *op. cit.* I, 107; II, 80, 110.
[2] *American State Papers*, 1832, Commerce and Navigation, vols. I and II.
[3] P. J. van Winter, *op. cit.* II, 112.
[4] Lord Sheffield, *Observations*, p. 252.
[5] P. J. van Winter, *op. cit.* II, 60.
[6] *Ibid.* I, 18; A. L. Kohlmeier, in *Indiana University Studies* (1925), nos. 66–8; D. McPherson, *Annals*, III, 428.

than English connexions. However, this heartening success in free competition against Hamburg was only temporary. Hamburg was developing rapidly even before the French conquest of Holland in 1795. In the early 1790's she was receiving an increasing proportion of American exports.[1]

In some respects, American independence was disadvantageous to Holland. From about 1750 the colonists' desire to escape from British mercantilist regulations led them to make use of Dutch services which were not needed afterwards. They gladly received Dutch tea, linen, gunpowder and gin either from Holland, or from the Dutch West Indies, or under cover of legitimate trade with Spain. Afterwards, they could fetch their own tea from China, and their trade in the East soon became a threat to the Dutch East India Company. Instead of Dutch eastern goods being smuggled into America, the Americans smuggled them out of the Dutch East Indies, or received them clandestinely from Dutchmen at the Cape of Good Hope. Before 1790, the Americans were supplying eastern goods to the Dutch West Indies, and to Europe, and were spoiling the market for the Dutch East India Company.[2] The Americans could fetch linens directly from Hamburg, and in any case were consuming more British cotton goods instead. American trade with the Dutch West Indies continued; but it now consisted merely of an exchange of American provisions and commercial goods for colonial produce, to the detriment of the motherland. Dutch planters sold sugar to the Americans in breach of agreements to send it to creditors in Holland. On the other hand, American consumption of Dutch gin certainly increased after independence.[3]

If the 1780's marked a decisive stage in the decline of Dutch commerce, the reason was not the fourth English war but rather that British economic expansion had accelerated. The volume of British imports and exports increased, capital accumulated rapidly in London, and the rate of interest declined in consequence. The gravitational centre in international trade shifted to London, which had now the pull of a larger scale of commercial operations than Amsterdam and could give more convenient, if not cheaper, credit facilities. For example, the Dutch lost their near monopoly of Archangel tar, and their whole trade in Scottish salmon, which now went mainly to London.[4]

The war left British commerce very powerful in the West Indies, and, with the help of London's attractive force, brought about what the French consul in Amsterdam described as a veritable revolution in the sugar trade.

[1] P. J. van Winter, *op. cit.* II, 30, 127–8.
[2] *Ibid.* I, 22–31; J. Gee, *The Trade and Navigation of Great Britain Considered; A new edition with notes by a merchant* (London, 1767), pp. 46–7, 87–94.
[3] P. J. van Winter, *op. cit.* I, 16, 22, 106; II, 46–8, 670–4.
[4] Lord Sheffield, *Observations*, p. 80; D. McPherson, *Annals*, IV, 35.

Formerly, cheap and plentiful supplies of West Indian sugar from France had given the Dutch a competitive advantage over the British refiners.[1] The position of the Dutch refiners now depended on the success of the Dutch and French authorities in preventing raw sugar from being smuggled out of their colonies; and it took time to re-establish colonial systems after the war. Meanwhile, British refined sugar was winning markets at the expense of the Dutch in Germany, Switzerland and Belgium. This was a serious matter, for the Dutch considered their West Indian trade to be even more important to them than that of their East Indian Company. The West Indian colonies had long been open to free Dutch enterprise, and much Amsterdam and Rotterdam capital had been invested in the plantations, whose produce was thereby assured to the port concerned. The Dutch West Indian trade was weakened by the difficulty of investors at home in maintaining control over the planters and by the fact that it had to bear the costs of the West Indian Company's administration, which was expensive, corrupt, and inefficient in maintaining order. Dutch colonies and trade had some benefit from the conveniences they offered for American smuggling in the British West Indies, but were much injured by British activities.

We are experiencing in America and even in our own colonies the damaging results of English competition, through their smuggling trade. They supply our colonies with much butter and salt meat. If our administration there is incompetent to prevent such inroads, what can we expect for our shipping and commerce? For the supply of provisions and other goods by the English gives them the opportunity to take produce in return, and what must be the result of that? Who cannot see in that an open door to many slippery tricks, to the disadvantage of our country and of all who are interested that the produce comes exclusively to this country, in accordance with the regulations of the High Government? The prosperity of the English colonies is another matter worth our attention....Their produce must reduce the price of that of the French colonies, of which Holland is in great part the stapling place. Our trade has drawn profit from the French West Indian possessions, but the English ones bring only harm to us. Every nation that keeps its whole trade in its own hands injures us directly or indirectly. The English do so...and no doubt their zeal is praiseworthy, although it deprives other nations, and ourselves especially, of advantages. But we have always to fear that they will abuse their superior sea-power in order to extend their trade; and that makes their competition dangerous.[2]

[1] J. Gee, *op. cit.* pp. 82, 201.
[2] E. Luzac, *Hollands Rijkdom*, IV, 188–9; J. B. Manger, *Recherches*, p. 35; cp. *The Cambridge History of the British Empire*, II, 65.

The Dutch share of French raw sugar had also declined. Colbert had protected French refiners in their home market, and after 1730 other mercantilist measures led to some export of French refined sugar. In the 1780's much more French, and also British, raw sugar was going to refineries in Hamburg.[1] All these tendencies had, however, been apparent before 1780.[2]

In the East Indies, the growth of the British-Indian 'country' trade in the 1770's had already undermined the Dutch system of monopoly, and had diminished the Dutch East India Company's local trade in the East, which helped to pay for its consignments to Holland. The Treaty of 1784 hastened matters by giving British ships freedom to navigate the seas of the Eastern Archipelago, thus making it difficult for the Dutch to prevent illicit trade. At the same time, Pitt's Commutation Act checked Dutch smuggling of tea into Britain, though it seems at first to have affected Swedish and Danish, rather than Dutch, sailings to Canton.[3]

In the 1780's, Haarlem and the Dutch linen trade were further weakened by the newly perfected method of bleaching by chlorine. This much reduced the time needed for the process and so reduced the need for working capital. The method was not adopted in Silesia, but the whole trade became more competitive, costs had to be cut, and often this meant passing the Dutch general market by. Capital, accumulated in Hamburg, served to finance bleaching and exporting. Between 1780 and 1794, owing to the growth of Hamburg's trade, direct dealings between Holland and Leipzig almost ceased.

The revival of Dutch trade after 1783 was hindered by continued political instability. International finance stimulated political intrigue at Amsterdam. France hoped for an armed Dutch neutrality in any future war. Intervention by the Great Powers in the struggle of Dutch factions led to a 'Patriot' revolution and a Prussian invasion in 1787. These bloodless events did not interrupt trade, but they undermined confidence and were blamed for Dutch decline by those who were unwilling to see the more permanent causes. William V was the chief scapegoat. In 1787, the Amsterdam magnates were alienated by the democratic tendencies of the 'Patriots', but they still refused to be reconciled with the Prince, or to give financial support in 1793 to prepare against French attack.[4]

[1] *A letter from a Merchant* (London, 1738) (Acton Library, Cambridge, d. 25. 1040), p. 32; E. Luzac, *Hollands Rijkdom*, IV, 362; G. Seelig, 'Hamburgs handelslage nach dem ersten Pariser Frieden', in *Annalen des Deutschen Reiches* (1902).
[2] B. Edwards, *The History, Civil and Commercial, of the British West Indies* (5th ed., London, 1819), II, 535, 581, 597-9; D. McPherson, *Annals*, III, 427, 430; IV. 538.
[3] D. McPherson, *Annals*, IV, 337
[4] S. E. Elias, *Het Amsterdamsche Regentenpatriciaat*, p. 257.

The recovery of the Dutch general market after 1783 was sufficient to persuade contemporaries that in more favourable political circumstances the old prosperity might return. The French consul in Amsterdam reported in 1785, after careful inquiries, that the low rate of interest was again attracting there many goods for which the final destination could not yet be determined, and even that much trade in the general market was being successfully conducted on Dutch account. In particular, the trade in Baltic grain remained important, and in 1789 the Amsterdam market was the centre of the speculation, and financial and political intrigue, to which a European harvest failure gave rise.[1]

Rotterdam had special reason for confidence. The same causes that weakened Amsterdam's general market increased Rotterdam's particular trades. These trades, Rotterdam knew, were based on geographical advantages, whereas Amsterdam's market was recognized to be an 'artificial' achievement of the Dutch spirit, like the dikes.[2] After 1750, Rotterdam felt the competition of Ostend, and after 1783, of Hamburg, in the trade of the hinterland. Nevertheless, Rotterdam's demand for labour for handling and improving merchandise continued to increase, thus saving her from the unemployment problems of other towns in Holland.

The development of Rotterdam slowed down after 1780, especially on the industrial side. The tobacco industry, for instance, which had been organized there on the domestic system by British merchants after 1750, suffered when Britain lost the monopoly of tobacco from her American colonies. Rotterdam could now draw raw tobacco directly from North America as well as from London, and became independent of British enterprise; but Hamburg obtained equal advantages, and made the most of them. Dutch exports of finished tobacco were confined more and more to the hinterland; in 1790, 80% to the hinterland, 13% to Hamburg, the remainder to Italy and northern Europe.[3] The gin industry was more fortunate. The number of distilleries at Schiedam rose steadily from 70 in 1750 to 160 in 1780 and 240 in 1800.[4] The gin was exported to England, and also smuggled, together with French brandy, with the encouragement of the Dutch authorities, in accordance with mercantilist ethics, but with less success than formerly. It was also exported to France, Spain, Portugal, and the colonies in general; but not much to the hinterland. The Dutch

[1] J. B. Manger, *Recherches*, pp. 42–3, 64–7.
[2] *Ged.* VI, 1366.
[3] *Ged.* VI, 1350, 1366; Z. W. Sneller, 'De toestand der nijverheid te Amsterdam en Rotterdam volgens de enquête van 1816', in *Bijdragen voor Vaderlandsche Geschiedenis en Oudheidkunde* (1926), pp. 139–40.
[4] *Ged.* V, 618.

themselves took to it readily enough.[1] The inhabitants of the hinterland could not be prevented from distilling spirits for their own use from their own grain, but the Dutch could do much to prevent them from obtaining raw sugar. Yet the development of sugar refining at Rotterdam was checked, probably by the growth of refineries in Belgium:

Number of sugar refineries[2]

	Amsterdam	Rotterdam	Dordrecht
1750	90	30	15
1799	108	30	12

After 1780, Dutch exports of sugar went almost wholly to the German hinterland.[3] Rotterdam's white lead continued to be exported to most parts of the world, though it was doubtful how long this could continue, since the raw materials were cheaper in England.[4]

(e) The Napoleonic wars

The Dutch supporters of an alliance with revolutionary France, and some French politicians and officials, hoped that in the event of maritime victory or of a favourable peace, the co-ordination of French productive capacity, the French and Dutch colonies, and Dutch shipping and capital could win much ground from British trade. Yet, during and after the negotiations for the Peace of Amiens, the 'Batavian' Republic found itself seeking British support for its independence and neutrality. The French had in fact abandoned their traditional support of Dutch neutral trade and adopted principles of economic warfare ruinous to the Dutch. Neither the Dutch nor the French supposed that this could be compensated by the growth of Dutch industry to compete against French. They foresaw rather that if the war continued long and the French policy were effectively imposed on the Dutch, impoverishment and depopulation would result in Holland.[5] Some Dutchmen long regretted that France had not allowed them neutral and contraband trade in return for loans of capital.

If Napoleon, instead of creating extraordinary and inquisitorial customs barriers, had given subsidies to young industries in order that they might

---

[1] *Ged.* vi, 1352; Z. W. Sneller, *op. cit.* p. 145; F. J. B. d'Alphonse, *Eenige hoofd-stukken uit het Aperçu sur la Hollande...* (The Hague, 1900) (*Bijdragen tot de Statistiek van Nederland*, n.s., no. 1), p. 263; D. McPherson, *Annals*, iii, 430, cp., however, *Post. Doc.* i, 34.

[2] Z. W. Sneller, *op. cit.* p. 135; C. Wiskerke, *De afschaffing der gilden*, p. 47; T. P. van der Kooy, *Hollands stapelmarkt*, p. 11.

[3] C. Wiskerke, *De afschaffing der gilden*, p. 68.

[4] Lord Sheffield, *Observations*, p. 32.   [5] *Ged.* iv, 336.

compete against the productions of the British Empire; if he had used for this temporary expenditure the incalculable sums spent on the customs service and its spies; if, like the British Government, he had admitted to his ports all flags, whether simulated or not, except the British flag: then the commerce of Europe would have been turned back without any catastrophe from the direction given to it by the genius of Queen Elizabeth during the tyranny of Phillip II, would have flowed more and more into the immense French Empire and have been established for ever under the protection of one who might have been the greatest of Emperors.[1]

The Dutch of the early nineteenth century knew that London's supremacy in international trade could not be challenged by economic means, and their hopes and fears were concerned more with the rivalry of Hamburg. Only in the mid-eighteenth century had Hamburg formed important commercial connexions with the world beyond the North Sea, but after that her trade in colonial goods soon led to a great development of the sugar, tobacco and calico-printing industries. At the end of the eighteenth century, Hamburg had 400 sugar refineries against about 160 in Holland, though no doubt Hamburg's were smaller, since less capital was available. After 1795, Hamburg's rise became spectacular, owing to the growth of a commission trade in British merchandise.[2] This seemed to many a temporary result of the war. Dutch capital, and, under false colours, Dutch ships retained a considerable share in the activity at Hamburg.[3] Certainly, an English observer in 1801 expected Hamburg to retain permanently much former Dutch trade:

It is a prevailing opinion that whenever peace comes, the adventitious commerce of Hamburg will revert to its own channels, and of course be very considerably diminished: but this may reasonably be doubted...for it is well known, new commercial relations are very slowly formed: it is as difficult to turn the current of trade as a tide.[4]

Hamburg, however, came under British blockade in 1803, and afterwards suffered more than Amsterdam from the chances of war. The Dutch naturally hoped to compete in the future at least as successfully as before 1795.[5]

The Continental System was not fully enforced in Dutch territory until 1810. From 1800 to 1806, activity at Amsterdam revived, partly at

[1] A. J. L. van den Bogaerde de Ter-Brugge, *Essai*, II, 170–1.
[2] G. Seelig, in *Annalen des Deutschen Reiches* (1902).
[3] A.R.A., Roëll 162 (ii)—memo. by Roëll, 1 March 1821, p. 16.
[4] *Hamburg—by a resident* (London, 1801).
[5] G. Seelig, in *Annalen des Deutschen Reiches* (1902); E. Baasch, *Geschichte Hamburgs 1814–1918* (Hamburg, 1924), I, 2.

the expense of Hamburg. The trade was dependent on neutral and especially American shipping, so that Dutch maritime industries and shipping continued to suffer unemployment, as did the manual servants of commerce, since the quantity of goods handled was less than before the war. The trade was risky, but the profits were high; and many Dutch merchants could congratulate themselves on their enterprising persistence in making the best of adversity. The grain trade remained active. Indeed, until 1811 the war was less effective in checking Dutch grain exports to Britain than the British Corn Laws subsequently proved to be. In the ten war-years from 1800 to 1810 the annual average was 186,000 quarters; in the ten years 1815–24 only 111,000.[1] The Amsterdam firm of Boissevain, dealing in grain, French wine and German linen, remembered these as years of 'good business' which comforted them for their losses in 1810 and after.[2] Observers commented with surprise on the continued display of wealth by many Amsterdam families. The price of merchants' town and country mansions remained high; though from 1802 many Amsterdam houses inhabited by workmen, master craftsmen and small shopkeepers were falling into disrepair as an unprofitable investment, and some were even seized and sold for quite small arrears in taxation.[3]

The Dutch, therefore, looking back in 1813 on events since 1780, saw much that seemed encouraging. If the recorded number of ships entering the Maas and the Zuider Zee from the open sea had given a reliable indication of the volume of trade at Rotterdam and Amsterdam, the following index would show its fluctuations in peace and war:[4]

	Amsterdam	Rotterdam
1775–7 (av)	100	100
1778–80 (av.)	155	96
1781–2 (av.)	99	47
1784–91 (av.)	153	108
1792–4 (av.)	153	125
1797–1801 (av.)	70	38
1802	174	113
1803–4 (av.)	123	49
1805–7 (av.)	60	29

[1] *Parl. Papers*, 1825, xx, 233–61.
[2] C. Boissevain, *Onze voortrekkers* (Amsterdam, 1906), pp. 73–4; J. T. Boelen, *Jacobus Boelen 1733–1933, Amsterdam* (Amsterdam, 1933), pp. 44–70. A. Hoynck van Papendrecht, *A. van Hoboken en Co. 1774–1924* (Rotterdam, 1924), pp. 37–62; J. Rogge, *Het handelshuis van Eeghen*, pp. 126–43.
[3] *Ged.* v, 606, 627–8.
[4] *Ged.* v, 258; vi, 1359; A. J. L. van den Bogaerde de Ter-Brugge, *Essai*, iii, 138; L. van Nierop, 'Amsterdams scheepvaart in den Franschen tijd', in *21ste Jaarboek van Amstelodamum* (1924).

The trend in the years of peace seemed healthy. A French official, who studied all the information and statistics available to the administrators of the Dutch departments in 1812, concluded that 'Dutch commerce could yet arise from its cinders if the sun of peace brought warmth again soon'.[1] Years that had been full of lamentation were now remembered for their prosperity. The export of capital in the eighteenth century, so often denounced as a sign of unenterprising spirit and a cause of declining trade, was now quoted as proving the continued vitality and profits of the general market.[2] Even the worst years, after Napoleon had annexed the Dutch provinces in order to prevent smuggling, were remembered with complacency by some: 'The profits of those favoured with Imperial licences can be judged from what others still gained by introducing English goods through the Baltic or the Adriatic and smuggling them through Germany and across the Rhine.'[3] Geography, it was argued, had not changed since the seventeenth century. Technical improvements in navigation since then were deemed insufficient to make Holland unnecessary as a stapling place for the Baltic. American trade to Holland, despite the war, appeared to have increased until 1807 and compared favourably to that direct to Germany.[4] It was hoped that after the war Holland would again be a main distributing centre for American produce, in order to quicken the return of United States ships.[5] A United States ambassador after 1814 foretold that it would.[6] A pamphleteer popular in commercial circles wrote in 1819:

Import from the sea and transport up the rivers, when trade was in its infancy, necessarily created a general staple market here, where all peoples, being less advanced in trade and navigation, could find and acquire what they needed.... We cannot compare our chances now even with those of the mid-eighteenth century. The rest of Europe, and America, have gained much experience while we were suffering loss and stagnation.... We have lost some of our best colonies.... But we still have the great advantages that fit our land permanently for trade; our location between North and South, our rivers a natural funnel for most of Germany.[7]

---

[1] F. J. B. d'Alphonse, *Aperçu*, pp. 4, 356.

[2] J. Scheltema (1816), *Knuttel* 24295, pp. 27–35.

[3] A. Warin, *L'Influence du commerce*, p. 23.

[4] J. McGregor, *Commercial Statistics*, III, 768–9.

[5] D. J. Garat, *Mémoire sur la Hollande* (Paris, 1805), pp. 27–35; E. Verviers, *De Nederlandsche handelspolitiek* (Leiden, 1914), p. 151.

[6] G. K. van Hogendorp, *Bijdragen tot de huishouding van staat van het Koninkrijk der Nederlanden*, ed. by J. R. Thorbecke (Amsterdam, 1859), VI, 378.

[7] F. A. van Hall (?), *Onpartijdige beschouwing van den toestand des koophandels binnen de Vereenigde Nederlanden* (Amsterdam, 1819–20), p. 46; pamphlet attributed to same author, *Knuttel* 24888, p. 42.

In 1814-15, the Dutch merchants filled their warehouses with their usual merchandise, and especially with British colonial and manufactured goods, and Baltic grain and timber. The Dutch government, at the end of 1814, boasted that the trade revival was beyond expectation. Continental purchasing power, however, proved disappointing. German shopkeepers bought stocks in the early summer of 1814, but did not replenish them as usual in the autumn, against the winter months when transport of goods still almost ceased. Prices were depressed by the desire of British merchants to get their colonial goods out of bond within the permitted term: and Dutch merchants who hoped that their stocks would serve an area beyond the hinterland found that the British were supplying every market directly and sending agents to seek out every unsatisfied demand. Only in the grain trade could the Dutch in 1816 still find solid reasons for optimism.[1] They preferred, however, to explain the failure of their hopes by political, and therefore remediable, causes, rather than admit that their general market was obsolete. Gogel, the great 'Batavian' financier, who had access to the Customs documents, made estimates in 1821 of Dutch trade in war and peace, to prove that some artificial impediment must be to blame:[2]

	1807	1809	1814	1815	1816
	Goods declared by value (£000)				
Imports	1,781	2,234	2,758	3,279	3,868
Exports	1,540	1,910	1,424	1,768	1,795
Transit	71	193	552	418	411
	Goods declared by weight (million lb.)				
Imports	127	35	102	135	132
Exports	150	112	108	118	132
Transit	4	2	4	7	8
	Goods declared by dry measure, mainly grain (thousand quarters)				
Imports	763	292	464	959	1,468
Exports	439	724	602	665	962
Transit	2	—	—	32	9

[1] W. L. D. van den Brink, *Bijdrage tot de kennis van den economischen toestand van Nederland in de jaren 1813-1816* (Amsterdam, 1916), pp. 46-51, 83; G. Seelig, in *Annalen des Deutschen Reiches* (1902).

[2] I. J. A. Gogel, *Bijvoegsel bij de memoriën en correspondentiën* (Amsterdam, 1844); N. W. Posthumus, *Nederlandse prijsgeschiedenis* (Leiden, 1943), I, ci.

Interested parties in London interpreted the situation with greater realism.[1] At the end of the eighteenth century, much Dutch trade had rested on custom rather than on clear economic advantages. War-time conditions had forced foreign merchants to seek new connexions. Their emancipation from the Dutch general market was thus hastened, and after a few years' interruption they were unlikely to return to the old ways unless they could see a positive advantage in them; but Holland, having lost touch with international trade during a period of rapid change, had lost her superiority of skill and information, and while capital had been accumulating in London it had wasted away in Amsterdam. After 1813, therefore, no Dutch revival could be expected even on the scale of that after 1783.

[1] *Parl. Papers* (1820), no. 300, pp. 87–9.

Table I. *British trade with the Netherlands, 1775–1824* *

Imports to Great Britain				
From:	Belgian Nether- lands	Dutch Nether- lands	North Germany	France
Official value (£000)				
1775–7 (av.)	117	617	701	70
Comparative indices (base 1775–7 av.)				
1775–7 (av.)	100	100	100	100
1778–80 (av.)	418	101	87	21
1781–2 (av.)	1,037	10	84	5
1784–6 (av.)	124	80	74	296
1787–91 (av.)	132	92	80	785
1792–3 (av.)	108	130	103	598
1794	66	165	114	—
1795–1800 (av.)	16	74	284	46
1816–24 (av.)	213	128	115	1,238
Exports from Great Britain				
To:	Belgian Nether- lands	Dutch Nether- lands	North Germany	France
Official value (£000)				
1775–7 (av.)	985	1,661	1,499	370
Comparative indices (base 1775–7 av.)				
1775–7 (av.)	100	100	100	100
1778–80 (av.)	124	81	79	4
1781–2 (av.)	211	12	86	2
1784–6 (av.)	84	83	88	137
1787–91 (av.)	95	84	107	299
1792–3 (av.)	92	91	154	197
1794	68	99	396	9
1795–1800 (av.)	18	62	570	89
1816–24 (av.)	201	139	568	339

* D. McPherson, *Annals*, III and IV; *Parl. Papers*, 1826, XXII, 121–43; 1828, XIX, 337; 1829, XVII, 255; 1830, XXVII, 255; 1849, LII, 129–33.

Table II. *British trade with the Netherlands, 1789–1826: imports* *

From:	Dutch Netherlands	Belgian Netherlands	Netherlands (total)	North Germany
Official value (£000)				
1789–92 (av.)	697	168	865	603
1797	530	10	540	1,576
1798	594	14	608	2,092
1799	200	12	212	2,820
1800	972	34	1,006	2,352
Comparative indices (base 1797)				
1797	—	—	100	100
1798	—	—	112	133
1799	—	—	39	178
1800	—	—	186	149
1801	—	—	195	130
1802	—	—	185	76
1803	—	—	120	58
1804	—	—	162	30
1805	—	—	135	20
1806	—	—	118	86
1807	—	—	167	11
1808	—	—	146	5
1809	—	—	319	66
1810	—	—	139	124
1811	—	—	5	13
1812	—	—	44	8
Comparative indices (base 1789–92 av.)				
1789–92 (av.)	100	100	100	100
1802	?	?	116	198
1814	?	?	250	119
1815	?	?	144	99
1816	94	46	84	46
1817	105	73	100	114
1818	163	340	197	210
1819	84	181	92	96
1820	81	59	77	106
1821	110	85	105	103
1822	118	155	125	127
1823	111	178	125	160
1824	157	279	181	250
1825	?	?	218	412
1826	?	?	161	264

* D. McPherson, *Annals*, III and IV; *Parl. Papers*, 1826, XXII, 121–43; 1828, XIX, 337; 1829, XVII, 255; 1830, XXVII, 255; 1849, LII, 129–33.

Table III. *British trade with the Netherlands, 1789–1826: exports* *

To:	Products of Great Britain			Colonial, Irish, and foreign products			Total	
	Dutch Nether-lands	Belgian Nether-lands	Nether-lands (total)	Dutch Nether-lands	Belgian Nether-lands	Nether-lands (total)	Nether-lands	North Germany
Official value (£000)								
1789–92 (av.)	760	370	1,130	734	661	1,395	2,525	1,837
1797	77	2	79	1,264	123	1,387	1,466	8,384
1798	6	—	6	932	17	949	955	10,689
1799	5	—	5	13	14	27	32	8,673
1800	21	40	61	3,208	768	3,976	4,037	12,665
Comparative indices (base 1797)								
1797	—	—	—	—	—	—	100	100
1798	—	—	—	—	—	—	65	127
1799	—	—	—	—	—	—	2	103
1800	—	—	—	—	—	—	274	151
1801	—	—	—	—	—	—	265	104
1802	—	—	—	—	—	—	300	95
1803	—	—	—	—	—	—	115	61
1804	—	—	—	—	—	—	159	16
1805	—	—	—	—	—	—	25	20
1806	—	—	—	—	—	—	79	67
1807	—	—	—	—	—	—	113	4
1808	—	—	—	—	—	—	24	18
1809	—	—	—	—	—	—	168	71
1810	—	—	—	—	—	—	33	26
1811	—	—	—	—	—	—	18	1
1812	—	—	—	—	—	—	21	2
Comparative indices (base 1789–92 av.)								
1789–92 (av.)	100	100	100	100	100	100	100	100
1800	3	11	5	434	116	284	159	689
1802	?	?	?	?	?	?	174	436
1814	?	?	?	?	?	?	351	532
1815	?	?	235	?	?	398	325	440
1816	194	235	207	319	287	304	261	473
1817	156	169	160	190	186	187	175	442
1818	139	189	155	135	185	158	157	473
1819	152	187	164	154	163	158	161	458
1820	159	187	169	114	129	121	142	539
1821	141	233	170	121	161	140	154	471
1822	160	270	195	109	128	118	153	492
1823	196	342	243	76	113	94	161	410
1824	178	310	221	91	162	125	168	411
1825	?	?	242	?	?	128	178	426
1826	?	?	233	?	?	167	196	483

* D. McPherson, *Annals*, III and IV; *Parl. Papers*, 1826, XXII, 121–43; 1828, XIX, 337; 1829, XVII, 255; 1830, XXVII, 255; 1849, LII, 129–33.

Table IV. *Ships of certain countries passing the Sound, 1772–1829* ★

Year	Dutch	British	Swedish	Russian	United States
1772	2,406	2,046	?	?	—
1774	2,447	2,385	1,227	36	—
1790	2,009	3,788	?	?	?
1791	1,736	3,720	1,816	34	45
1814	551	2,319	2,795	495	—
1815	740	2,397	2,156	576	128
1816	876	1,848	2,042	399	168
1817	1,305	4,172	2,000	387	136
1818	600	5,052	1,745	323	128
1819	834	3,078	1,559	356	89
1820	853	3,597	1,519	242	169
1821	589	2,819	1,439	300	196
1822	391	3,097	1,214	259	216
1823	461	3,016	1,133	306	158
1824	399	3,540	1,303	369	167
1825	630	5,186	1,319	335	230
1826	637	3,730	1,280	328	158
1827	814	5,099	1,389	384	191
1828	1,066	4,426	1,324	407	221
1829	1,120	4,796	1,132	359	181

★ *Parl. Papers*, 1828, XIX, 463; 1830, XXVII, 49; D. McPherson, *Annals*, III, 561; IV, 229.

Table V. *Dutch trade with the United States, 1789–1822* *

Exports and re-exports to certain countries: average annual values ($ million)			
To:	England	The Hanseatic ports	The Dutch Netherlands
1789–92	5·3	0·4	1·3
1796–1801	14·2	11·5	4·9
1802–7	12·9	4·3	11·2
1808–10	5·6	1·2	1·3
1811–12	7·5	—	—
1813–14	—	—	
			The Netherlands
1815–22	22·6	2·9	4·8

Imports from the Dutch Netherlands: average annual quantity

	Spirits (thousand gallons)	Cheese (thousand lb.)
1789–92	220	7
1795–6	197	205
1797–1808	849	310
1809–14	20	2
1815–19	519	69

Imports of white and red lead: average annual quantity (thousand lb.)

	Dutch	British
1805	42	1,669
1806	108	2,401
1807	58	2,593
1816–22	125	3,035

* *American State Papers* (1832), Commerce and Navigation, vols. I and II; A. Seybert, *Statistical Annals* (Philadelphia, 1818); T. Pitkin, *A statistical view of the commerce of the United States of America* (New York, 1817). Exports to the Austrian Netherlands were recorded for 1789–92, but were negligible.

34

Chapter II

THE DUTCH PEOPLE AND THEIR OCCUPATIONS

(a) Industry

The difficulties of old-established urban handicraft industries in the face of cheaper rural labour were specially serious for Holland, whose civilization was irremediably urban. Conditions were unsuitable for the development of the new sources of power which revived urban industry elsewhere in the early nineteenth century, so that any new growth of Dutch industry, apart from occupations ancillary to commerce, was likely to be attracted by the cheap rural labour of the eastern provinces, and to leave the most pressing Dutch problem unsolved.

The Napoleonic wars hastened the decline of Dutch commerce, but did not promote any significant industrial growth. Indeed, it was said that, while in 1806 the Dutch general market was still full of vitality, Dutch industry, with certain exceptions, was almost extinguished.[1] This showed that industrial decline had been due not merely to the commercial policy of the Republic, nor to the predominance of the merchants, but rather to the economic facts which determined Dutch opportunities as the international division of labour increased. The Dutch territory offered no important industrial raw materials except flax, coarse wool, hides, peat and madder; water power was absent or inadequate. Dutch industry could prosper only by taking advantage of its favourable location for the supply of foreign raw materials and for access to foreign markets. It was necessary and inevitable that Dutch industry should share the fortunes of Dutch commerce. Industries could not be preserved, revived or created, on a scale sufficient to maintain the urban population, by isolating the small Dutch home market from foreign trade. Contemporaries, other than those personally interested in particular protectionist measures, rightly considered that it would be absurd to seek to restore the material basis of Dutch urban civilization by a policy of self-sufficiency. Dutch agriculture could not well supply the necessary food, much of the land being best suited for the specialized uses which commerce had made possible. Without foreign trade, it was supposed, Holland and Zeeland must return to a swampy state of nature.

Cut off from the sea, as an outlying part of a Continental empire, at a time when war conditions made the transport of raw materials specially

[1] Ged. v, 258; A. J. L. van den Bogaerde de Ter-Brugge, Essai, ii, 160.

expensive, the Dutch provinces had nothing to attract industrial enterprise. Furthermore, until 1811 they were excluded from the French customs area, which robbed them of traditional markets as more and more of their hinterland was annexed behind increasingly prohibitive import duties; and by 1811 the 'prosperity phase' of Napoleonic industrialization was over.

The effect of the war on existing industries varied, but was often unfavourable. The tanners complained of declining business for lack of imported hides. Even the brickyards were influenced by the fortunes of maritime trade, for Holland bricks served as a marketable outward ballast to the colonies, and Frisian yellow bricks to the Baltic. The war checked building in the towns of the maritime provinces, and stimulated it only in certain agricultural districts.

The beer and bottle industries were two examples of how the general market fostered a scale of operation large by Continental standards. A Rotterdam bottle firm, for instance, was still employing fifty workers in 1807. Both industries had worked for colonial demand and for the provisioning of ships, and both had used Newcastle coal. Dutch beer, which to English taste 'seemed to be made chiefly of spice',[1] had long been losing ground to coffee, tea and gin. The war brought a modest revival, for the high price of colonial goods made beer again a necessity to many; since urban water, including that carried daily into Amsterdam by boat, was unpalatable and often considered unwholesome. On the other hand, bottle-making was a vigorous young industry which became important only in the second half of the eighteenth century. It suffered by the interruptions to maritime trade, especially to that in wine, and by 1809 several firms had closed down. The distillers, too, suffered. They were especially indignant that the authorities, in trying to comply with the French policy of preventing communication with the enemy, interfered with smuggling to England. The island of Walcheren was most concerned; there were said to have been over 2,000 British residents there before the war.[2]

It is arguable that mercantilist devices, and the manipulation of import and export duties, were responsible for the survival of some Dutch industries in the second half of the eighteenth century;[3] others relied on traditional privileges which the rulers would probably have abolished, if they could, as contrary to the general interest. The position of such industries in a time of war and revolution was highly precarious.

---

[1] *Grandfather's Letters to Marianne* (Bungay, 1826), p. 65.

[2] *Ged.* VI, 1320–1, 1334, 1356, 1383; D. McPherson, *Annals*, III, 428, 697.

[3] C. Visser, *Verkeersindustriën te Rotterdam in de tweede helft der achttiende eeuw* (Rotterdam, 1927), p. 17.

The silk industry had flourished in the early eighteenth century at Amsterdam, Haarlem, Utrecht, Naarden and other towns because the Dutch Mediterranean trade, the sales of the Dutch East India Company and especially the Dutch-Russian trade in Persian produce made Amsterdam the main European market for raw silk. High Dutch costs and mercantilist measures by foreign governments nearly destroyed the industry in the 1780's, but strong pressure compelled the Dutch East India Company to keep the price of raw silk low and to find markets in the east for Dutch velvets and other specialities. The loss of these advantages after 1795 proved disastrous for the few thousand workers still employed, mainly in Amsterdam.[1]

The Amsterdam shipyards in the eighteenth century relied on municipal regulations which forced Amsterdam merchants to employ them. They remained active until 1807, though presumably engaged by then mostly on repair work. Afterwards, work almost ceased, except in suburban yards that worked for inland navigation. The situation was not much better in 1816, for the French administration of 1810–13 and the cessation of trade resulted in the effective abolition of the old privileges, which had probably continued in practice long after all such regulations had been officially abrogated by the Dutch constitution of 1798. Dutch shipbuilding and repair work were costlier than foreign, so that after 1813 the use of foreign shipyards and the purchase of foreign ships were essential in order to create as soon as possible a competitive Dutch merchant fleet. The subsequent fate of the industry depended on government policy. Meanwhile, Amsterdam shipbuilders maintained a minimum staff, and waited.

Many urban craftsmen, shopkeepers, and employees of commerce such as brokers, crane-operators, wagoners, boatmen and lightermen, had been members of gilds. These broke up gradually after 1798, for at first effective action was taken only against obnoxious ones like those of Amersfoort or weak ones like those of Leeuwarden. Even in 1811, there were still 14,071 members of officially extant gilds in Amsterdam. Many of their old powers had been removed, but were said to be exercised still in practice, particularly against hawkers. Only in 1812 did the French authorities succeed in establishing effectively the right of every citizen to set up in any trade on payment of a simple patent tax. After the war, the demand for the restoration of the gilds was strong, both from the former members, and from the municipal governments of Amsterdam and other towns. William I and his advisers, however, feared that such restoration would raise costs and so hinder the return of the general market. Indeed, the Amsterdam gilds of master ships-carpenters and those of their journey-

[1] *Ged.* v, 620.

men, entrenched behind their municipal privilege, must have raised shipping costs. No doubt, too, the candle-makers' gild, whose members had worked mainly for home demand and in the provisioning of ships, though also for a modest export trade to Spain, Portugal and the West Indies, raised shipping and office costs for the Amsterdam merchants. William I, therefore, only authorized the restoration of the gilds of boat-men, and harbour and market workers, in order that sworn men might always be ready, under municipal regulation, to serve commerce honestly, and also to facilitate the collection of dues and duties. The boatmen's monopolies concerned only their work as common carriers; merchants with large consignments were at liberty to own or hire barges for their sole use. The boatmen's gilds may have raised costs, but at least they pro-vided a punctual and efficient, if slow, public service, much admired by foreigners for 'a precision which resembles mechanism rather than animal motion'.[1]

Delft in the eighteenth century lived largely on the presence of a Chamber of the Dutch East India Company, originally established there for political reasons. The town was privileged to supply provisions and chandlery for the Chamber's expeditions, and the return cargoes of colonial goods were auctioned there, whereby storage and transport work was gained and merchants were attracted. Officials of the Chamber lived at Delft and many who had served it in the Indies retired there with their savings. The least satisfactory or successful members of worthy Delft families were given places in the Indies, and the moral advantage to Delft of this arrangement was defended with frankness. Apart from these privileges, which were lost for ever in 1795, Delft was merely a market town for the neighbouring agricultural and fishing villages, and especially an assembling market for butter, which was casked there under municipal supervision. Only two cloth firms remained, one of which, however, employed 1,000 domestic workers towards the end of the eighteenth century; they depended on military and East India Company orders.[2]

Delft ware was typical of many minor, luxury, products, dependent on the general market. Although in the seventeenth and eighteenth centuries it was to be found, purely for display, in the homes of Dutch peasants, the industry could not be maintained by home demand. Its decline in the second half of the eighteenth century was ascribed to high costs, especially in the supply of raw materials, for which Delft was unsuitably located, and

---

[1] W. Jacob, *A View of the Agriculture, Manufactures and Statistics of Germany and parts of Holland and France* (London, 1820), p. 20; *Ged.* VI, 912; C. Wiskerke, *De afschaffing der gilden in Nederland.*
[2] *Ged.* VI, 1373–80.

to foreign mercantilist measures. The high costs were certainly not due to a high standard of living of the skilled artists and craftsmen. The loss of export markets in which quality had once been more important than price, ruined the industry. The English potters had discovered and exploited a wide and elastic demand, and the coming of their ware into actual, common use diminished the prestige of Delft, which had no advantage except the reputation of its outmoded and uncompetitive products. English imports after 1760 showed that Dutch demand too was elastic; but although some Delft firms tried to exploit it by adopting English methods and employing English enterprise and labour, the attempt failed. The industry only employed a few hundred workers at the end of the eighteenth century, as against 2,000 at the beginning. The political plates with which it welcomed the 'Batavian' revolution proved its swan song, and not even the war's impediments to English imports revived it.[1]

Enkhuizen owed its remaining importance in the eighteenth century to the presence of a Chamber of the East India Company, and to its privilege to provide part of the fleet and governing body of the College of Deep-sea Herring Fishery. Its woollen, rope and netting industries depended on these privileges. The war and the principle of 'equality' therefore brought unrelieved distress, and after the war

Everywhere the finest houses have been demolished; and those still upright threaten to fall, or stand like mourners in a churchyard. Sheep, horses and cattle graze where once proud buildings stood; the warehouses of the once prosperous East India Company no longer exist. Only one family, which lives mostly at Leiden, still keeps a carriage and horses, whereas in 1800 eighteen did so.[2]

After the war, the making of nets and rigging was revived by a Burgomaster and his relations, as a partly private and partly public enterprise. Nearly 200 men, women, and children were employed in this institution, and more as out-workers.[3]

The Dutch cotton industry was among those that gained by the war. In the eighteenth century, Amsterdam was the chief Continental market for raw cotton, and cotton yarn was imported by the Dutch East India Company. Thanks to this, an industry grew up at Amersfoort to make 'bombazine', using a linen warp. The gilds of Amersfoort, however, being exceptionally strong, successfully excluded the half-finished products

---

[1] H. Havard, *Histoire de la Faïence de Delft* (Paris, 1878), pp. 149–88; *Le commerce de la Hollande*, I, 313.

[2] J. van Lennep, *Nederland in den goeden ouden tijd, zijnde het dagboek...in den jare 1823*, ed. M. E. Kluit (Utrecht, 1942), p. 33.

[3] J. van Lennep, *Dagboek*, pp. 36, 49.

of rural industry, restricted the number of apprentices and impeded technical change. The industry accordingly shifted to Twente, where cheap and suitable rural labour was available. It was a district of rural linen-making, organized by local merchants who bought local or German linen yarn, put it out to weavers, especially in and near Almelo, and had it bleached locally or at Haarlem. They exported much linen, some of which they bought from independent rural weavers, to the West Indies, and supplied bleached linen yarn to Amersfoort and to British importers. They received payment for their maritime exports from their Amsterdam and Rotterdam commission agents largely in the form of colonial and other goods for local consumption. From 1728, they organized their own bombazine industry at Enschedé. During the Napoleonic wars, the linen industry lost more than it gained by the interruption of maritime trade, but there was an improved home demand for bombazine. The spinning jenny and other manual machines were accordingly introduced from Germany after 1796, and small factories were set up, in each of which about twenty workers were employed on the machines under supervision. During the war, apart from stoppages owing to lack of raw cotton, the industry prospered. After the war, plentiful imports stimulated greater activity than ever, until a sharp depression set in towards the end of 1816.[1]

The success of the bombazine industry in a rural, inland district was matched by failures in the ancient cities. Attempts to overcome high labour costs in Utrecht by the use of water power for silk throwing, and for cotton spinning, with the water-frame, were made in the last two decades of the eighteenth century, but, perhaps because the water power was too weak, they were abandoned soon after 1795. The only way of keeping the silk and cotton industries alive in the cities proved to be the use of pauper labour subsidized by charitable organizations or the municipal authorities. Such enterprises employed 200 adults and children in Utrecht in 1811. Since their purpose was charity rather than profit, they did not attempt to introduce labour-saving machines.[2]

The spinners and weavers of wool in the maritime provinces were also largely paupers. Blankets, camlets, polemites and military cloths were made by urban weavers in Holland, some of whose organizations were strong enough to prevent the flooding of their trades by unemployed from other branches of the industry. Rural weaving in Holland, which had existed surreptitiously in the eighteenth century, increased when the 'Batavians' removed the old restrictions. For the rest, charities and local authorities contracted to supply entrepreneurs with the labour of prisons,

[1] J. A. P. G. Boot, *De Twentsche katoennijverheid, 1830–73* (Amsterdam, 1935).
[2] *Ged.* VI, 1332.

workhouses and orphanages, and subsidized others to employ urban spinners and weavers, mostly in sweat-shops. Some of the entrepreneurs were philanthropists who did not seek a profit. The system reduced the cost of poor relief by enabling the spinners and weavers to remain at work and by providing a labour test to reduce mendicancy. It also made possible the maintenance of a labour reserve against the temporary revivals that occurred in the industry from time to time. The 'allowance' system of relief in aid of wages for large families was also used. By the end of the eighteenth century, supporters of industrial protection considered that the spinners and weavers were too demoralized by charity to work well at the wages even a protected industry might afford, and therefore recommended the continuance of forced pauper labour, under a stricter discipline, with measures to prevent the seasonal departures of the women to clean herring, pick fruit, or lift turnips. They feared, too, that without effective protection the craftsmen of the cloth-finishing industries might soon find it impossible to live on their wages, and either leave the trade or become paupers.[1]

The war stimulated those branches of the wool industry that worked for home demand, but under the rule of 'equality' the benefit went to rural rather than urban industry and to North Brabant rather than Holland. The demand was for cheap cloth, and Leiden's reputation and commercial connexions were of little advantage, though her political influence was still valuable in securing public contracts.

The cloth merchants of Amsterdam and Rotterdam had long ceased to be industrialists, though they still sometimes owned finishing workshops in their respective cities. In Leiden, large finishing establishments had ceased to justify themselves, and the wealthier employers had withdrawn from the industry. They had been replaced by entrepreneurs with no pretension to the status of merchants, who put out work to the masters of small workshops sometimes as agents for Amsterdam or Rotterdam merchants.[2] In North Brabant, the production of unfinished cloth had been organized on the putting-out system by commission agents at Tilburg, the centre of the main district, on behalf of the clothiers of Leiden and other towns in Holland. The development of the finishing industries at Tilburg gradually made the commission agents into independent capitalists, and led some Leiden clothiers to migrate thither. The process quickened after 1795, for the Tilburg cloth that still needed Leiden finishing was mainly for export by sea, especially to the Levant.

Leiden gained from the war, especially in the first years of the nineteenth

[1] N. W. Posthumus, *Bronnen*, VI, 267–70.
[2] N. W. Posthumus, *Geschiedenis van de Leidsche lakenindustrie*, II, 816, 1033–4.

century. Her output of cloth for the home market increased.[1] Her pole-mites and camlets, which were designed specially for China, no longer enjoyed the reliable patronage of the East India Company, but were exported by American merchants.[2] In 1803, the municipal debt had been paid off, and pauperism was much diminished. From 1805, however, supplies of Spanish wool became expensive and uncertain, and export opportunities for fine cloth became rare.[3] Leiden was less able than Tilburg to compete against imported and smuggled cloth in the home market. Annexation to the French Empire ended the need for special Dutch uniforms, and led to the cancellation of contracts and difficulties in securing payment for cloth already supplied. In 1811 the Maire of Leiden reported that his city was the most unfortunate in Holland. The portions destroyed by an explosion in 1807 were still not being rebuilt and the number of firms in active business was less than in 1794.[4] This does not accord with the view of the French authorities that Leiden was more prosperous than before the war,[5] but certainly the war period as a whole did not halt the decline in her population. Afterwards, she had few advantages either in the home or the foreign market. Half her inhabitants were said to be dependent on charity in 1816.[6]

The revival of the commercial industries after the war was incomplete, owing to broken relations, to the development of industry in former im-porting countries, and to increased British exports. Dutch calico-printing, still prosperous in 1765, was now of small importance. In Amsterdam only sixty sugar refineries started up after the war, and only eighty in Hamburg. No doubt in both cases the reduction was due to concentration, as well as to British competition. Amsterdam refiners were at least helped by the return of some of the Dutch West Indian colonies, though many of the planters were now British, with a right secured by treaty to maintain their British trade connexions.

Apart from textile firms, few Dutch enterprises employed above fifty workers, fewer indeed than in the eighteenth century, owing to the decline of the shipbuilding and calico-printing industries. A few paper firms employed over fifty workers (including children), mostly in the Zaandam area, but with one at Groningen which worked only for the eastern Dutch provinces. The largest of the surviving bleaching firms of

---

[1] O. Pringsheim, 'Beiträge zur wirtschaftlichen Entwicklungsgeschichte der vereinigten Niederlande im 17 und 18e Jahrhundert', in *Staats- und Sozialwissen-schaftliche Forschungen* (Leipzig, 1890), p. 72.

[2] *Ged.* VI, 1392.

[3] A. R. Falck, *Ambtsbrieven, 1802–42* (The Hague, 1878), p. 28.

[4] *Ged.* VI, 1368. [5] *Ged.* VI, 1317, 1378.

[6] P. J. Blok, *Eene Hollandsche stad in den nieuweren tijd* (The Hague, 1918), pp. 110–11.

Holland employed forty-one workers in 1816, mainly women. Most industrial work was done in quite small workshops, or in the workers' homes. In the inland provinces, a good deal of linen was made for household or for purely local use. Such machines as existed relied on human or animal power; or on windmills, the one source of power in which the Dutch had a natural advantage, and which were used for pressing oil from Baltic and home-grown seeds, for drainage, for sawing timber, for grinding corn, for crushing dye-woods and tan-bark, and for making paper and cement. Only about four men could work at each mill.[1]

(b) *The fisheries*

The fishing industry drew its raw materials, including hemp, timber and salt, from the general market. It was useful to commerce, for salt was a convenient ballast cargo for return voyages from France, Spain and Portugal, and beneficial for 'seasoning' new ships. Freight charges were therefore low. Fishing was also valuable as a school for seamen, and one reason for the low operating costs of Dutch ships was that the seamen came from fishing villages and left their families there, so that their wages were not affected by the urban cost of living. Fishing was an export industry, and so did not come into conflict with commerce about import duties, although imports of whale products, dried cod and pickled salmon threatened some of its branches. The merchants were willing that the industry and its secrets should be protected by the prohibition of the export of nets, vats and other equipment, and from 1775 subsidies were granted, owing to the loss of certain foreign markets.

Dutch fishing was handicapped by the College of Deep-sea Herring Fishery, which represented, in the usual oligarchic manner, the owners of busses in certain privileged towns, and which controlled not only the movements of the herring fleet but also the prices of early herring at least, the admission of vessels to the fleet, and the nature of the technique and materials used. The fleet, which included many busses from towns not represented in the College, had a monopoly of gutted salt herring, and the College kept up the price as well as the quality in a manner that did not assist exports. The 'coastal' fishermen, who used vessels that could be beached on the sandy shores, were permitted to sell other kinds of herring, and exported many, especially bloaters, to the Belgian Netherlands. The vessels were often owned, like the busses, by sedentary capitalists, but the skippers and crews enjoyed a traditional share of the catch.

[1] I. J. Brugmans, *De arbeidende klasse in Nederland in de 19de eeuw* (The Hague, 1925).

In the eighteenth century, Dutch salt herring faced increasing Scottish, and later English and German, competition in its German export markets. The owners of busses sought relief not by changes in method or organization, but by demanding subsidies, compulsory consumption of salt herring in charitable institutions, and a stricter enforcement of the regulations. All Dutch salt herring had to be inspected and casked in the United Provinces before it was re-exported, and no catches were permitted before 24 June. In 1609, Hamburg had accordingly been persuaded to bind herself by treaty to admit no early herring until sufficient days had elapsed after the 24 June for the Dutch procedures to be completed. All through the eighteenth century, the Dutch struggled ineffectually to get this enforced against Scottish early herring. With great reluctance, the Dutch College began in 1752 to license each year the marketing in Hamburg, directly from the fishing grounds, of small quantities of uninspected early herring, but its regulations continued to impede exports.[1]

The 'Batavians' changed the officers of the College, but not its spirit; for the new regulations of 1801 were even stricter than the old, since they gave formal sanction to monopolistic practices adopted in the eighteenth century in the struggle to maintain prices. The College also obtained fuller powers over coastal fishing. The regulations could not be enforced in war-time, when Dutch trade in salt herring was maintained only by packing foreign fish in casks with the Dutch control marks and by salting fish from the Zuider Zee; and the French administration abolished the corporate system in 1810. Nevertheless, as soon as the Dutch regained independence, they reverted to the old ways, and the regulations of 1801 were revived in January 1814. However, lack of vessels and of skilled hands led to the nationalization of foreign busses whose owners were attracted by Dutch subsidies, and to the employment of foreign hands. This made it difficult to re-establish traditions, and complaints continued for some years that the College was even less successful in maintaining quality than in maintaining prices. Herring, it was said, were being kept overnight before being gutted, instead of being thrown back if more were caught than could be handled. The consequent decline in the reputation of Dutch herring was blamed for its failure to win back its foreign markets. The difficulty might have been overcome if the surplus fish could have been preserved by some other method to meet the demand of the lower classes in Holland for cheap food; but this would have infringed the prerogatives of the coastal fishers, and could not be permitted at a time when a rather bitter struggle was in progress to repress salt-curing by the coasters, which

[1] A. Beaujon, *Overzicht der geschiedenis van de Nederlandsche zeevisscherijen* (Leiden, 1885), pp. 82–105.

had been encouraged by the French.[1] This was an old subject of dispute, for the coasters needed to salt some of their fish temporarily for subsequent smoking, and precise control was difficult. The policy of the College after 1814 was less liberal than in the eighteenth century, yet spokesmen of Dutch free-trade supported it in the States General, with some misgiving, against the complaints of the coasters.[2]

In the eighteenth century, Dutch whaling declined in the face of German and Scandinavian competition. Its weakness was increased by laws which required the whole catch to be brought to Dutch ports and so prevented avoidance of the costs of the general market. At the end of the eighteenth century, the industry was kept alive by subsidies and by the investments of merchants who profited rather by supplying provisions and ships' stores than by the direct results of whaling. Provisions consumed on whalers, including wine and spirits, were exempted from excise after 1750, and it was said afterwards that the opportunities for fraud thus created were more profitable than the pursuit of whales. The industry seemed quite dead in 1814.[3]

When the post-war reorganization was complete, nearly 4,000 men were employed in various kinds of fishing during the season; about half of them in the deep-sea herring fleet, which contained about 160 vessels against 196 in 1794.[4]

(c) Agriculture

Any re-orientation of the Dutch economy to replace the decaying general market by new sources of wealth implied adaptation to the fact of British expansion. Those who thought in these terms saw little hope in industry, but much in agriculture. Butter, cheese, and madder were promising exports. In 1764, Holland still imported Irish butter, but this was ceasing, partly because Dutch provisioning of the West Indies was declining but mainly because Irish supplies were taken up by an expanding English demand.[5] Dutch output increased to meet home needs, and in the second half of the eighteenth century for export to London, whose caricaturists began to imagine the typical Dutchman as a butter merchant.

Study of agricultural technique in the eighteenth century suggested that much waste land in the inland provinces could be reclaimed, and that

---

[1] A. Beaujon, *op. cit.* pp. 210–16, 226–8.
[2] *Ibid.* pp. 231–8.
[3] *Ibid.* pp. 143–5.
[4] E. Baasch, *Holländische Wirtschaftsgeschichte*, pp. 58–74; A. J. L. van den Bogaerde de Ter-Brugge, *Essai*, IV, 54; *Le commerce de la Hollande*, I, ch. v.
[5] J. Gee, *The Trade and Navigation of Great Britain Considered*, pp. 48–9; D. McPherson, *Annals*, III, 429.

surplus industrial workers from the maritime provinces might be settled on it for subsistence farming. The capital outlay, however, would be considerable, and the grazing rights of existing villages stood in the way. The poor peasants necessarily opposed the division of the waste land. Little was done, apart from a few benevolent schemes by exceptional landlords, and some piecemeal extension of the holdings of rich peasants who farmed for the market with hired labour. Progress was speeded by high corn prices during the war, and laws of 1809–10 granted new tax exemptions for reclaimed land and made it easier to overcome obstruction from a minority of the owners of common rights. Capital for reclamation was provided by merchants who hoped for profit and amenity from a country estate, and especially by influential or ambitious officials of the various régimes after 1795. Rotterdam capitalists, sometimes in syndicates, showed renewed energy in promoting drainage schemes in South Holland and Zeeland.[1] Land reclamation and the desire for war-time profits helped to overcome conservative instincts, and often led to an improved rotation of crops, enclosure, and an increased use of manure, including night-soil from the towns and military camps. Districts out of contact with the market were unaffected, but enough was achieved to impress British travellers after the war. 'I have seldom passed a district in any country, in which such great and recent steps towards improvement have been made', one wrote of Gelderland, noting the pine plantations, the rotation of buckwheat, rye and turnips, and the neat, new buildings.[2]

The new land was not settled by urban poor. Some was allotted by landowners to cottagers of the district. More often, the result of reclamation by landowners was the creation of tenant farms large by Continental standards. Many rich peasants used the profits of war time to meet the cost of minor encroachments on the waste land. To an English traveller after the war, the 'substantial' holdings, and brass and pewter utensils, of the richest peasants seemed 'very ordinary'; and the largest farm-house seemed literally 'a great barn of a place', not to be compared to 'the spacious halls, boarded floors and carpeted parlours of a wealthy English farmer'.[3] Dutch travellers nevertheless blamed the farmers of the grain districts for using their profits for expensive houses and furniture, and for sending their children to French boarding schools.[4]

Peasants in the western provinces had long been accustomed to individual, commercial farming. Few traces of feudalism remained there,

---

[1] *Ged.* VI, 1345, 1404–11.
[2] W. Jacob, *View*, pp. 51–2.
[3] *Grandfather's Letters to Marianne*, pp. 35–7.
[4] J. van Lennep, *Dagboek*, p. 101.

apart from dues sometimes paid to the lord of the polder for ancient windmills, probably no longer in use. Farming was conservative, and little of the experimental spirit had yet penetrated. A valuable tradition had been inherited, and crop rotation and manure were well understood; but, like the comparatively efficient cultivators of reclaimed land in the eastern provinces, the farmers of Holland, so English travellers reported, had not learned to hoe their turnips. They had a good knowledge of weights and measures, and were described as 'merchants through and through, who know wonderfully well how to use their soil and location to the best advantage for supplying the needs of the commercial towns in their vicinity or to which transport is easy'.[1] Those in the Schiedam area, for instance, like many of the distillers, used the offal from the distilleries for feeding pigs to provide pork for ships' provisions. Pigs' manure was found specially valuable for tobacco cultivation, and Rotterdam needed home-grown tobacco for mixing with American.[2] The farmers of the Waterland specialized in producing milk which went by boat daily into Amsterdam in white vats. The madder growers of South Holland and Zeeland were experts, and often were partners in ovens for processing it. In some districts there existed specialist flax cultivators, who hired suitable land over considerable distances just for one year and sent their own work-people to raise and prepare the crop.

Independent farming was usual also among the cultivating proprietors of Groningen and the tenant farmers of Friesland, and in some other eastern districts with good transport facilities. In Drenthe, and in parts of Gelderland, Overijssel and North Brabant population was still sparse and isolated, and farming was still mainly for direct subsistence.[3] There was little trace of serfdom, but many seigneurial privileges remained and the village system of scattered strips continued. The influence of the market was felt only through local middlemen, such as the shopkeepers and usurers of North Brabant who organized linen weaving, collected butter and rye to sell at Rotterdam, and supplied goods from the market in exchange. Other North Brabant peasants were more independent, and brought their butter and linen to the open market at such towns as 's Hertogenbosch.

The general market influenced all except very backward areas. The urban population stimulated commercial agriculture and market gardening, as did the activity of merchants on their rural estates, especially in Utrecht province. In the eighteenth century landowners in all provinces invested in securities which were administered for them in Holland. This

---

[1] *Ged.* v, 629.   [2] *Ged.* VI, 1382.
[3] J. van Lennep, *Dagboek*, p. 128.

strengthened the 'harmony of interest' between commerce and land. The Napoleonic wars disturbed this harmony, by forcing agriculture to adapt itself to diminution of foreign trade. In the process, agriculture gained more in the home market than it lost in exports. This was less true of Holland, where not enough grain was produced to supply even the rural population, and specialization and dependence on exports and urban consuming power were greatest. Producers of butter and cheese depended on maritime trade both for their main markets and for their supply of salt. The war did not, however, damage these interests much until 1810. In the eight war-years from 1801 to 1809, an average of 68,000 cwt. of Dutch butter and 80,000 of cheese was imported into Great Britain: in the first eight years of peace from 1814, an average of 72,000 and 88,000 cwt. respectively.[1]

In Holland, the prosperity of agriculture depended on that of the urban consumer: in the eastern provinces the prosperity of the towns depended on that of the surrounding agricultural district. In town and country in the east, war profits encouraged investment. In the Arnhem district, farmers began to grow sugar-beet and tobacco, and the landowners built barns for drying and storing the tobacco, and factories to make sugar, with stalls for cattle to eat the offal.[2] In some towns, factories were built to prepare chicory as a substitute for coffee. There were still six in Leeuwarden in 1816, employing 150 adults and children in the season. Peace necessarily reduced the value of such investments. At first, grain prices remained high, but it was clear that the revival of international trade was likely to cause a fall later. This would threaten the considerable investments that had been made in arable land, and the prosperity of many east Dutch towns and villages. In that case, their interest would conflict with that of Holland's commerce.

In fact, the war had seen the growth of new economic forces in the inland provinces, including the woollen industry of Tilburg, the bombazine of Enschedé and the more intensive farming. All were based on home demand and were threatened by foreign competition. If these interests combined in an anti-commercial movement, they might challenge the hegemony of the merchants of Holland, as the 'Patriots' had challenged the Regents. They might take up again the familiar idea of an economic re-orientation to foster new sources of prosperity to replace the decayed general market. Previously, the idea had lacked practical force, because the only new growth that had accompanied the decline of commerce had been commercial, namely the growth of the gin, tobacco and butter trades.

Parl. Papers 1826–7, XVIII, 2–7.　　² W. Jacob, *View*, pp. 51–60.

(d) Paupers and poverty

After the war, Dutchmen sometimes boasted that they had no Poor Rate, and attributed this to the stability of their old-fashioned ways, and to the harmony of interests by which all classes had some share of the benefits of the general market, diminished though it was.

> Under the laws of our ancestors, we not only made wealth, but wealth so widely distributed that it could really be called prosperity. Then for years all sources were petrified.... Nevertheless we remained on our feet, we revived at the least breathing space, and our paupers are proportionately fewer than in that country which has made itself master of our trade and by force and artifice has raised its production so excessively.[1]

Certainly, the official returns of expenditure on poor relief do not suggest a problem as serious as that in England at the time. An English visitor supposed that pauperism was prevented by thrift and by the lack of a Poor Rate:

> The working classes will subsist on saltfish and herrings, or on anything that is digestible, in order to be on the gaining hand; and hence there is scarcely any such thing as absolute poverty or wretchedness among them, or so much as a beggar to be seen in the streets.[2]

Comparisons with England were invalid, however, for English pauperism was largely the product of agrarian changes. Dutch villages, even where individualistic farming had long been the rule and little remained by way of common rights, still had a social cohesion which enabled their poor to be maintained without official assessments. The Dutch pauper problem was urban.

There was widespread poverty. Van Hogendorp estimated that a quarter of the Dutch people was poor, in the sense that it did not eat meat or wheaten bread and consisted of families with an annual income of about £13 or less, when employment was normal.[3]

In the inland provinces, the poor included wretched squatters on waste land, and small peasants who subsisted on cottage gardens, common grazing rights, agricultural wage labour and domestic industry. In the maritime provinces, individual farming and alienable property had long ago created a rural proletariat which lived by day labour or service in husbandry, and ate mainly potatoes, or a porridge of buckwheat and skimmed milk,

[1] Van Alphen in 1820—*Knuttel* 24916, p. 46.
[2] *Grandfather's Letters to Marianne*, p. 113.
[3] G. K. van Hogendorp, *Lettres sur la prospérité publique, 1828–30* (Amsterdam, 1830), p. 50.

according to the season.[1] In the west, the position of the rural wage-earners was weakened by the organization of hutted camps for urban harvest workers and in the east by the employment of Germans during the harvest and peat seasons. In Groningen, a labour shortage in the late eighteenth century, caused by the extension of arable farming after an outbreak of cattle disease, had led to the adoption of a horse-driven threshing machine.

Urban poverty had grown steadily with the industrial decline since 1730. Already in 1740 an English ambassador had declared that the lower orders had forgotten the taste of bread and ate mainly buckwheat porridge.[2] During the Napoleonic period, buckwheat millers complained of loss of trade, because the poor could now afford only potatoes; they were reluctant to eat large potatoes, however, for these were considered tasteless and rather disgusting.[3] The urban poor were demoralized and in the main docile. They sometimes roamed in gangs into the neighbouring countryside in order to intimidate farmers, or even rural labourers, into giving them a few potatoes. This continued throughout the first half of the nineteenth century.[4] Strikes were rare. Even in the eighteenth century, they had been confined to skilled and better paid groups such as the cloth-shearers of Leiden. In the 1820's, organized agitation, such as that of the Amsterdam diamond-cutters against the introduction of horse-driven machines, was unusual; as was sporadic violence, such as that in the North Brabant woollen industry against the steam-engine in 1827.[5]

The need for new charitable institutions continued. In 1818, for instance, a workhouse was set up in Amersfoort which employed 400 in picking tow, and making horse-rugs and various textiles. Charitable organization was always local and therefore impeded the mobility of labour. Local authorities were reluctant to permit the settlement of potential paupers, especially when a law of 1818 laid down the principle that four years' residence should qualify for relief. There was considerable variation in wage rates between towns and between occupations, and no sign of a levelling tendency. In 1820 the British Ambassador reported that 'it does not seem to be the general practice here to vary the wages of workmen with the greater or lesser degree of activity of the manufactory'.[6] This conservatism was no doubt due to recent memory of the

---

[1] W. Jacob, *View*, pp. 6–7.
[2] P. Geyl, *Revolutiedagen te Amsterdam (Augustus–September 1748)* (The Hague, 1936), p.10.   [3] *Ged.* VI, 1377, 1386.
[4] Z. W. Sneller (ed.), *Geschiedenis van den Nederlandschen Landbouw 1795–1940* (Groningen, 1943), p. 432.
[5] I. J. Brugmans, *De arbeidende klasse in Nederland*, p. 184.
[6] *Ged.* VIII (1), 144.

gilds and of the municipal regulation of wages. It may explain the presence in Amsterdam, despite local unemployment, of many young German workers, especially in the baking, brewing, distilling and building trades. They were preferred to the Dutch as better workmen, stronger and free from military obligations. In the pauper industries, the municipal authorities still had influence over wage rates. Their principle was that the entrepreneurs should pay as nearly a living wage as they could afford; just as in the eighteenth century, the Leiden Regents had compelled the protected blanket makers to pay the full official rates, even though they recognized that other weavers could not be protected from deductions.[1]

[1] N. W. Posthumus, *De Leidsche lakenindustrie* II, 1092–3.

Table VI. *Population of Dutch provinces, 1815, and
statistics of relief, 1822**

	Inhabitants of towns with urban suffrage (thousands)	Rural population (thousands)	Total population (thousands)	Paupers relieved out of doors in 1822 (thousands)	Spent on outdoor relief in 1822 (£000)
North Brabant	63	230	293	22	16
Gelderland	65	189	254	19	17
North Holland	241	116	357	} 90	100
South Holland	205	186	391		
Zeeland	36	76	112	7	16
Utrecht	51	57	108	6	15
Friesland	47	129	176	16	38
Overijssel	29	118	148	6	9
Groningen	28	108	136	6	15
Drenthe	8	39	46	2	3
Total	773	1,250	2,022	176	229
Dutch Limburg	37	119	155	?	?
Total (1839 frontier)	809	1,368	2,178	?	?

* *2de kamer*, 1822–3, B, 851; J. C. Ramaer, 'Het Koninkrijk der Nederlanden
(1815–1931)', in *Geschiedkundige atlas van Nederland*, no. 17 (The Hague, 1931).

Table VII. *Population of Dutch towns of more than 6,000 inhabitants in 1795, 1795–1840* *

	1795 (thousands)	1815 (Jan.) (thousands)	1840 (thousands)
NORTH HOLLAND			
Amsterdam	221·0	180·2	211·3
Haarlem	21·2	17·4	24·1
Zaandam	10·1	8·4	11·1
Hoorn	9·6	7·5	8·7
Alkmaar	8·4	7·9	9·8
Enkhuizen	6·9	5·2	5·0
SOUTH HOLLAND			
Rotterdam	53·2	58·6	78·1
The Hague (with Scheveningen)	41·3	42·3	63·6
Leiden	31·0	28·5	37·5
Dordrecht	18·0	17·4	21·0
Delft	14·7	12·8	17·0
Gouda	11·9	12·0	14·7
Schiedam	9·3	9·9	12·4
ZEELAND			
Middelburg	20·1	13·1	15·9
Zierikzee	6·1	6·3	6·9
UTRECHT			
Utrecht	32·3	33·7	48·5
Amersfoort	8·6	8·7	12·9
FRIESLAND			
Leeuwarden	15·5	17·0	23·4
Harlingen	7·5	6·9	7·9
GRONINGEN			
Groningen	23·8	27·8	33·5
OVERIJSSEL			
Zwolle	12·2	12·9	16·9
Deventer	8·3	9·6	14·4
Kampen	6·2	7·0	9·1
GELDERLAND			
Nijmegen	12·7	13·3	21·2
Arnhem	10·1	9·6	16·8
Zutphen	6·9	7·6	11·6
NORTH BRABANT			
's Hertogenbosch	12·9	13·1	22·0
Tilburg	8·5	9·9	14·0
Breda	8·2	9·0	15·4

* J. C. Ramaer, *loc. cit.*

Table VIII. *Indices of Dutch population** (1815 = 100),
1795 and 1840

	1795	1840
TOTAL (excluding LIMBURG)	95	131
North Holland—urban	121	122
North Holland—rural	101	128
South Holland—urban	99	134
South Holland—rural	98	135
North Brabant	89	129
Zeeland	102	134
Friesland	91	129
Groningen (province)	85	130
Drenthe	85	156
Gelderland	88	136
Utrecht (province)	90	135
Overijssel	91	134
TOWNS		
Amsterdam	123	117
Rotterdam	91	133
Leiden	108	131
Schiedam	93	125
Utrecht (city)	96	144
Groningen (city)	85	120
Leeuwarden	97	137
Tilburg	86	142
Enschedé	76	155
Almelo	97	129

* J. C. Ramaer, *loc. cit.*

Table IX. Employment in certain industries, Dutch towns and provinces, 1794–1819*

	Firms					Workers				
	1794	1806	1811	1816	1819	1794	1806	1811	1816	1819
AMSTERDAM										
Sugar-refining	108	—	—	60	—	—	1,160	95	600	—
Shipbuilding	—	35	—	40	—	—	3,000	350	405	—
Tobacco	—	100	—	1	—	—	1,800	200	2	—
Rope	—	—	—	—	—	—	—	—	60	—
Timber	—	—	—	—	—	—	—	—	328	—
Ships' biscuit	—	—	—	—	—	—	—	—	80	—
Distilling	—	—	—	—	—	—	—	—	78	—
Calico-printing	—	—	2	1	—	—	—	16 (a)	59 (a)	—
Cotton-spinning	—	—	—	4	—	—	—	—	26 (a)	—
Brewing	—	—	7	7	—	—	—	158	130	—
Dyeing (wool and woollens)	—	—	15	8	—	—	—	28	10	—
Dyeing (cottons)	—	24	18	—	—	—	80	42	—	—
Coppersmiths	—	—	68	68	—	—	—	38	35	—
Vinegar	7	—	3	3	—	—	—	50	38	—
Gold and silver thread	—	—	5	2	—	—	—	22	100	—
Book-printing	—	—	34	28	—	—	—	113	87	—
Goldsmiths and silversmiths	—	—	129	38	—	—	—	311	121	—
Candlemakers	—	—	103	80	—	—	—	89	100	—
Lacemakers	—	—	18	2	—	—	—	96	90	—
Dyestuffs	—	8	6	—	—	—	70	14	—	—
Military buttons, etc.	—	1	1	—	—	—	80	20	—	—
Hats	—	14	14	—	—	—	44	28	—	160
Silk-throwing	—	—	5	—	3	—	—	250	—	—
Velvet, satin, gauze, etc.	50	6	2	—	—	3,000	—	—	—	—
Wool-weaving (coarse)	—	2	2	—	—	—	220	130	—	—
Porcelain	—	1	1	—	—	—	65	6	—	—
Coppersmiths and braziers	—	85	75	—	—	—	112	52	—	—
Bronze ornaments	—	12	4	—	—	—	50	10	—	—

ROTTERDAM										
Shipbuilding (b)	7	—	4	—	—	550	—	—	225	—
Tobacco	50	—	—	—	—	3,500	—	200	1,200	—
Rope	4	—	4	—	—	70	—	35	110	—
Calico-printing	1	—	1	—	—	100	—	25	—	—
Timber	24	—	—	6	—	—	—	—	130	—
Brewing	12	—	—	14	—	—	—	—	65	—
Sugar-refining	30	—	—	29	—	700	—	—	200	—
Distilling	26	—	—	—	—	180	—	—	150	—
White lead	16	—	1	15	—	30	—	—	146	—
Cloth dyeing and finishing	—	—	—	—	—	—	—	—	45	—
Tan mills	3	—	—	—	—	—	—	3	—	—
DORDRECHT										
Smalt	—	—	—	—	—	—	—	30	—	—
Sugar-refining	12	—	—	—	—	—	—	—	—	—
HAARLEM										
Silk	—	—	—	—	6	—	—	—	—	86
Linen tape, thread, etc.	—	—	—	—	2	—	—	—	—	270
ZAANDAM										
Timber	—	—	—	—	82	—	—	—	—	328
Oil mills	—	—	—	—	59	—	—	—	—	177
DELFT										
Delft ware	10	—	8	—	—	—	—	—	—	—
KROMMENIE										
Sail	—	—	—	—	13	—	—	—	—	550
NORTH AND SOUTH HOLLAND										
Paper	—	48	48	—	52	—	569	372	—	1,142 (c)

* *Ged.* VI; Z. W. Sneller, in *Bijdragen voor Vaderlandsche Geschiedenis en Oudheidkunde*, 1926; I. J. Brugmans, *De arbeidende klasse in Neder-land in de 19de eeuw*; J. A. P. G. Boot, *De Twentsche katoennijverheid*. Information fragmentary and unreliable.

(a) Largely children.　　(b) Private enterprise only.　　(c) Includes 333 children.

Table IX (cont.)

	Firms					Workers				
	1794	1806	1811	1816	1819	1794	1806	1811	1816	1819
SOUTH HOLLAND										
Rope	—	40	32	—	—	—	1,492	247	—	—
Peat-digging	—	—	226	—	—	—	—	5,200	—	—
Tanning, etc.	—	97	56	—	—	—	880	470	—	—
Sugar-refining	—	28	—	—	—	—	200	—	—	—
Madder-preparing	—	31	30	—	—	—	244	140	—	—
Bottles	—	7	2	—	—	—	170	60	—	—
Tobacco pipes	—	—	36	—	—	—	—	2,900	—	—
Bricks	—	49	49	—	—	—	994	864	—	—
Potters	—	49	44	—	—	—	440	360	—	—
Gunsmiths	—	1	1	—	—	—	117	200	—	—
Oil mills	—	—	21	—	—	—	—	200	—	—
Brewing	—	20	27	—	—	—	250	300	—	—
Distilling	—	292	224	—	—	—	939	396	—	—
Calico-printing	—	3	—	—	—	—	—	—	—	—
Dye-wood mills	—	25	19	—	—	—	—	—	—	—
NORTH HOLLAND (excluding AMSTERDAM)										
Calico printing	—	9	4	—	—	—	110	27	—	—
Silk- and linen-weaving	—	2	2	—	—	—	300	65	—	—
Peat-digging	—	29	22	—	—	—	2,235	1,835	—	—
Brewing	—	—	—	—	9	—	—	—	—	153
Carpets	—	5	5	—	—	—	100	60	—	—
Bleaching (linen)	—	3	3	—	—	—	200	132	—	—
Bleaching (cotton)	—	7	7	—	—	—	111	51	—	—
Sail	—	24	20	—	—	—	106	48	—	—
Oil mills	—	119	109	—	—	—	260	240	—	—
GELDERLAND										
Paper	—	—	—	—	115	—	—	—	—	466 (d)

	1	2	3	4	5	6	7	8	9	10
UTRECHT (province)										
Calico-printing	54 (e)	—	—	—	—	1	—	—	—	—
Peat-digging	—	—	2,327	2,716	—	—	—	219	275	—
Bricks	—	—	332	406	—	—	—	17	18	—
Tiles	—	—	164	366	—	—	—	12	22	—
Buttons	—	—	150	300	—	—	—	1	1	—
Silk- and wool-weaving	—	—	150	400	—	—	—	1	1	—
FRIESLAND										
Peat-digging	—	—	4,400	334	—	—	—	—	—	—
Potters	—	—	137	563	—	—	—	37	43	—
Bricks	—	—	543	—	—	—	—	19	19	—
Wool-spinning	—	—	365	—	—	—	—	27	—	—
Distilling	—	—	86	—	—	—	—	71	—	—
Brewing	—	—	42	—	—	—	—	28	—	—
NORTH BRABANT										
Linen-weaving	953	—	—	—	—	839	—	—	—	—
Wool-spinning	570 (f)	—	—	—	—	26	—	—	—	—
Wool-weaving	2,930 (g)	—	—	—	—	126	—	—	—	—
TWENTE										
Linen-weaving	132	—	—	—	—	529	—	—	—	—
Table linen	60	—	—	—	—	5	—	—	—	—
Cotton-spinning	965 (h)	—	738	649	—	51	—	39	30	—
Bombazine	6,341 (i)	—	4,700	4,093	—	87	—	65	53	—
Wool-spinning	—	—	1,156	650	—	—	—	12	8	—
AMERSFOORT AND DISTRICT										
Wool-spinning	—	—	1,052	1,137	—	—	—	90	101	—
Bombazine	—	—	250	—	—	—	—	45	—	—
LEEUWARDEN										
Knitting	250 (j)	—	—	—	—	11	—	—	—	—

(d) Includes 132 children.   (e) Includes 16 children.   (f) Includes 2,020 children.   (g) Includes 90 children.

(h) Includes 511 children.   (i) Includes 150 children.   (j) Includes 869 children.

Chapter III

FREE TRADE AND PROTECTION IN
THE DUTCH NETHERLANDS

(a) The Propositions of 1751

The harmony of interest between those who sought income in various ways from the general market was not complete enough to prevent controversy in the Republic about commercial policy. Argument was in mercantilist terms, with but little theoretical elaboration. Each interest pressed its own claims in its own city. Only the gilds of cloth-merchants and cloth-finishers for a time created a formal provincial organization in Holland; though no doubt the larger capitalists of all kinds frequently discussed policy with correspondents in other cities. The Regents judged what was desirable for their own city as a whole, and then argued and bargained on a provincial or federal level. It was a conflict of interests, not of classes; and the demands made were similar to those heard in other countries. All industries desired high export duties on their raw materials, and those unable to compete in the export markets desired high import duties to protect their finished products. Since the raw materials of some were the finished products of others, the claims of industrialists often conflicted. They all desired measures to prevent the hinterland from securing either raw materials or foreign finished products. Controversy always concerned particular cases, and since all depended directly or indirectly on the general market, each group was easily persuaded that trade in general must be free and that its own need for protection was strictly exceptional. This prevented those who claimed more protection than the merchant oligarchy would allow from joining forces in an anti-commercial agitation. Thus, Leiden and Haarlem usually voted with Amsterdam and Rotterdam, and supported them loyally in their disputes against the inland provinces in the States General.[1] The decisions of the ruling oligarchy too were often inconsistent, and certainly not influenced by any theoretical free-trade principles. Thus in 1769 the brewers obtained the prohibition of the import of foreign beer, but in 1738 the pleas of the hatters for a protective duty elicited merely an exhortation to all Regents and officials to wear Dutch hats.[2]

There was no clear-cut division between industrial and commercial

[1] P. Geyl, *The Netherlands Divided* (London, 1936), p. 164.
[2] O. Pringsheim in *Staats- und Sozialwissenschaftliche Forschungen* (1890), pp. 35, 37.

interests in the Republic, and in the eighteenth century many industries dwindled without any serious political fight. The reason was that industrial organization was dominated by merchant capitalists. Every successful industrialist used his accumulated capital to seek commercial profits, and these could be obtained by dealing in foreign as well as native products. The Dutch general market had created a Dutch industrial apparatus more highly developed than home demand could justify, so industrial success and expansion were usually only possible by exporting. The main interest of industrial capitalists was therefore to keep down costs, and this was incompatible with protectionism as a general principle. In the eighteenth century, low costs could usually only be attained by importing foreign half-finished products, to be finished by Dutch craftsmen for the sake of Dutch skill, reputation and trade names. Thus the interests of merchant-industrialists and finishing craftsmen were in conflict with those of the rest of their industry. The native industries evolved into commercial ones and the proportion of Dutch labour in the final product diminished as technique improved elsewhere. Natural disadvantages made this inevitable, unless the Dutch were to become poor and self-sufficient, and to relapse to a lower level of economic organization. Dutch capitalists were blamed for sending funds abroad that could have given employment at home, but their reason for doing so was that they had learned by experience the unprofitability of industrial investments at home. The low Dutch rate of interest ensured at least that established industries were kept alive as long as any profit could be earned in them, and perhaps longer, if charitable motives intervened.

Dutch protectionists on the whole recognized the dependence of Holland on foreign trade, and framed their demands accordingly. Protectionist proposals in 1683, for instance, provided for the total and effective exclusion of foreign finished cloth and an import duty of 25% *ad valorem* on butter and fish; but only 8% on unfinished cloth, and still lower rates for the varieties most needed by the finishing industries, and for Silesian linens.[1] The exclusion of foreign linen, whether bleached or not, might have diminished the export of Dutch, since export consignments were mostly mixed.

The Dutch of the eighteenth century, unworried by theoretical inconsistencies, readily accepted the polite formula of agreement that trade must be free and both trade and industry must be protected. The merchants desired only such freedom as was necessary to themselves, and were willing to admit restrictions at the expense of foreigners. Their demand for freedom grew steadily more extensive, but this was due to practical

[1] O. Pringsheim, *loc. cit.* p. 90.

experience rather than to any change of outlook. As the Dutch general market declined in relation to the volume of international trade and as the competition of Hamburg grew fiercer, it became necessary to attract trade by concessions, and the merchants preferred that it should be at the expense of the customs revenue rather than of their profits and commissions. The majority of duties in the tariff enacted by the Placaat of 1725 were fiscal rather than protective, at about 5% both for imports and exports. The merchants were content with this so long as they were strong enough to ensure that their foreign correspondents bore the whole burden, except that which was passed on to the home consumer. Between 1730 and 1750, however, it became difficult to shift the burden on to foreigners, so the merchants looked for a way to ease it and discussed such measures as making Amsterdam a free port. At the same time, many industries found difficulty in exporting and therefore pressed for protection in the home market. A compromise seemed possible. If purely fiscal duties were abolished or reduced, increased protective duties might be conceded and the freedom of trade as a whole might be increased as well.

Such a compromise was attempted in 1751 by the 'Propositions' of William IV for a 'limited Porto Franco'. All duties were to be much reduced, except those on imports that competed with Dutch industry, or that were mainly consumed at home and so could bear a fiscal duty without injury to trade. Export duties on raw materials were not to be favoured as a form of protection, since they discouraged plentiful imports. In order that protective import duties might be reconciled with commercial interests, some system of bonding or drawbacks was to be introduced to exempt re-exports from the burden. These proposals, for more protection and freer trade, prefaced by a remarkably realistic assessment of the situation, were much praised, and continued for generations to be quoted in support of both causes. Nothing was done, however. One reason, no doubt, was the constitutional difficulty of changes. The inland provinces opposed the Propositions, owing to their traditional desire for the maximum customs revenue. Possibly merchants who would otherwise have seen material benefit in the scheme opposed it because the Stadtholder was the proposer. They may have had a reason which could not be publicly expressed; namely, that they had already established a limited *porto franco* by systematically declaring only about half the real value or quantity of their goods. This 'indulgence' was tolerated by the Admiralties because it had become necessary to commerce, and was distinguished from 'fraud', which was also said to be prevalent. The Propositions would have made the tariff more liberal on paper, but implied a strict enforcement: and although William IV postulated that the new duties on commercial goods must not merely be lower than the existing rates but substantially below those actually paid, the merchants may have been sceptical of this. The Propositions asserted that even the duties actually paid were causing diversion of trade, but the merchants may have known that other costs were more to blame, and so have preferred to retain a system which at least gave them a privilege over foreigners, who could only obtain the indulgence of the customs officers by employing a resident commission agent.[1]

Among the most outspoken opponents of the Propositions was the town of Campvere, which, its representatives admitted, would sink to a mere fishing village if it lost its privilege as the Scotch Staple. Scotsmen had the ancient right to import there free of duty woollen and linen goods, hides, salmon, tallow, oils, salt meat, butter and leather. If the duty on these were reduced below the level of the Placaat, the value of the privilege would be lost, and the Scots burghs and British government could no longer be expected to maintain their contract to prevent Scotsmen from carrying these goods to other Dutch ports. The staple had been inconveniently situated since the commercial decline of Zeeland. Auctions were no longer held there, but the goods were removed to Holland after the necessary legal formalities. Some Scotsmen already preferred to import regularly to Rotterdam and other ports, pay the ordinary duties, and in addition pay special dues to the Conservator of the Staple in consideration that he should withhold prosecution. The town authorities asked that if the Propositions took effect there should be no reduction in the duties on the staple goods, and argued that this must be to the interest of the Republic since 'the Scotch Staple subsisted while the trade of the Republic was in the most flourishing condition'. A committee of the States of Zeeland supported them:

The Scotch Court hath subsisted with consent and agreement of the sovereigns of this country, long before duties upon goods outward and inward were brought under the direction and government of the States General. And when these duties were given up to be regulated by them, it can never be supposed that any province or particular town, being members of the State, have renounced any of their privileges, which they were legally possessed of before, or that they have submitted or yielded to the taking of them away in prejudice of their own interest: far less can it be done without their consent....It cannot be reconciled with the principles of common equity and justice, that the town of Campvere, because of any pretended inconveniences to the public, and by the commission of some frauds alleged to arise from their aforesaid privileges:

[1] E. Luzac, *Hollands Rijkdom*, IV, 363, 375, 385–6; *Le commerce de la Hollande*, II, 301; III, 65–8.

that therefore they must be deprived of all their rights and liberties, and totally ruined. For besides these, there are several other customs and staple duties, that must be considered as no less hurtful to the common good, but they must, notwithstanding, be preserved and sustained as the privileges or prerogatives of respective provinces or towns.[1]

Whatever the motives of opposition, the vague hopes of the unprivileged classes that William IV would so reform the Republic's structure and policies as to halt the decay of its power and the impoverishment of many inhabitants, were disappointed on the economic side as well as the political.

(b) The woollen industry

The woollen industry was the subject of the most serious disputes over tariff policy. In the seventeenth century, the gilds of cloth merchants formed a national organization to face their suppliers, the English Merchant Adventurers, as equals and also effect the exclusion of interloping foreign cloth merchants from the Dutch markets. The Dutch cloth merchants were interested in the finishing of English white cloth, and not in the protection of Dutch spinners and weavers. They desired the exclusion of foreign dyed and finished cloths, and obtained this, with certain exceptions, in 1614 as a measure of reprisal against English restrictions on the export of unfinished cloth. This prohibition became part of the established order. It was supported by the woollen interest as a whole, and cloth merchants who circumvented it rarely spoke openly against it. It was retained in the Placaat of 1725, when the mildly protective specific import duties of the seventeenth century on combed wool, spun wool, and white unfinished cloth were reduced respectively to 1, 2 and 3 % *ad valorem*. The exceptions to the prohibition had perhaps originally admitted only cloths which did not compete with the Dutch finishing industry, but they made possible the mitigation of the law by interpretation, until only cloth dyed in the piece was excluded. Under a lax administration, this afforded small protection, though lawsuits about the character of particular cloths, and the confiscation of illegal imports, continued to occur. Leiden's agitation for strict enforcement was perhaps what prevented the prohibition from becoming a completely dead letter.[2]

The keenest protectionists in the eighteenth century were the masters of workshops for finishing cloth. They desired the free import of unfinished and the prohibition of all finished foreign cloth. The capitalists who employed them were pulled in different directions by their interests as

---

[1] J. Yair, *An Account of the Scotch Trade in the Netherlands* (London, 1776), pp. 312, 314, 316, 324, 337, 353, 370, 396.

[2] N. W. Posthumus, *De Leidsche lakenindustrie*, Deel II.

industrialists and as dealers in foreign goods. As Dutch costs grew less competitive, they imported more finished cloth and became less interested in the protection of the Dutch finishing industries. In 1753, the cloth merchants of Amsterdam and Rotterdam still opposed the admission of certain finished cloths which they were accustomed to import unfinished and themselves dye in the piece; but the list of broadcloths, bays and worsteds concerned was short, and they asked that all other finished, coloured cloths should be admitted at ½% *ad valorem*. They complained that the 2% duty on cloths dyed in the wool or the grain suggested in a draft tariff put forward by the Stadtholder's government would finally kill their trade in English cloth, which was now confined to the hinterland and would, they freely admitted, be dead already if the Placaat of 1725 had been 'exactly and impartially enforced'. The English cloths concerned, they added, were at least 15% cheaper than the Dutch equivalents, so that the 2% duty would have no protective value; and even a higher duty would achieve nothing, for in that case the Dutch employers would probably soon be compelled to grant an equivalent rise in wages.[1] Other merchants, with no industrial interests, had always opposed the prohibition of any foreign cloths.

The situation was complicated by the existence of the cloth industry of North Brabant. In most respects, the Lands of the Generality were treated as a conquered territory retained only for strategic reasons; they were excluded from the Dutch customs union and so, largely, from the benefits of the general market. The Dutch clothiers, however, desired the advantage of cheap labour and in 1687 obtained the admission of cloth from the Tilburg district as though it were Dutch. This encouraged the Leiden clothiers to send their wool, after it had been washed at Leiden, to Tilburg to be made up for finishing at Leiden. The Leiden authorities were puzzled how far to allow this necessary evil. In 1736, thanks to the prohibition of the import of blankets, they were able effectively to prohibit the finishing in Leiden of interloping blankets. At the same time, they forbade the removal from the city of unspun wool; but the only effect of this was that the clothiers sent their wool direct to Tilburg, and either had it washed there, or bought it already washed at Amsterdam or Rotterdam. In 1738, therefore, Leiden again permitted the removal of wool, on oath that it would be made up in Holland. In practice this meant total abandonment of the regulation, and the authorities resisted all pressure to revive it. They continued to oppose the admission of North Brabant cloth as Dutch. This concession was of value to North Brabant as giving some protection against Verviers and Aachen. As far as un-

[1] E. Luzac, *Hollands Rijkdom*, IV, Bijlage C and D.

finished cloths were concerned, it did little damage to Leiden, since the import duties were too low to be useful to her. On the other hand, the prohibition of cloth dyed in the piece at least ensured that certain cloths from the hinterland destined for export through Holland, especially to the Levant, had to be dyed and finished in the United Provinces, and this was of real value to Leiden, even though the varieties concerned were not very important in the home market. The development of finishing industries at Tilburg as well as at Verviers was therefore damaging and caused Leiden to agitate more strenuously against all concessions to North Brabant.[1]

In Holland, a provincial organization of the cloth-finishing gilds had existed since the seventeenth century. It was originally dominated by the capitalist employers and its purpose had been concerted action in each town against combinations of journeymen. In the eighteenth century, the industrial activity of the cloth merchants diminished and the gilds came to represent only the small masters. From 1737, they took up the fight for protection, and demanded the prohibition of all imports of finished cloth by sea and high duties on those from the hinterland, including North Brabant. This agitation, together with discussion among some merchants about the desirability of making Amsterdam a free port, provoked the official inquiry and 'Propositions' of 1751. The gilds also kept a watch to prevent any finishing of cloth in Holland outside the walls of towns and, rather less energetically, pressed for the suppression of rural weaving, lest it should lead to finishing as well. They were careful, however, to make it clear that they were opposed only to finishing in North Brabant, not to weaving there. Their efforts achieved little. By 1790, the gilds in Dordrecht, Gouda and Haarlem had died with the industry. They were not even in agreement on precisely which processes should be protected. In 1741, the journeymen in Leiden refused to handle cloth shorn abroad, though not objecting to that shorn in North Brabant. The majority of the masters replied that foreign shearing was cheaper, so that if Leiden refused the cloth in question, she would merely lose the finishing of it altogether. The town government agreed, but suggested that the cloth ought not to receive Leiden markings. In the end, the masters, though supported by police measures, accepted the journeymen's demand; but probably the increasing quantities of shorn cloth imported to Leiden continued to include German and Belgian as well as that of North Brabant.[2]

---

[1] N. W. Posthumus, *Bronnen*, VI, 27.
[2] N. W. Posthumus, *Bronnen*, VI, 458–88; N. W. Posthumus, *Bescheiden betreffende de provinciale organisatie der Hollandsche lakenbereiders* (*Werken uitgegeven door het Historisch Genootschap te Utrecht*, 1917), pp. 133–8, 141, 174, 182, 187, 207, 229, 243.

The protection of the Dutch finishing industries extended to the inward as well as outward trade of the hinterland, for the export duty on unfinished cloth was higher than on Dutch-finished, and this encouraged Dutch finishing of English cloth for the hinterland. By the mid-eighteenth century, the Dutch industries became too weak for such protection to be effective; English merchants, furthermore, were financing exports by other routes and English houses at Rotterdam were learning to mitigate the severity of Dutch customs duties. The lack of capital in the hinterland, however, implied greater possibility of effective protection in the outward trade. If goods were sent to Hamburg or Ostend to avoid Dutch territory, transport part of the way was by land. Goods for the Levant were likely to wait longer than in Dutch ports for cargo space, and might have to sail under a flag less well protected than the Dutch against Algerian pirates. The Leiden shearmen, and those masters who agreed with them, used such arguments to prove that, if the Dutch refused to handle cloth shorn in the hinterland, all the cloth for maritime export would be shorn in Holland. The other masters, and the merchants of Amsterdam, replied realistically that the result would rather be to foster Levant trade at Hamburg and Ostend, since Dutch ships would soon respond to any persistent demand there for freightage, and thus to injure Holland as a general market for cotton, figs, goats' hair and so on, and as a collecting centre for outward cargoes to the Levant. In that case, 'the Leiden manufacturers concerned with these types of cloth would be done for'.[1]

As the use of Dutch labour for improving foreign cloths diminished and tended to be confined to the purely commercial work of pressing, packing and carrying, it became unprofitable to handle them except at Amsterdam and Rotterdam. The number of Leiden capitalists interested in foreign trade accordingly diminished. Those who remained in the woollen industry mostly supplied coarse cloth for the home market, and especially for purchasers amenable to pressure and influence, such as the governors of orphanages. Leiden accordingly became thoroughly protectionist, and any inhabitants who voiced the usual arguments for the primacy of the commercial interest were reproached for subservience to Amsterdam and disloyalty to their own city. A vigorous agitation began in 1791 and, for the first time, took the aspect of a general protectionist movement; its leaders claimed to speak not merely for the cloth finishers but for the whole woollen industry, and sought to act in concert with other industrial interests.

One of Leiden's demands in 1791 was for higher export duties on raw

[1] N. W. Posthumus, *Bronnen*, VI, 469–88.

wool. Leiden had often made a similar demand in the seventeenth century, but the town authorities had dropped it about 1750, owing perhaps to the Austrian government's efforts to develop Ostend as a port for Belgian industry. By 1791, much Spanish wool was indeed passing the Dutch market by and going direct to the French, Belgian, German and English industries; more German wool was being made up in Germany instead of coming to the Dutch market; and Dutch wool was being sent, often on Dutch account, to France for working, or had been at least until the recent revolutionary disturbances. The Dutch woollen industry could no longer see its best hope in the continuance of the Dutch general market in wool. The Leiden authorities therefore pressed for a 25% export duty at least on Dutch wool, a measure which would have hurt the agricultural interest more than the commercial. Leiden entrepreneurs who still sent wool abroad for working, and especially those who produced fine cloths for export, were doubtful of the wisdom of this demand, but supported it in the hope that the protectionist agitation would win benefits for all branches of the industry.[1]

Probably the protectionists of 1791 did not really hope to win drastic changes in the Dutch commercial system at the expense of foreign trade, but only secondary, less controversial concessions. When their agitation led to practical bargaining, they pressed the authorities in Holland to ensure that the Admiralty, the military contingent and the public charities of the Province, all who received official salaries or pensions and their families, and the East India Company, should use only cloth made in Holland, or at least finished in Holland and woven in Dutch territory; and to obtain from other provinces similar measures in favour of Dutch cloth. Subsidies were demanded for cloth prepared in towns in Holland under municipal supervision.

These proposals involved a difficulty. Leiden had a system of markings to show that each stage of production had been controlled and inspected for quality. Foreign cloth finished at Leiden received a special mark. Foreign finished cloth which entered Leiden was also marked, in order to show that toll had been paid and to facilitate searching for cloth withheld from supervision. This affixing of the town arms helped the export of foreign cloth as Leiden manufacture. In the late eighteenth century, counterfeit markings were also commonly used, by manufacturers who wished to avoid irksome controls, and by those who wished to pass off foreign cloth as Dutch, especially for military supplies. In 1778, the Leiden authorities were compelled to issue special certificates to prove that

[1] N. W. Posthumus, *Bronnen*, VI, 162, 267; N. W. Posthumus, *De provinciale organisatie der Hollandsche lakenbereiders*, p. 250.

cloth was really what its markings pretended. The concessions demanded in 1791 were to apply only to cloth thus certified by a municipal authority.[1]

The agitation of 1791 caused the Stadtholder's government to hold a serious inquiry into the means to 'quicken new life in the miserably weakened body' of the Dutch economy, but nothing was done. The challenge to the predominance of commerce was but feeble. The protectionists did not engage the free traders in a general controversy. Rather, all negotiations continued to yield a polite formula of agreement in principle, and a deadlock in regard to any practical proposals for reform.[2]

(c) The 'Batavians'

The 'Batavian' revolutionaries of 1795 were not anti-commercial, but they sought the support of all who were discontented. Like the adherents of William IV in 1748, they were inspired by vague and contradictory hopes. They blamed the old régime for exclusive pre-occupation with commerce, and took up the argument that new sources of wealth must be sought to replace the decayed branches of the general market. They proclaimed a new era for agriculture and industry, a new and more genuine harmony of interests, in which none should be sacrificed to others as the cloth industry had been to the general market.

The woollen interest pressed its claims with new confidence. 'We have had enquiries before', wrote a Leiden manufacturer, 'but the commercial party always brought them to nought; under former governments, only the merchants had anything to hope for.'[3] Among the leading 'Batavians', P. Vreede, a Leiden clothier who had moved to Tilburg in 1790, was a specially active protectionist. Other interests pressed conflicting claims. The maltsters asked for a high import duty on malt, which was much opposed by the brewers and distillers. In fact, the old difficulties still impeded practical decisions. No general revision of the 1725 tariff was attempted, although more protectionist amendments were enacted. In 1802, the prohibition of foreign dyed cloths was renewed and a strict interpretation was promised. This was the chief victory of the protectionists, and it provoked a vigorous counter-agitation by the merchants.

Vreede was theorist, and he proposed national self-sufficiency as an ideal. He conceded the necessity of retaining the general market as long as possible; but so far as cloth was concerned he doubted whether it still existed. The traditional trade in English cloth having vanished, he supposed

[1] N. W. Posthumus, *Bronnen*, vi, 573.
[2] A.R.A., Goldberg 221 (iv)—reports to van Spiegel in 1793; *Ged.* v, 311; D'Alphonse, *Aperçu*, p. 250.
[3] A.R.A., Goldberg 221 (iv)—Van Heukelom to Goldberg 23 Oct. 1800.

that the Amsterdam agitation for free trade in cloth was the work of foreigners and Dutchmen who imported for the home market, and that respectable First Hand merchants had only joined it from fear that Vreede and his friends were hostile to the general market as a whole and especially to the still valuable trade in Spanish wool. This he denied. He was not hostile to the First Hand, only to the Dutch shopkeepers who evaded the old laws by retailing foreign dyed cloths and thus robbed Dutch families of their bread. Industry could be protected without injury to the First Hand if the general market could be separated from ordinary importation by a bonding system, with special low duties for goods that came merely to be re-exported. To the merchants' argument that the decline of Dutch native industry was natural and inevitable, Vreede replied that England and France had even created new industries by protection, whereas the Dutch woollen industry was still as well equipped as it had been during its prosperity before the Peace of Westphalia.[1]

When the war was renewed after the Peace of Amiens, the Dutch Government was moderate and no longer inclined to revolutionary experiments. Its main concern was to keep Dutch trade alive despite the prospect of a long war, and it no longer assumed that this aim was compatible with protectionist measures denounced as ruinous by the merchants. A few recent measures were revoked. The import duty on nails, for instance, was reduced in 1807 to the former level. The remaining protective measures had little effect. Even in 1802 Leiden and Tilburg complained that the customs administration was treating the new prohibition of foreign dyed cloth in the traditional manner, and that the government seemed to have enacted it merely for show, without any real intention of enforcement.[2] The government ignored these complaints, and in 1803 the Prussian ambassador reported that the merchants of Amsterdam and Rotterdam had finally 'won the fight between commerce and the cloth-makers'.[3] The manufacturers complained that English coloured cloth was impudently displayed even at Leiden itself.[4] It was probably true. When British cloth exports direct to Holland were interrupted in 1795, those to Germany at once increased by an equivalent amount.[5] War-time smuggling from Germany was long remembered in Groningen as a source of unexampled prosperity, by ships-carpenters, for instance, who built small vessels for the purpose.[6]

[1] P. Vreede, *Vervolg der proeve om...'t fabrijkwezen te vereenigen met...den koop-handel, zeevaart en landbouw* (The Hague, 1803), pp. 6-20, 37-40, 58.

[2] P. Vreede, *loc. cit.* p. 58.

[3] *Ged.* IV, 192.   [4] *Ged.* IV, 408, 582; V, 404.

[5] D. McPherson, *Annals*, IV, 489.

[6] J. van Lennep, *Dagboek*, pp. 97-101.

The King of Holland, Louis Bonaparte, sympathized with the protectionists:

Why are our manufacturers so inferior? We need a general directorate to encourage good enterprises and weed out bad ones, to excite emulation by effective incentives without permitting one enterprise to harm another, to encourage products whose raw materials are found here or in our colonies.... We cannot hope much from treaties of commerce, for influence is now more than ever proportionate to power,...so the first thing to do is to prohibit all foreign imports that compete against our industries and to relieve the latter of taxation.[1]

He did not do much to put these ideas into effect. They were incompatible with his main purpose, to protect Dutch trade and smuggling by passive resistance to his brother's policies of economic warfare. Gogel, his Finance Minister, was loyal to the commercial interest.

After 1803, the protectionists felt that commerce was again supreme, and modified their demands accordingly. They made little effort to secure the continuance of the prohibition of foreign dyed cloths when it expired in 1808. Instead, a compromise was reached in 1809 by a combined committee of merchants and cloth-manufacturers:[2]

1. The import duty on all kinds of cloth should not exceed 5% *ad valorem*.
2. Manufacturers should always be represented at official discussions, in order that industry and commerce might understand each other better.
3. A system of national markings should be introduced, the army and other public institutions should use only cloth marked as wholly Dutch in origin, and all citizens should be exhorted to do likewise.
4. Exports should be encouraged by treaties of commerce. Consuls and colonial officials should collect useful information for manufacturers.
5. There should be general subsidies for manufacturers in proportion to their wage costs, and special subsidies for the introduction of foreign machines.

Thus the woollen industry exacted tribute in return for abandoning its demand for tariff protection. The government feared that subsidies might encourage manufacturers to delay necessary technical changes which it expected to follow from the abolition of the gilds, but the subsidies for machines were intended to remedy this conservatism. The annexation of the Kingdom of Holland by Napoleon in 1810 prevented any action to carry out these proposals.

[1] *Ged.* v, 425.
[2] A.R.A., Goldberg 221 (iv)—report of Prof. Tollius, 1809.

After the 'Uprising' of 1813, the commercial interest attempted to reassert its supremacy. The merchants demanded a return to the wisdom of their ancestors, as embodied in the Placaat of 1725, and the revocation of the protectionist measures introduced since 1795. They petitioned, for instance, against the 6% import duty on hosiery,

enacted in 1797 at the demand of a few petitioners who hoped to start or extend factories, or perhaps only to celebrate the exaggerated spirit of that time, whereby the greatest advantages of commerce and of the commonwealth were sacrificed without the least attention to the warnings of many interested and well-informed persons against the destructive flood. Experience soon showed however that such novel undertakings did not yield the measureless profits foreseen by heated minds; almost all the factories then set up with great capital outlay quickly disappeared.[1]

The woollen interest was content to press for the fulfilment of the 'friendly compromise' of 1809. Vreede and others petitioned for subsidies, national markings and government contracts. 'In accordance with the spirit of the times'—a phrase which covered recognition of the need to placate British public opinion for diplomatic reasons—they even agreed that foreign cloth should be admitted to the Dutch colonies when they were restored, and merely asked that it be excluded from government supplies. This earned a marginal comment from Goldberg, the Minister of Commerce, who supported the commercial interest, 'completely liberal, could not be better'.[2]

The impoverishment of Holland during the French time discredited the experiments of the 'Batavians'. Commerce, it seemed, could not be replaced as the source of urban prosperity, and a return to tradition seemed to offer the best hope of its revival. Van Hogendorp, the leader of the 'Uprising', proclaimed: 'The sea is open. Commerce will revive.' On this promise were focused the hopes of all who had shared in the old harmony of interests. The restoration of the Placaat of 1725 was therefore inevitable. Van Hogendorp wished to restore it innocent of 'Batavian' amendments, but William I insisted that those in force in 1810 should mostly be retained.

[1] A.R.A., Goldberg 130—J. F. Schmole and others to the Sovereign Prince, 7 May 1814.
[2] A.R.A., Goldberg 221 (i)—P. Vreede and others to the Sovereign Prince, Oct. 1814, and the Governors of the Lakenhalle at Leiden to the Sovereign Prince, 20 Dec. 1813.

(d) 'The spirit of the Placaat'

Experience after 1813 forced the commercial interest to re-examine its policy. It had adopted the Placaat of 1725 as a rallying cry to express its demand for as much freedom of trade as the general market needed; but conditions had evidently changed since 1725, for even duties that had not been amended now proved irksome.[1] An explanation was easily found. The wisdom of the forefathers, it now appeared, lay less in the actual terms of the Placaat than in the manner in which those terms had been systematically disregarded. The Placaat laid down that Dutch commerce and navigation must be protected and the honest merchant tenderly treated; customs officers were threatened with dismissal if they acted otherwise. Dutch merchants accordingly claimed as a right that inconvenient duties should be 'winked away', as they had been in the eighteenth century when the Admiralties vied with one another in laxity of customs administration.

One purpose of this 'spirit of the Placaat' was to protect Dutch merchants by preventing direct trade by foreigners over Dutch territory. Only resident merchants knew how to handle the customs officials, so foreign merchants found it advisable to employ Amsterdam commission agents and use the complicated services of the general market in the conventional manner. Such was Gogel's explanation of the relatively high duties included in the Placaat: 'It had indeed its rigorous sides, but they were turned against the foreigner, while its loopholes were all to the advantage of our own merchants.'[2]

A customs official of the old régime, who had studied the archives, asserted in a pamphlet in 1816 that this development had been deliberately planned. The growth of English and French trade, he wrote, had convinced the authorities at the beginning of the eighteenth century that customs duties could no longer be regarded as a tax on foreigners for the privilege of access to the general market, and that fiscal concepts must be altered accordingly; foreigners must be enticed from rival markets, and the honest Dutch merchant must therefore be given such latitude that, by paying less duty than the foreigner supposed, he could offer apparently better terms than merchants elsewhere. What the State lost by thus allowing the under-declaration of goods would be made up by the increased volume of trade. In order to carry out the policy, the customs had to be taken out of the hands of farmers and entrusted to the Admiralties,

---

[1] H. H. Huijbers, 'De zee is open, de koophandel herleeft', in *Sociaal-Economische Geschriften* (1919).
[2] *Ged.* VIII (2), 226.

against the strenuous opposition of the inland provinces which desired to get the maximum revenue, by granting the farms to the highest bidders. The Placaat achieved what was intended; and it therefore became undesirable that the official rates of duty should be reduced, for the Dutch merchant would then lose part of his concealed preferences. That, the pamphleteer believed, was the true reason for the shelving of the Propositions of 1751, though it was kept out of the records. He recommended that the benefits of Dutch free trade should still be partly reserved for Dutch merchants:

Some say that it is undignified for a Government to enact laws which it deliberately intends to carry out only in part. But it is not really so strange that the Government, while making foreigners pay in full, should remit a part for our own commerce, in the general interest, for the good of the commission trade, and in order that the honest merchant may come to market with the smuggler.[1]

Dutch merchants were wrong in supposing that foreign clients could long be kept ignorant of such practice. They were, in fact, a subject of complaint by the 1760's, despite Dutch secretiveness. Dutch merchants supposed that by disguising their profits they could attract clients, but when foreigners realized that they could not rely on the accuracy of such items in their accounts as customs and weighage duties, warehousing costs, and tares, they gave it as a reason for transferring their business to Hamburg, where they knew what commission they were really paying and did not feel always that they were being defrauded.[2]

The difficulties of Dutch trade in 1816 were nevertheless explained away as the result of the 'French spirit' in which the restored Placaat of 1725 was administered by customs officials who had learned under Napoleon to carry out regulations literally. Gogel contrasted this with the time when he, as Finance Minister, had kept alive the 'spirit of the Placaat' despite the French and preserved a healthy Dutch trade, even in wartime, until 1808.[3] But although many cherished the 'spirit of the Placaat' as a 'trade secret' that could still be valuable,[4] others, including Van Hogendorp, admitted that the principles of the new age demanded an exact and honorable application of the laws.[5] Falck, a minister who had

---

[1] *Knuttel* 24295 (J. Scheltema), pp. 13–20, 31, 66, 70–1; *Ged.* VIII (3), 385–8.
[2] *Le commerce de la Hollande*, II, 364–7; III, 70–1.
[3] *Mem. en cor.* p. 65.
[4] J. van Ouwerkerk de Vries, *Verhandeling over de oorzaken van het verval des Nederlandschen handels en de middelen tot herstel* (Haarlem, 1827), p. 121.
[5] W. L. D. van den Brink, *Bijdrage tot de kennis van den economischen toestand van Nederland in de jaren 1813–16* (Amsterdam, 1916), p. 28.

had experience of French administrative methods under King Louis, described the 'spirit of the Placaat' as 'a malpractice best forgotten for the honour of our ancestors'.[1]

(e) The transit problem

In the eighteenth century, when the Scheldt was closed, and the free trade policy of the north German ports was partly frustrated by the complicated frontiers of Germany, which, though not permitting effective mercantilist barriers, resulted in the multiplication of fiscal exactions, much of the trade of the hinterland could be forced into the channels of the Dutch general market. A system of bonding and low transit duties would have provided a way of escape, so the merchants did not welcome the suggestion of some protectionists that such a system would make high customs duties innocuous. The merchants were willing to give Dutch industry a preference in the Belgian, German and Swiss markets by obstructing the passage of raw materials and foreign finished products across the inland frontiers; and were anxious that the commercial industries they themselves invested in should have such protection. Clearly, however, if the sum of the Dutch import and export duties exceeded the difference in transport and other costs between the Dutch and the alternative routes, trade would be diverted. In that case, either the duties must be reduced, or a special transit duty would become a necessary evil. The commercial interest did not oppose the institution in 1688 of a special duty for transit trade with the southern Netherlands, to be equal in each case either to the import or to the export duty, whichever were the higher. In 1752, the same concession was extended to certain German goods, mainly of iron and linen, in transit to Spain. This was intended to increase the cargoes for Spain from Dutch ports, in competition with Ostend and Hamburg.[2] In general, however, the Dutch merchants preferred that in such cases the import and export duties should be reduced: if foreign merchants could not be compelled to use the general market, they should at least not be encouraged by a special transit system to arrange with other foreigners for direct trade through Dutch territory.

In 1802, the 'Batavian', Appelius, believed that the general market could never again be the main source of Dutch prosperity and that direct trading could not be wholly prevented in the nineteenth century. As a corollary to 'Batavian' protectionism, he introduced facilities for the bonding of

---

[1] *Ged.* IX (2), 879.
[2] *Ged.* v, 668; J. Ratté, *De Nederlandse doorvoerpolitiek en de vrije vaart op de internationale Rijn* (Rotterdam, 1952), pp. 18, 27–8.

transit goods and their exemption from either the export or the import duty, whichever were the lower. This unimpressive concession was denounced by the commercial interest as revolutionary folly. Gogel, however, retained it as a necessary evil for so long as it should be a mitigation to the Continental System. The Rotterdam Chamber of Commerce, which in 1806 was still urging the abolition of the transit system and confident that trade could thus be held in the channels of the general market, in 1811, when the French spirit had triumphed in the customs administration, asked for easier bonding, in the hope that this would at least help to check the fall in the value of real property such as warehouses and wine cellars.[1]

After the war, it was still found impossible to abolish the transit system, although both Van Hogendorp and William I disliked it. The Allied occupation authority in Belgium reverted provisionally to the former Austrian policies, which included a liberal transit system. In the new competitive conditions of the nineteenth century, the Dutch government, unable now to close the Scheldt, was forced in 1814 to reduce its transit duties to half the higher of the normal duties. The Dutch merchants, of course, argued that since the Dutch government would now have influence again in Belgian affairs, Belgian transit policy might be brought into line with the principles of the Placaat of 1725; but a few years' experience showed that in any case a special transit system would be needed unless import and export duties could be reduced, in practice if not in theory, considerably below the level of the Placaat. The merchants' attack on the transit system therefore took the form of agitation for a general tariff reduction that would make it unnecessary. They recalled that in 1807 the import duty on nails had been reduced in order 'to revive trade on Dutch account in this article, which had recently been dispatched through our territory only in transit to Spain and Portugal'.[2]

In 1814, the Amsterdam Chamber of Commerce asked for a general downward revision of duties. It foresaw that Hamburg, Bremen and Antwerp would be much more dangerous competitors than in the eighteenth century, and feared that Emden, now it had fallen into 'English' (i.e. Hanoverian) hands, might become a distributing centre for English merchandise.[3] Gogel agreed that Dutch legislation must take account of changed circumstances, for Amsterdam prices were no longer locally determined and dominant in international trade, but depended on

[1] *Ged.* v, 637, 676; J. H. Appelius, *De staatsomwenteling van 1795* (Leiden, 1801), pp. 224–5.
[2] A.R.A., Goldberg 130—Canneman to the Minister of the Interior, 4 April 1814.
[3] A.R.A., Goldberg 130; B. C. E. Zwart, *De Kamer van Koophandel en Fabrieken te Amsterdam...1811–1911* (Amsterdam, 1911), pp. 65, 73.

the interaction of London, Hamburg and other markets, so that it was no longer foreigners only who bore the weight of the Dutch customs system.[1] Rotterdam was largely concerned with English trade and, it was estimated, three-quarters of her business was on commission;[2] so her merchants had every reason to be aware of the increasing need for speed, simplicity and low costs in commerce, and criticized the Dutch customs system accordingly. One of them, Smeer, addressed the government vigorously in 1814: 'The English do not expect troublesome formalities in a country famed for its moderate system. It is not surprising that they send their next consignment to Hamburg, Bremen, Antwerp or Emden.' Yet, at the same time, he bitterly opposed the idea that low transit duties could win back trade from other ports, and seemed unaware of any danger that existing Dutch trade might be lost unless allowed to transform itself into transit trade. The transit trade, he said, degraded the Dutch commission agent into a mere dispatch-clerk, prevented him from using and improving his special knowledge and skill, and robbed the Second Hand, the brokers, the weighers, and so on, of their livelihood. No true Dutchmen could have introduced a system so contrary to that of the Placaat, and in fact it had not been freely adopted in 1802 but imposed by France for the sake of her Rhineland territories.

The special character of our trade lies in the speculative purchase by the Second Hand of goods imported here or sent on commission, which are then stored until the Germans, Swiss or others come to market. It was our own active trade that made us the staple market of the world, and it can do so again. But if the Germans, Swiss and others are given the opportunity to place orders directly in England, France, Spain, Portugal and America, what will be left for the Dutch merchant to do?[3]

In 1816, the Rotterdam Chamber of Commerce grudgingly admitted that unless drastic tariff reform could be accomplished a transit system was necessary, but added that bonding should be strict and should be refused for goods requiring Dutch warehousing as well as transport facilities.[4] The whole commercial interest agreed that in any case the transit duty must be as high as was possible without driving trade away. Calculation

[1] *Mem. en cor.* p. 78.

[2] *Knuttel* 24691 (F. Frets, 1818), p. 11.

[3] A.R.A., Goldberg 130. According to J. Ratté (*op. cit.* p. 51), the die-hard attitude of the Rotterdammers was due to confidence that traffic which passed their way would continue even if the transit system were abolished, since the Rhine was still indispensable for much of the hinterland. Amsterdam felt more strongly the need for low duties on all goods that passed through the Netherlands.

[4] W. L. Groeneveld Meyer, *De tariefwetgeving van het koninkrijk der Nederlanden 1816–1819* (Rotterdam, 1924), p. 72.

showed that a general rate between 2.20 and 3.00 florins per 100 kg. would not be too high, since it was rather less than the difference in transport costs between the Rotterdam and the Hamburg route for goods going from the Channel to the German interior.[1] Antwerp could be ignored in this calculation, in view of the impending fiscal unification of the whole Netherlands. The commercial interest aimed at reducing the sum of the import and export duties to this level for most commodities. In that case, foreigners, though not compelled to use the general market, would at least be given no inducement to avoid it, and would no doubt learn by experience that the old ways were best. If, on the other hand, import and export duties remained high but transit duties were unnecessarily low; or if, in the definitive regulation of the navigation of the Rhine called for by the Treaty of Vienna, the Great Powers, by a rigorous interpretation of the Treaty, forced the Netherlands to give up its right to levy a sufficient duty on river traffic; then indeed old Holland would be ruined, for she would lose the main advantage of her location, namely her trade, active or on commission, with the continental interior.[2]

Some Dutch firms, by adopting new methods, found profit in the transit system. The trade in English cotton yarn for German industry, which arose towards the end of the eighteenth century, rather than adapt itself to Dutch ways, had always used the North German ports. Having a temporary advantage over their German competitors in early 1814, some Amsterdam firms tried to take up the trade, but found it impossible under the Dutch tariff. In 1815, they secured administrative action which enabled them to hold goods in 'fictitious' bond, unsealed in their own warehouses, and diminished both the cost and the delay of passing them through the customs. The trade increased to a value of 2,000,000 florins in the first year, though this was still small compared to Hamburg's 25,000,000. The difference in transport costs was said to be barely in Holland's favour, for the German manufacturers could not give as much as six weeks' notice of their requirements, so river transport was too slow. The Amsterdam firms therefore declared that a duty above $\frac{1}{2}$% would be fatal; conditions, they explained, had altered in the last thirty years, and competition had become so severe that they had to be content with very low profits and make good by a large and frequent turn-over. Trade of the old Second Hand type being in this case impossible, they supposed that there could be no objection to their methods or to the low transit

[1] W. L. Groeneveld Meyer, *op. cit.* p. 100; Ged. VIII (3), 270; F. A. van Hall, *Onpartijdige beschouwing van den toestand des koophandels binnen de Vereenigde Neder-landen* (Amsterdam, 1819–20), p. 153.
[2] *Ged.* VIII (ii), p. 51.

duty they needed.[1] The older, and still very much predominant, species of Dutch merchant regarded such trade with horror. Such were the Amsterdam merchants who in 1836 still considered a railway to Cologne unnecessary because their forefathers had desired no such speed and had welcomed the interruption of transport in the winter as an opportunity for making out accounts and balancing their books, and because merchants and shopkeepers had no right to be in business unless they had enough capital to practice the art of speculation and buy beyond immediate needs.[2]

In 1816, most Dutch merchants met the challenge of the new age in the spirit of fifteenth-century Venice[3] rather than of nineteenth-century Hamburg; they desired a *porto franco* which was limited by all possible restrictions in favour of Dutch commercial profits and traditions.

[1] A.R.A., Staatssec. 12 Feb. 1824, no. 67, pt. IB, 15 Feb. 1820 (address by Jaeger and others of Amsterdam, 1 Feb. 1820).

[2] T. P. van der Kooy, *Hollands stapelmarkt en haar verval*, p. 80.

[3] J. W. Thomson, *Economic and Social History of Europe in the later Middle Ages* (New York, 1931), p. 204.

Chapter IV

THE DUTCH EXCISE PROBLEM

The tariff question was not the most important or the most keenly contested point at issue between commerce and industry. Of more importance was the question why costs were too high and how they could be so reduced as to enable Dutch industries to compete in the export markets. Many supposed that the native industries had been ruined, perhaps unavoidably, by the effect on the cost of living and therefore on wages of the high taxation necessitated by the Republic's position in Europe. Adam Smith for example:

It ought to be remembered that, when the wisest government has exhausted all the proper subjects of taxation, it must, in cases of urgent necessity, have recourse to improper ones. The wise republic of Holland has upon some occasions been obliged to have recourse to taxes as inconvenient as the greater part of those of Spain.... In Holland the heavy taxes upon the necessaries of life have ruined, it is said, their principal manufactures, and are likely to discourage gradually even their fisheries and their trade in ship-building.[1]

In the days of Dutch prosperity, however, a contrary effect was often attributed to the system of taxation:

The Dutch have brought their poor under such regulations that there is scarcely a beggar to be seen in the whole United Provinces; for, that no other nation may underwork them, they take all imaginable care to keep all materials for manufactures as low as possible, and lay their taxes upon such things as the people cannot subsist without; as eatables, firing, etc., very well knowing that cold and hunger will make people work to supply their necessities.[2]

Freedom from inconvenient taxation was always a major item in the programme of the commercial interest. In order that commerce should be free, it was necessary that revenue should be raised mainly by taxes on real property, foodstuffs, and luxury. This did not mean that the merchants were unwilling to pay their share. On the contrary, Holland assumed more than her fair share of the burden and purchased thereby the acquiescence of the inland provinces in the political leadership and fiscal

---

[1] *The Wealth of Nations* (Everyman ed.), II, 387, 411.
[2] J. Gee, *The Trade and Navigation of Great Britain considered...a new Edition with notes by a Merchant* (London, 1767), p. 72.

policies of the merchants. Holland even established a tradition, unusual at the time, that honour required honest payment of taxes on real property and personal expenditure. This tradition did not, however, apply to taxes that touched business interests, for such taxes were tolerated only as a necessary evil, which should be mitigated by the ingenuity of the tax-payer and the benevolence of the revenue authorities.

There was no persistent opposition to this system from the agricultural interests, partly because until the nineteenth century the inland provinces were undertaxed and partly on account of laxity in the collection of all except the Land Tax in rural areas. The industrial opposition was naturally more serious, since the excises on meat, salt, flour and fuel, the capitation and window taxes, and the multifarious municipal taxes were supposed to cause high labour costs. Partly in order to compensate urban industry for this situation, the governments supported the efforts of the gilds to suppress rural industry; but this was of little use, when no protection was given against foreign industry. The difficulty of making any fiscal change prevented the governments of the eighteenth century from attempting to relieve the burden on wages. Even the idea of special tax reliefs for workers in depressed industries was rejected, on the ground that the workers might not understand the need for an equivalent reduction in wages. The only convenient remedy, one to which the commercial interest had no objection in principle, seemed to be the granting of subsidies to manufacturers to offset the direct and indirect taxes borne by their workers; but this was never attempted on a large enough scale to have much result.[1]

The merchants, afraid that any remission of existing taxes would lead to inconvenient new imposts, argued that high industrial costs were due not to taxation but to inefficiency, and those who were influenced by contemporary economic thought blamed the gilds, the municipal regulations, and the prohition of rural industry. 'Batavians' such as Gogel, who were loyal to the traditional primacy of commerce, believed that industry could be sufficiently encouraged by the abolition of restrictions; others proposed subsidies for progressive enterprises, and perhaps, as an exceptional measure, patents of monopoly.[2] Thus technique could soon be raised to the English level, and only incompetent manufacturers would languish. Entrepreneurs who hoped for subsidies flattered this confidence. One Leiden clothier, who boasted that his son had studied machines in England, promised great results, if he received adequate subsidies, and was

---

[1] A.R.A., Goldberg 221, Report to van Spiegel, Sept. 1793; *Ged.* v (i), 311; F. J. B. d'Alphonse, *Aperçu*, p. 250.
[2] C. Wiskerke, *De afschaffing der gilden*, p. 172.

protected against detraction and conspiracy by less energetic manufacturers, and if farmers were compelled by heavy penalties to breed more
sheep.[1]

In general, it does not appear that high real wages in Dutch towns can
be blamed for the weakness of Dutch industry, though no doubt owing
to lack of mobility of labour they were high in some cases. In so far as
labour costs were to blame, therefore, the cause was taxation and the
necessary expenses of urban life. The excise problem therefore attracted
the attention of those 'Batavians' who recognized as inevitable at least
a partial decline of the general market and who accordingly desired a re-
orientation of the economy and the commercial policy of the Republic.
Among them was Appelius, Gogel's chief rival as 'Batavian' financial
expert.

The heavy taxation in the old Republic was largely due to legitimate
public debts, which were widely held by the middle classes and by charitable institutions. The 'Batavians' had no wish to repudiate these debts,
and could not avoid the new burdens due to revolution and war; so the
question at issue between Gogel and Appelius concerned the method, not
the amount, of taxation. This question was the most fiercely contested
matter of economic policy in the early years of the nineteenth century,
when the Dutch were striving to preserve the precarious remnants of their
prosperity. The British Ambassador reported in 1802:

> While passing through France and Flanders the traveller is rendered
> melancholy by the desolate state of the houses of the great, and is impor-
> tuned and disgusted by the swarms of mendicants that infest the roads, in
> Holland he perceives no vestiges of the ravages of war, no marks of
> a stagnated industry. With the exception of a few individuals of the
> lowest classes in the Hague, who suffer by the absence of the Stadtholder's
> court, the people appear, as formerly, well fed, well clothed, busy and at
> ease. In their buildings, public and private, not a brick seems to be out of
> its place... but those who are intimately acquainted with the state of the
> country, affirm that it would be imprudent to draw important con-
> clusions from this appearance.... The general diminution of capital is not
> the less real and alarming in its consequences, and the load of taxes imposed
> with a view to supply the public exigencies... is felt to be oppressive in
> an extreme degree.[2]

Appelius was the leading member of a committee that in 1800 had to
consider a plan prepared by Gogel, as Agent for Finance, for a uniform
national system of taxation. Gogel proposed drastically to rationalize the

[1] A.R.A., Goldberg 221 (iv), Van Heukelom to Goldberg, 23 Oct. 1800.
[2] *Ged.* IV, 319, 325.

existing system, but to abide by its principles, including the taxation of food and fuel. The committee rejected the plan and put forward instead proposals drawn up by Appelius. The food and fuel taxes, its report asserted, and the excess of money brought into circulation by commerce had ruined industry by high wages. Former governments had done nothing, because they cared only for commerce. The whole common-wealth had been burdened with debt by wars and other expenses under-taken solely for the sake of commerce. The new government must look the facts in the face. The Dutch general market was in decline, and was kept alive only by the abundance of capital at Amsterdam. The nation must seek new ways in agriculture and industry, 'in order to achieve a less dependent prosperity, which can maintain the commonwealth even if it should prove impossible to restore foreign trade to its former level'. Appelius proposed that the government should clear the way for this re-orientation by abolishing all taxes on barley, oats, rye, small beer, firewood and low quality peats, and by leaving untaxed potatoes, peas, beans and green vegetables, which were said to complete the list of articles necessary for a labourer's subsistence. Then, perhaps, without damage to commerce, the government would find itself easily able to achieve a thing impossible to its predecessors; namely, so to promote industry, without excessive regulation, as to ensure the high quality and low price of its products; provided that it could overcome the national obstinacy, prejudice and lack of adaptability. The remitted taxes were to be replaced by new ones on the domestic consumption of foreign imports such as tobacco, coffee, sugar, tea and chocolate.[1]

Van Hogendorp, still a supporter of the House of Orange, published a pamphlet in reply to this anti-commercial proposal, which, he said, was the work of envious revolutionaries from the agricultural and industrial middle classes. He admitted that the food taxes had ruined some industries, but regarded this sacrifice to the needs of commerce as inevitable. Trade was not artificially retained by capital saved from former profits, but was natural to the Dutch character and location; and only industries, such as sugar refining, that fitted in with this trade could survive. Fortunately, there were many such, and probably they employed more men than the native industries had ever done. The majority of common men knew very well that the rich, and especially the merchants, provided the livelihood of the poor and must not be hindered by bad taxes. Food taxes were the best for everybody, because their incidence passed imperceptibly through society in all wages and prices. The rich and the merchants, he added,

---

[1] *Besluiten der eerste kamer van het vertegenwoordigend lichaam des bataafschen volks* (The Hague, 1800), pt. 24, 9 July 1800, Bijlage.

could be relied upon to understand the principles on which Dutch prosperity depended, and government should be left to them. They would decide all questions of politics, war and taxation according to the interests of commerce, which was identical with the common good.[1]

Even before 1795, there had been excises on certain articles of consumption which were also articles of foreign trade, such as wine, spirits, salt and soap. Great care was taken that the tax should fall only on home consumption and that the merchants, especially those of the First Hand, should suffer no inconvenience. Responsibility for the payment of the tax was therefore confined to the retailers. The Second Hand was submitted merely to a mild documentation. The excise service was entirely separate from the customs and had no control of goods imported by sea. It could check fraud only by the control and inspection of traffic within the country, a system that was facilitated by the organization of the common carriers and the retail shopkeepers in gilds regulated by the municipal authorities. Fraud was widespread. One way of dealing with it was to farm out the tax to those who had most incentive to fraud; the Amsterdam gild of wine merchants, who combined wholesale and retail trade, farmed the wine excise until popular agitation caused the abolition of all tax farming in 1748; afterwards, the authorities soon found it best to negotiate terms of agreement with the leading 'smokkelbazen', who were said to have organized the insurance of gild members against fines for excise offences.[2]

The 'Batavians', who, as van Hogendorp admitted, were but half-hearted revolutionaries, showed the utmost tenderness for commerce in their plans for fiscal reform. Appelius rejected the idea of levying excise at source or at the First Hand. Such a system, he said, would destroy the precarious general trade still remaining to Holland in the goods concerned, for the inconvenience and cost of the controls would reduce the advantages that commissioners could offer to foreigners. The burden of advancing cash for the excise would also be hard on the small Schiedam distillers, who already had to give credit to the retailers. He proposed to tighten the existing system by closer control of the Second Hand and by requiring the customer, who had less motive for fraud, to pay the tax instead of the retailer, who would not be allowed to hand over the goods until given the excise receipt. If this system could be made to work well, he hoped that the new excises on imported goods would, together with some increase in the Land Tax, yield enough to replace the food and fuel taxes without injury to foreign trade. Similar proposals had in the past been made by

---

[1] G. K. van Hogendorp, *Gedagten over 's lands finantiën* (Amsterdam, 1802).

[2] *Le commerce de la Hollande*, II, 351–6; C. Wiskerke, *De afschaffing der gilden*, p. 172.

sensible men who were loyal to commerce and far from being revolutionaries;[1] but the merchants now raised a great outcry, on the ground that the internal and general trades could not be separated, and that therefore any tax on commercial goods would be injurious.

The 'Batavians' did not succeed in introducing a unified, national system of taxation until 1805. By then, power was in the hands of moderates. Gogel, the Finance Minister, had himself been in business at Amsterdam for a time. He wished to retain existing principles, but to increase the revenue by efficient administration. His proposal in 1800 was therefore for excise levied at source or at the First Hand, with only a limited term of credit, on the articles traditionally liable. The goods would be subject to control until they were exported or the duty paid. A full drawback or write-off would be allowed on exports. The internal circulation of goods on which tax had been paid could then be free of all control and impediment, as seemed logical if the advantages of a uniform, national fiscal system were to be reaped. The merchants, however, protested as vigorously against these proposals as against those of Appelius, and the system of 1805 was accordingly much less drastic. The excises continued to be levied from the retailer. Documentation was extended to the First Hand. Taxable goods held by the Second Hand became liable to inspection and the Second Hand became liable for duty on any that went astray. Internal traffic in the goods continued to be subject to tiresome formalities.[2]

During their annexation to France, the Dutch departments were brought into the French fiscal system. The food taxes were abolished and the traditions of Dutch administration discarded. After the Uprising of 1813, however, Gogel's system was restored, though certain minor French taxes were kept on for extra revenue. The system proved more annoying to the inhabitants than before, for the officials had been trained by the French to carry out regulations literally and rigorously, and the new government encouraged the continuance of the French spirit by demanding the maximum revenue. Before long official reports began to come in from rural areas and agricultural market towns of popular discontent against interference with internal traffic by the excise officers, and especially against the flour tax.[3]

[1] E. Luzac, *Hollands rijkdom*, IV, 407.
[2] *Besluiten der eerste kamer, loc. cit.*; *Mem. en cor.* p. 303; J. T. Boelen, *Jacobus Boelen 1733–1933 Amsterdam* (Amsterdam, 1933); H. T. Colenbrander, *De Bataafsche Republiek* (Amsterdam, 1908), pp. 183–4.
[3] *Rec. Fin.* pp. 671–9.

Chapter V

THE BELGIAN PROVINCES

In the Hapsburg territories in the South Netherlands, the rising capitalism of the sixteenth century had been checked by the consequences of war, and backward economic arrangements had grown rigid. In the sixteenth century, new industries had been organized in the towns by capitalists, often with municipal support; but later, when the industries took root, the small masters secured the establishment of gilds for them with the usual regulations. The towns protected their own industries and so hampered trade within the provinces. The gilds retained political power in the towns and the towns in the Provincial States. In order not to endanger the voting of subsidies, the Hapsburg governments avoided offending the gilds. Rural industry, capitalist methods, and technical changes were impeded. This made it easier for the Dutch to keep the South Netherlands in commercial dependence by the closure of the Scheldt, by mercantilist tariff policies, and by a diplomatic veto against efforts by the Hapsburg governments to protect Belgian industries from foreign imports.

The Bishopric of Liége, under pacific clerical rule, offered more favourable conditions for capitalist development, especially in the cloth and armament industries. The government was not helpful, for only the nobles and clergy had influence, fiscal duties were levied impartially on the import and export of both raw materials and manufactured goods, and co-ordination with the neighbouring territories of public works for land or water transport was proudly refused. However, the suppression of the gilds after the troubles of 1684 cleared the way for the development of capitalist industry in town and country. Coal, and water-power, were available. Merchant-manufacturers organized the arms industry by putting out the materials in turn to a number of specialist small masters, often through middlemen. Nail-making was similarly organized. The collieries by the mid-eighteenth century were already capitalist undertakings, some employing several hundred men, while the pits in the Austrian Netherlands were still mostly exploited by small partnerships of working miners. The woollen industry in the Bishopric was organized by capitalists of Verviers, some of whom put out work to several hundred families, and had their own water-driven fulling mills.

The merchant-manufacturers of the South Netherlands depended on the Dutch not merely for their access to maritime trade, but also for credit. Only the landowners and ecclesiastical institutions had great wealth. They certainly accumulated liquid funds, but did not make them available to commerce or industry, apart from mining and metallurgical works on their estates. Rather, they bought more land, or lent on mortgages on land, or to public authorities, including in the eighteenth century the French government. Some Belgian merchants acted as private bankers, but their resources were inadequate and their charges high. Rather than discount bills or borrow locally on merchandise, Belgian merchants consigned to Dutch commission houses the products of Belgian industry, whether or not it was capitalist in organization. The widespread Flemish linen industry, which employed over 200,000 persons, was, apart from a few urban weavers' gilds, a rural winter occupation, often organized by the peasants who grew the flax. The peasant weavers remained independent and sold their linens to merchants at the regulated open markets at Ghent and elsewhere. The merchants undertook the bleaching of linen not fine enough to require the services of Haarlem, but consigned most of their supply to Holland. So did the nail merchants, who collected their wares directly from the working masters to whom they put out the raw material. The Dutch advances, however, served only for working capital; and even when Belgian capitalists had control over the processes of production there was little extension of fixed capital. The iron industry of Namur remained in the eighteenth century much as it was in the seventeenth. The landowners and merchants provided the fixed capital but left control of the workshops to the working masters. The foundries employed about ten men each and the forges not more than forty, though the number employed in supplying charcoal and iron ore might reach several hundred. Several workshops might belong to one integrated enterprise. Less than 10,000 persons were employed in the whole industry, including nail-making, and a similar number in the metallurgy of Liége.

From 1748 to 1789 Belgium enjoyed peace, and economic revival began. Population increased. The gilds, however, were by then thoroughly oligarchic, so that the expansion of urban industry implied more journeymen, but not more masters. The old limitations on the numbers of apprentices and journeymen tended to be disregarded. Otherwise, the economic revival was insufficient to cause much modification of gild organization. The governments of Maria Theresa and Joseph II were influenced by physiocratic theory, but achieved little against the vested interests. They supported the attack on the limitation of apprentices and journeymen, authorized the employment of rural workers in the towns and showed vigour against the reactionary efforts of the journeymen's organizations.

The journeymen resisted with some success, however, especially the hatters, who in some towns continued to enforce the closed shop principle even under the Napoleonic administration. The government's attempts to reduce the power of the gilds were even less successful. Small ones, often mismanaged and in debt or in trouble with their town authorities, were suppressed or amalgamated with others as opportunity arose. The more ambitious reforms of Joseph II in the years 1784–7 were designed to prevent the gilds from engaging in litigation, from controlling technique, from contracting loans and from monopolizing the local retail trades. These measures swelled the discontent caused by Joseph II's religious policy, and had to be withdrawn.

The government's efforts to promote freedom of internal trade were cautious, partly in order not to offend local protectionism and particularism, and partly because political rigidity made it difficult to replace any revenues that were given up. Progress was achieved rather by granting privileged exemptions than by any radical reform of the various barriers to trade. Even the measures adopted were not always effective. For instance, the boatmen continued to insist on the transshipment of goods at Ghent long after a decree of 1784 had declared it to be no longer obligatory. The system of collecting customs revenue at offices in the interior, which involved administrative control of all internal traffic, was a great hindrance to the formation of a single national market, and when administrative efficiency was improved by the reforms of Joseph II the hindrance became worse, though the aim of increased revenue was achieved. The method of customs administration could not be changed because it had the support of the towns; for it hampered rural trade and industry, and strengthened the position of each town in its local market.

Under the terms of the treaty of 1748, and in view of the decline in Dutch power, Maria Theresa's government was able cautiously to begin protecting Belgian industry against foreign imports. Import duties on finished goods and export duties on raw materials were raised gradually and one at a time, in the hope that the maritime powers would not notice. Each province had its own customs duties, but goods from other provinces were liable only to the extent to which a higher rate of duty might be involved. The privileges of the Dutch enclaves in Austrian territory in the East Netherlands diminished the effectiveness of the protectionist measures even when they became more open and efficient under Joseph II.

The new industries fostered by the government were, for political reasons, set up in the towns. They were started by capitalists, often foreigners with foreign artisans, aided by subsidies from the government and from the provincial and municipal authorities, by the grant of monopolies, and by certain fiscal immunities. Such enterprises were for making glass, carpets, porcelain, paper, camlets, bombazine, pins, ribbons, playing cards, and soap, for refining sugar, printing calicoes, and preparing tobacco. Industries which competed against Dutch ones were in special favour. Some of the establishments were on quite a large scale; a calico-printing firm at Ghent, for instance, was employing 500 workers in 1777.[1] Saw-mills and oilseed-mills on the Dutch model were set up in the Ostend district, which was windy and convenient for the import of Baltic raw materials.

After a time, the government found that the physiocrats were right, and that its outlay in subsidies was not justified by the results, for much was wasted by intrigue and fraud. From 1766 few special favours were given to individual capitalists and reliance was placed on general measures of protection, transport improvement and internal reform. The results were modestly encouraging. Rural industries increased, their markets widened and the influence of the merchant capitalists extended, partly because the increased number of wholesalers and their travellers made cottagers feel that they could get fair remuneration for their products without troubling to carry them to the organized market. New rural industries were created by merchant capitalists, including tobacco-working and new kinds of lace-making. The most important was a woollen industry in Limburg similar to that in the neighbouring district of Liége; at first it provided mainly unfinished cloth for Holland, but soon after 1750 the capitalists set up small finishing workshops and were able to build up an eastward export trade, especially to the central European Hapsburg territories where they were given tariff preference. Coal production was stimulated by the increase in population, the growth of industry and by certain official measures to check the depletion of the forests. Landowners and merchants combined to provide capital for deeper pits. Nineteen Newcomen engines were operating in mines in the Austrian Netherlands in 1776. More coal was exported to France, and in time of war to the Dutch Netherlands, though in time of peace even the western Belgian provinces still used English coal. New items began to appear on Belgian export lists, such as printed fabrics, carriages, spirits and cigars.

The only means by which Belgium could be freed from dependence on Dutch trade, or by which the Dutch could be compelled to trade on more favourable terms, was the development of Ostend as a sea-port. Physical and fiscal measures were taken for this purpose. Public works reduced the cost of transport to the interior. By decrees of 1751 and 1755 special transit duties ranging from $\frac{1}{2}$ to $1\frac{1}{2}\%$ were introduced for goods passing

[1] V. Fris, *Histoire de Gand* (Brussels, 1913), p. 283.

in bond to foreign destinations by specified routes. This enabled Ostend to compete for the trade of the industrial areas of Liége and the nearest Rhinelands. Decrees of 1781 and 1783 made Ostend a free port for re-export by sea, and abolished there, alone of important towns in the Austrian Netherlands, all power of the gilds to interfere with wholesale or retail trade. This policy was strongly supported by merchants, especially in towns which enjoyed warehousing privileges. The transit arrangements, however, facilitated smuggling into the home markets, and so were bitterly opposed by industrial interests at Ghent and elsewhere. In the 1780's, the merchants were annoyed by increases in the duties on the import of finished goods and the export of raw materials, and more especially by Joseph II's stringent administrative measures against fraud, which were blamed for a decline in transit trade more probably due to the restoration of peace between Britain and the United Provinces. In the last years of Joseph II, the tariff quarrel acquired some of the heat of the political and religious disputes of the time.

The modest industrial growth in Belgium after 1750 did not keep pace with the growth of population. A high rate of pauperism in the towns resulted, especially in view of the continued decline in the urban cloth industries. This was perhaps a reason for the willingness of the government to support certain gilds against the introduction of labour-saving techniques.[1]

At the end of the old régime in Belgium, the industrial development made possible by available natural resources and needed by the increasing population was still being held up by the lack of capital in the hands of persons who would use it for industry, by lack of internal free trade, by antiquated institutions and ideas, and by Dutch mercantilist policies. If the situation was not yet urgent, this was mainly due to the possibility of employing more hands in agriculture, both by reclamation and by intensi-fication. This was especially so in Flanders, where there was a long tradition of intensive, individual farming and of 'tenant right'. The established peasants prospered, as was shown by their taking up more land despite the fact that rents and the price of land rose more than the profits of farming. Noble and ecclesiastical landlords were mostly unwilling to sell land, but urban capitalists who had investments in rural land were tempted to sell by the high prices, in order perhaps to employ the capital in trade or industry. Small-holding and peasant proprietorship slowly increased, methods slowly improved and artificial grasses spread eastward into Limburg. Rural industry helped to maintain the increasing number of poor cottagers. In the Walloon country the soil was inferior, and

[1] H. van Houtte, *Histoire économique de la Belgique à la fin l'Ancien Régime*, p. 47.

traditional methods, especially communal grazing practices, hindered reclamation and farming in severalty, despite decrees of 1757 and 1767 which facilitated the division of common and the withdrawal of land from common grazing during the customary fallows. There was great poverty among the cottagers, who were a source of cheap labour for industry, especially in Liége.

The increasing Belgian population being employed mainly in agriculture, the supply of corn increased more rapidly than the demand for it. From about 1750, the Flemish harvests not only yielded enough to fill the deficit of Wallonia but often a surplus for export to the Dutch corn market. The landowning and commercial interests therefore demanded freedom to export corn; though they were divided in regard to the export of flax according to whether or not they were interested in the linen industry. The supporters of free export, like the supporters of the transit system, used physiocratic theory to support their case. They were opposed by most urban opinion, which was still exceedingly sensitive about food supplies. In the majority of years, accordingly, the export of corn was prohibited, although licences could often be obtained. The local authorities also imposed their own local embargoes. The industrial capitalists were necessarily against the free export of corn, and those who had created the new urban industries of the eighteenth century wanted all the favours and subsidies they could win from the governments; they were therefore not attracted by physiocratic theory and had no objection in principle to restrictions on enterprise, though they attacked particular gild regulations inconvenient to themselves.

In the last decade of the eighteenth century, Belgium again became the battleground for several campaigns and was greatly plundered by the French. The towns experienced great difficulty in obtaining food and raw materials. Pauperism increased. Banditry became widespread and recurred periodically until 1810. Wolves reappeared, owing perhaps to conscription. The peasants no doubt made good, by profiteering, part of what they lost by plunder and requisition; but they hoarded much grain, and local famines occurred, in 1802 for instance. The prohibition of the export foodstuffs to Holland, even in years of good harvest, disorganized the market, for transport costs to French markets were high. Export licences were sometimes obtainable, but expensive.

During the wars, Belgian industry suffered from the difficulty and costliness of maritime trade through either Dutch or Belgian ports, though much grain, lace, linen, and other produce was said to be smuggled to the Dutch provinces in return for raw wool, cotton and colonial goods in general. Eupen and Verviers had to get much of their wool by circuitous routes, and their eastward exports were often hindered by Continental campaigns. The linen industry suffered from impediments to its exports to Spain and her colonies and from a higher export duty. The tobacco, calico-printing, steel, cutlery, leather and copper industries suffered similar inconveniences. Even the Liége arms industry did not prosper, apart from the state workshops, for much valuable trade in sporting weapons was lost, war contracts were given only grudgingly to Belgian private firms and many bankruptcies occurred before the end of the Empire. French fiscal methods discouraged transit trade; and put out of operation many small breweries and distilleries, which were said often to have been a significant source of rural prosperity.

On the other hand, when order was re-established about 1800, conditions were more favourable to capitalist development than ever before. The gilds were abolished, customs barriers banished to the frontier, and many tolls removed. Previously, the formation even of a national Belgian market had been impossible, but now the Belgian economy was thrust into the wide market of a re-organized Continent and as part of France enjoyed considerable privileges as a result of the commercial policies imposed on conquered territories. Mobile capital had become available in the hands of the profiteers of war and revolution, especially of those who speculated in confiscated ecclesiastical property, which religious scruples prevented the peasants from buying until after the Concordat. Ecclesiastical premises were often suitable for factories. Unemployment, high prices, and the disruption of many traditional occupations had made available a labour force which, under a strong civil government, could be set to work for low real wages on unfamiliar and unpopular tasks. The government was willing to grant subsidies, though not large ones, and, more important, it encouraged officials and contractors to curry favour by investing in industry.

Napoleon was at first anxious that cotton industries should be created to rival Lancashire, though when the Continental System proved incompatible with this aim he found it convenient to argue that linen and silks should be preferred by good Europeans, as needing no materials from outside the Empire.[1] Flanders could offer the cotton industry a labour force with experience in handling the similar material, linen. Water-power was not available in Flanders, except at Ghent; and there only when the tide was out, so that although long used for fulling mills it was unsuitable for cotton-spinning. Until steam could be introduced, the new industry had to rely on manual power and cheap labour. Workhouses were accordingly set up by the public authorities in which paupers and

---

[1] E. F. Heckscher, *The Continental System* (Oxford, 1922), p. 277.

beggars were forced to learn the new techniques. In due course, these forced trainees were permitted to transfer themselves to free employment by private entrepreneurs, but the *livret* system still tied them to their jobs. L. Bauwens, the most enterprising cotton manufacturer of the time, was given the management of three prisons in order that he might transfer the inmates, after training, to his own factories. The yarn spun in factories in Ghent and other towns was mostly put out to former linen weavers in the country. Difficulty in obtaining raw material after 1807 caused employment to fluctuate considerably. The crisis of 1811 caused the bankruptcy of many manufacturers who had been relying on bank credit, often in the form of bills repeatedly renewed.[1] Bauwens struggled on in the difficult conditions of 1812 and 1813, but failed before William I assumed the government of Belgium. 13,000 workers from cotton factories were said to be unemployed at Ghent in 1813.[2] The whole industry appeared to have been created by temporary political circumstances and its future seemed precarious.

The woollen industry could rely during the war on military orders and so enjoyed prosperity, using more German instead of Spanish wool. The manufacturers of Verviers responded to their opportunity by technical change, by setting up spinning factories and by calling into existence a specialized machine-making industry. The firm of Cockerill in the first decade of the nineteenth century established a healthy organization for supplying throughout the Empire manual or water-driven carding, combing and spinning machines, and looms equipped with the flying shuttle. By 1811, the firm was able to undertake the equipping of factories with gas. The firm then employed 500 smiths and 1,500 carpenters, many of the latter being out-workers. Its early operations were financed partly by the woollen manufacturers and partly by the firms which supplied the wrought and cast iron parts, and were thus much aided by the previous growth of capitalism in the bishopric of Liége. The firm was often paid for its services by shares in the textile partnerships concerned and so it acquired interests in many parts of Europe. Its main customers were the woollen manufacturers of Verviers, of whom there were said in 1810 to be eighty-six, employing 25,000 persons in all. An outbreak of machine-breaking occurred at Verviers in 1810.[3]

Belgian industry at the end of the Empire was therefore well equipped by Continental standards. In 1814, the Prussian government sent a

---

[1] R. Bigo, *Les banques françaises au cours du XIXe siècle* (Paris, 1947), p. 234.

[2] V. Fris, *Histoire de Gand*, p. 327.

[3] E. Mahaim, 'Les débuts de l'établissement John Cockerill à Seraing', in *Vierteljahrschrift für Sozial- und Wirtschaftsgeschichte* (1905); *Post Doc.* III, 41–2.

technical mission to western Europe to take advantage of the allied occupation by gathering information useful to Prussian industry for its future competition against British; and its attention was directed mainly to Belgium.[1] The future of Belgian industry seemed, however, very doubtful. Only the woollen industry seemed capable of competing against the British in unprotected markets. In the long run, exports were necessary for the fuller utilization of Belgian natural resources and cheap labour, and so Belgian industrialists might be expected to be free traders; meanwhile, however, they were accustomed to rely on help from the government of the day and were vociferous in demanding it. They could be sure of a hearing, for the government knew that there now existed an urban proletariat dependent on capitalist enterprises serving more than a local market and therefore liable to dangerous vicissitudes. Industrial capital was scarce and timid, and after the collapse of the Continental System it could only be coaxed forth by government favours. Most manufacturers wished only to keep their existing equipment in operation, not to embark on the improvement and expansion which would be necessary in the long run to compete against the British; until political events should favour them by the coming of a new Continental System, they accordingly limited their hopes to the markets of the reunited Netherlands in which their new government could give protection.

The opening of the Scheldt enabled Antwerp during the war to attract a share of neutral trade, mainly limited to the needs of the part of her hinterland within the French customs area. In the year of peace in 1802, nearly a thousand sea-going vessels entered Antwerp, despite the inconvenience of French customs arrangements as compared with those of Rotterdam. After the fall of Napoleon, the revival of Antwerp began in earnest. It might therefore have been expected that a class of Belgian merchants would arise as allies of the Dutch in the struggle for free trade. Commercial capital, however, was scarce in Antwerp; and the new foreign trade, which was mainly transit trade for Germany, was financed by foreigners who settled in Antwerp or sent representatives there. This cosmopolitan society had no roots among the population. It certainly desired free trade, but it did not share the reverence of Dutch merchants for the traditions of Dutch mercantilism. The native Belgian merchants were not interested in foreign trade in the sense of the Dutch 'general' trade, but mainly in importing raw materials and goods for consumption in Belgium and in exporting Belgian products. Antwerp's industrialists were engaged not so much in commercial industries of the Dutch type as

[1] W. Treue, 'Eine preussische technologische Reise in den besetzten Gebiete im Jahre 1814', in *Vierteljahrschrift für Sozial- und Wirtschaftsgeschichte* (1935).

in producing textiles, soap, spirits and so on for a limited local market.[1] In fact, Antwerp had no affinity with Amsterdam and Rotterdam which could mitigate the inevitable jealousies caused by her revival.

Table X. *Population of Belgian provinces, 1815, and statistics of relief, 1822**

	Inhabitants of towns with urban suffrage (thousands)	Rural population (thousands)	Total population (thousands)	Paupers relieved out of doors in 1822 (thousands)	Spent on outdoor relief 1822 (£000)
South Brabant	129	312	442	100	31
Liége	73	285	358	55	9
East Flanders	140	475	616	57	26
West Flanders	136	380	516	75	29
Henegouw	109	380	489	103	21
Namur	20	144	164	23	4
Antwerp	97	194	292	8	18
Luxemburg	31	183	214	2	1
Limburg	52	235	288	37	9
Total	787	2,588	3,379	460	148
Dutch Limburg	37	119	155	?	?
Total (1839 frontier)	750	2,469	3,224	?	?

Table XI. *Estimated population of certain Belgian towns, 1784–1840† (thousands)*

	1784	1790	1800	1803	1805	1807	1811	1812	1814	1815	1829	1840
Brussels	—	60	—	72	—	—	—	—	75	—	112	—
Ghent	51	55	—	—	—	55	—	61	—	60	95	—
Antwerp	—	—	55	—	59	—	—	60	—	—	77	—
Liége	—	50	45	—	—	—	48	—	—	—	65	—
Verviers	—	10	—	—	—	—	—	—	—	—	—	20

[1] A. J. L. van den Bogaerde de Ter-Brugge, *Essai*, II, 168–9.

* *2de kamer*, 1822–3, B 851.

† H. Pirenne, *Histoire de Belgique* (Brussels, 1907–32), V, 360; VI, 164; P. Verhaegen, *La Belgique sous la domination française* (Brussels, 1929), IV, 126, 562; J. McGregor, *Commercial Statistics*, III, 66.

Chapter VI

DUTCH-BELGIAN FISCAL UNION:
THE SYSTEM OF 1816

(a) The government of William I

The British government was anxious that the constitutional powers of William I should be adequate to ensure that the new kingdom fulfilled the strategic purposes of its creation; and assurances were received that 'the sovereign is quite sensible that if the object cannot otherwise be brought about, a recourse to institutions of equal harshness, though perhaps less odious than existed under former governments will be indispensable'.[1] The king inherited the centralized administration that had been established by French domination in both the Dutch and Belgian Netherlands; and his own autocratic temperament ensured that this Napoleonic machinery would not be allowed to rust. In view, however, of the intransigent opposition of the Belgian Catholics, the only possible way of gaining a foothold on Belgian opinion was by winning the support of the Liberals; the king attempted to do this without surrendering any of his authority and without destroying his popularity among the Dutch. He was aware of the value of the States General for testing public feeling and preparing it for changes in policy. Having insisted that his ministers should be responsible only to himself, he was content to respect the legislative powers of the States General and to exercise the patience necessary to impose his will without violating the constitution. Being of an experimental turn of mind, he pondered other methods in case the States General should prove unmanageable; but he was not hasty in his decisions, and even if such action became necessary he intended to postpone it until the States General put itself in the wrong. The nature of his rule was shown by the method of incorporating Belgium in the kingdom. Consent was desired, so the constitution was submitted to assemblies of notables; but the majority was hostile, and 'Dutch arithmetic' was accordingly used to get the desired answer. Some administrators considered the methods of the French time more practical.

Having been long in exile, the king needed time to feel the pulse of Dutch opinion, and at first selected his ministers from all the old parties, in an unnecessary anxiety to avoid giving offence. Some, the French ambassador reported, were 'puritans of equality', others 'adherents of the

[1] H. T. Colenbrander, *Ontstaan der Grondwet* (The Hague, 1908–9), II, 50.

Elector of Hesse and the King of Spain'. None were taken fully into William I's confidence. He transacted business privately with each minister and soon gave up the practice of holding cabinet meetings. The royal secretariat was the main channel of interdepartmental communication and ministers became chary of consulting together except by the king's special order. The king thought it necessary to impart his decisions only to those required to act on them, except in the case of such Royal Decrees as were for general publication. In this, he followed the principles and practice of King Louis Bonaparte.[1]

The king had no objection to taking counsel, and tried to decide each question on its merits. The minister concerned always had plenty of time to prepare his proposals, which were then often sent to and fro for the comments of other ministers. At length, the king might either issue a Royal Decree, or pass the documents to the Council of State, whose advice he was constitutionally bound to hear before proposing legislation to the States General. Decrees and draft laws were usually based on the advice of the minister concerned. That advice might be influenced by the known wishes of the king, but the ministers were not obsequious and were often unimpressed by the tentative suggestions of their master. The king liked to see his advisers put their own ideas to the test, even when he expected in the end to convince them of the need for bolder measures of his own devising. In this 'Government of Departments', the policy of giving each minister his head, although he might be ignorant of much that his colleagues were doing, sometimes led to inconsistency.

The government, led by a king who was cautiously feeling his way, for many years felt itself to be too preoccupied with day-to-day problems to formulate permanent policies.[2] In economic matters, it was also aware of the inadequacy of its information. The collection of statistics had been resisted with some success by the Dutch local authorities in 1810 as a new-fangled innovation of the French.[3] William I's government continued the efforts of the French, but without much success until 1825, when a special statistical bureau was formed.[4] In earlier years, the ministers ordered statistical returns, but to little purpose. The industrial surveys of 1816 and 1820, for instance, were intended to assist the revision of the tariff, but seem not to have been used. Ministers mostly gave only *a priori* advice, even about the effect of past policies; they protested the impossibility of giving

[1] *Ged.* VIII (1), 150; (2), 235–7; A. R. Falck, *Gedenkschriften* (The Hague, 1913), pp. 127–8; J. A. Sillem, *De politieke en staathuishoudkundige werkzaamheid van I. J. A. Gogel* (Amsterdam, 1864), p. 60.
[2] *Ged.* IX (2), 5. [3] F. J. B. d'Alphonse, *Aperçu*, p. 224.
[4] J. A. Drieling, *Bijdragen tot een vergelijkend overzigt van Nederlands zeevaart en handel* (Amsterdam, 1829), p. 7.

factual evidence and referred inquiries to the Chambers of Commerce. The latter had emphatic opinions but were vague as to the supporting evidence.[1]

William I's methods of government were partly determined by the fact that there was very little desire either among the Dutch or the Belgians that the union should succeed. The king and a few of his closest advisers wished to create a centralized state containing all the Low Countries, in order not to be condemned to diplomatic impotence like that of the Republic in the eighteenth century; but most of his subjects and many of his ministers regarded union as a necessary evil, and wanted as little of it as possible. The king, therefore, made a show of reluctance in accepting Belgian territory, although he used all his influence with the Allies to bring the union about. The Eight Articles, which laid down that the union should be 'complete and intimate', were drawn up by Falck, the king's secretary; but they were published as an act of the Allies in which the Dutch government had no part, and were afterwards treated as sacrosanct and as imposing a special responsibility on the king, beyond that of a constitutional monarch.[2]

In imposing on the Dutch and Belgians a bargain that neither desired, the government tried to convince each side that it was receiving compensations for its sacrifices. The Dutch were compensated for the inevitable opening of the Scheldt by the pooling in a single budget of their large national debt with the much smaller Belgian one. The Belgians were compensated for this burden of debt by sharing the advantages of the Dutch colonies and naval power and by free access to the Dutch market. The colonies were also weighed in to justify the granting of half the seats in the States General to the Dutch, in spite of their smaller population; though a scruple was felt that this counting of the colonies twice might seem unfair to the Belgians.[3]

Since few of his subjects were interested in the survival of the union and both ministers and members of the States General had mostly a narrow sectional outlook, the king had a special and unique responsibility for balancing impartially the conflicting arguments and ensuring that decisions conformed to the interest of the kingdom as a whole. This was made all the more necessary by the fact that, for lack of suitable Belgian candidates, most of the ministers remained Dutch. Procedures in the States General accorded with this special function of the king. Legislative projects were drafted by the government and submitted to the States General for

---

[1] *Post. Doc.* I, 178, 335, 352; I. J. Brugmans, *De arbeidende klasse*, p. xviii.

[2] *Ged.* VII, 19; A. R. Falck, *Gedenkschriften*, pp. 139–44; G. J. Renier, *Great Britain and the Netherlands 1813–1815* (London, 1930).

[3] A. R. Falck, *Gedenkschriften*, p. 162; *Ged.* IX (2), 456–8; *Knuttel* 24158.

acceptance or rejection without any possibility of amendment. They were, however, first submitted to small committees, or 'Sections', of the States General, which were free to make observations. The government replied to each of these observations and took them into consideration before presenting the draft law in its final form for voting in full session. As a Dutch member remarked in 1829:

> After consideration by the Sections, it is then the task of His Majesty to judge whether concessions can be made to meet their criticisms. For he alone is in a position to review the whole matter, whereas this or that Minister can only have his own Department in mind.[1]

(b) The system of 1816

The government postponed the Dutch-Belgian fiscal union until the political union was completed, and then allowed time for consultation, so that both Dutch and Belgian opinion meanwhile became resigned to union and aware of some of its economic implications. In 1814 and 1815, Appelius, as head of the Excise Department, was responsible for the temporary fiscal arrangements in Belgium. He respected Belgian interests and wishes, but had it in mind to introduce in Belgium a system that could later be extended to the whole kingdom. He consciously intended to use the opportunity of fiscal union in order to accomplish in the Dutch provinces reforms that he had long regarded as necessary.[2] For Belgian opinion desired free internal traffic, and the avoidance of taxes likely to raise wages or annoy the private citizen; and preferred excise to be levied on inessentials and at source, so that the consumer and the retailer need have no contact with the tax officials. One of the more popular features of the new régime was the relief it brought from the odious *droits réunis* by which the French authorities had raised revenue arbitrarily to meet the needs of the last years of the Empire; but once these exceptional taxes had been abandoned, the Belgians were well content with the French fiscal system. Appelius preserved it. When the time came in 1816 for fiscal union, he proposed to extend it to the Dutch provinces. The Dutch commercial party protested vigorously. The Belgians, it was said, had no experience of political independence; and must not claim to interfere with the arrangements of the old-established nation to which they had been joined, but must respect its wisdom and seniority. Belgian industry, it was assumed, was largely an artificial product of the Continental System, so the Belgians should be grateful to be allowed to share the beneficent

---

[1] *2de kamer*, 1829–30, A 145.
[2] A.R.A., Staatssec., 5 June 1819, E4—report from Appelius, 6 Feb. 1819.

influence of Dutch trade, which would help them in making the necessary painful adjustment to peace-time. The balance of foreign payments in the new kingdom as in the old Republic would depend on commercial earnings, and the Dutch fiscal system must be imposed on the Belgians, for their own good, even though the 'necessary taxes on food' would preclude the existence of healthy industries other than those serving the needs of general trade. Other Dutchmen argued that these taxes would not raise industrial costs because they would force workers to work harder and longer for their subsistence.[1] However, the complicated controls involved in the Dutch system reminded the Belgians of the *droits réunis*, and they were unimpressed by the benefits of general trade, for whose sake the Dutch were willing to submit to these inconveniences.

The Belgian industrial crisis after the collapse of the Continental System made the tariff problem urgent. Manufacturers attributed all their troubles to the foreign competition to which the new political order exposed them and had a habit of telling dismissed workers to blame the government. The tariff introduced by the allied occupational authority in June 1814 was primarily fiscal, and was designed to avoid offence to allied governments. The import duty on manufactured goods was only 8%, though some industries were helped by the prohibition of exports of such raw materials as rabbit skins, tan-bark, hides, oilseeds, bones, flax, raw or combed wool, and scrap iron. When the Dutch government took over control, it quickly introduced a new Belgian tariff in which the import duties on most manufactured goods ranged from 10 to 20%. This tariff was welcomed by moderate Belgians as 'the least imperfect so far', in comparison, that is, mainly with eighteenth century tariffs that were influenced by diplomatic considerations. It was even held to prove that in promoting Dutch-Belgian union 'England protects us without destroying our independence since the tariff is calculated according to our interest against hers'. It could not of course please everyone. Nail-makers and other users of pig-iron complained loudly of the effect of the high import duty on the price of their raw material.[2]

When fiscal union was under discussion in 1816, the Dutch commercial party argued that this Belgian tariff was to be regarded as a temporary measure in an industrial emergency, while the Belgian industrialists insisted that it had been presented to them as a permanent embodiment of the principle of protection and that as their business plans had been based

[1] G. K. van Hogendorp, *Bijdragen*, I, 113–41; G. K. van Hogendorp, *Lettres sur la prosperité*, p. 86; F. A. van Hall, *Onpartijdige beschouwing*, p. 45; W. L. D. van den Brink, *Bijdrage*, p. 8.
[2] *L'Observateur* (Brussels), 6 Feb., 2 April and 20 April 1815.

on its continuance the government was bound in good faith not to reduce the duties. The government always sought to disarm criticism by declaring that its policies would be adjusted by trial and error, and the details of the tariff were certainly regarded as experimental, for the king took great personal interest in them, was constantly considering changes, and was accustomed as soon as one tariff had been enacted to call upon his ministers to propose revisions. The policy of moderate protection, however, was intended to be permanent, and to be extended to the whole kingdom. This evoked a protest from Van Hogendorp, who argued that Dutch traditions were suitable for the whole kingdom and that 'the true principles of commercial policy must be made known in Belgium'. In a marginal comment on Van Hogendorp's memorandum, the king emphatically rejected this educative programme. Finding himself unable to modify policies of which he disapproved, Van Hogendorp gradually withdrew from governmental functions and passed into opposition.[1]

In 1816, the government asked for the advice of the Chambers of Commerce and Manufactures before it drew up a single tariff for the whole kingdom. This stimulated public controversy, and the Dutch protectionists, encouraged by the changed political situation, abandoned the compromise of 1809 and agitated for protective import duties. The woollen and bombazine interests took the lead. Leiden manufacturers asked for a 15% import duty on all cloth and for rigorous enforcement.[2]

The Dutch protectionists received no support at this time from the Belgian woollen manufacturers, who were confident that they were fully competitive and up to date at least in their own special lines, and that they could command a ready market on the Continent from Spain to Kiatka in North China by the overland route. Since the separation of Belgium from the French Empire, they had been badly hit by the high French tariff, but at least their eastward exports were still unimpeded. They feared that if the Netherlands abandoned free trade, the German states might retaliate by higher duties on cloth. Verviers was not averse to a high export duty on raw wool, nor to retaliatory import duties on English and French cloth and other goods, since both countries excluded Belgian cloth by high duties: but otherwise, and as a general principle, she supported free trade. This attitude was shared by other exporting manufacturers, such as the glass and arms makers of Liége.[3] The most important,

[1] A.R.A., Staatssec., 5 June 1819, E4—report from Appelius 6 Feb. 1819; *Ged.* VIII (2), 26–7; G. K. van Hogendorp, *Brieven en gedenkschriften* (The Hague, 1866–1903), V, 391–2.

[2] P. J. Blok, *Eene Hollandsche stad in den nieuweren tijd*, p. 112.

[3] A.R.A., Goldberg 217—report from the Council of State, 3 May 1822; *2de kamer* (1827–8), A239; W. L. Groeneveld Meyer, *De tariegwetgeving*, p. 61.

but least articulate, Belgian industry, linen, was not interested in import duties, but desired a high export duty on flax. Some landowners wished to profit by the French demand for flax, but the agricultural interest as a whole preferred that it should be used by Belgian rural industry.

Despite the complexity of the tariff problem, the protectionism of the coal, iron, cotton, and a few other industries took the appearance in 1816 of a Belgian national cause. It was attractive to all who desired to score off the Dutch by flouting their traditional policies and to many who were interested in the general prosperity of Belgian towns or worried by the unemployment among the cotton operatives. Most Belgian Liberals were protectionists.

The Dutch merchants regarded Belgian protectionism as an attempt to prolong the Continental System. In a sense, they were right, for the movement was directed mainly against Britain, of whom in the late eighteenth century a Belgian mercantilist had already remarked:

Our trade with England is ruinously unfavourable and there seems no reason to hope for a change. We ought therefore to try to have the least possible trade with that kingdom, to diminish our imports of English manufactures and to seek elsewhere the merchandise which the English re-export to us.[1]

The Netherlands government was aware of its debt to British diplomacy, and, at the beginning, cited British support as one of its main claims to public confidence in both the Dutch and Belgian provinces. Its agents in Belgium tried to use British troops for purposes of Orangist propaganda. One British diplomat even asserted that the Belgians had only been reconciled to union with the Dutch by the illusion of becoming part of the British Empire through the marriage of the heir to the Dutch throne with Princess Charlotte. It is probable, however, that much of this popularity was due to the fact that the British occupying forces behaved better than the Prussians or the Cossacks: and it did not last long. Moderate Belgian liberals continued to admire the British constitution, but showed their Continental outlook by demanding that British maritime pretensions should be openly discussed by the Concert of Europe. The more extreme liberals, being vaguely Bonapartist in sentiment, accused Britain of aspiring to world domination and of treating Europe as the British East India Company treated India.[2]

The influx of British goods in the immediate post-war years provoked

[1] H. van Houtte, in *Vierteljahrschrift für Sozial- und Wirtschaftsgeschichte* (1910), p. 365.
[2] *L'Observateur*, 23 Feb. and 23 March 1815; *Ged.* VIII (I), 28–9; G. J. Renier, *Great Britain and the Netherlands.*

strident protest. In quantity, these imports seem to have been much less than the outcry suggested, but in the circumstances even small quantities of cheap imports could have a serious effect on Belgian prices. It was believed that British goods were being deliberately sold at a loss in order to ruin Belgian industry. Britain was thus blamed for much of the distress due to the loss of the markets of the French Empire and for the effects of the international post-war crises. This belief added to the effectiveness of protectionism as a focus of national feeling. Belgium, it was said, having been disposed of by right of conquest, was now tributary to the British government which had been bribed by the Dutch in order that they might avoid much of the burden of their national debt:

> Vous en payerez les deux tiers,
> Ainsi l'ordonne l'Angleterre;
> Mais la représentation
> Aura une autre proportion....
>
> Ne faites plus, on le désire,
> Des draps, basin ni casimir!
> Vos amis d'Angleterre
> Pour vous sauront les faire.[1]

This anti-British agitation had an effect on the government, which was sensitive to such criticism. The Dutch government and public understood the lesson of history, pointed out by Van Hogendorp in a pamphlet in 1802, that wars against France, unless they ended in utter defeat, left the sources of Dutch prosperity untouched, but that wars against Britain were invariably ruinous.[2] The unpleasant necessity was generally admitted of making whatever sacrifices might be necessary for good relations with Britain; but there was also a desire for real and demonstrable independence. The king shared this attitude; and the behaviour of the British ambassador after 1813 was not such as to make him alter the opinion he expressed in 1800 that 'whenever the British interest had been prevailing in Holland, an ambassador from that country had constantly assumed the style and dictature of a Lieutenant in an English country'.[3] He had admired Napoleon and during the war had sometimes seemed to regret that it was impossible to re-establish the fortunes of his House by a French rather than a British connexion. Many of his ministers had been accustomed under previous governments to justify every proposal by the pretext that it would injure Britain; and for those of them who wished to reconcile Belgium to the union and who were not passionate adherents of the

---

[1] *Ged.* VIII (2), 5–6, 82, 91.   [2] G. K. van Hogendorp, *Gedachten*, p. 31.
[3] H. T. Colenbrander, *Willem I, koning der Nederlanden* (Amsterdam, 1931–5), I, 96.

Dutch commercial tradition, a moderately protective tariff was an attractive way of asserting independence of British influence.

The government also saw political advantage in a tariff war with France. The French tariff seemed specially designed to remind the Belgians of what they had lost by separation. The French import duty on glass, for instance, was said to enable the French producers so to raise their home prices that they could afford to sell in Belgium at a loss in order to destroy the Belgian industry. Pro-French sentiments were very common, even among Belgians who disliked the political and religious character of the restored Bourbon government. Some saw in the effects of the French tariff an additional reason for desiring a new Customs Union with France, or at least a commercial treaty. In 1817, a prominent Belgian protectionist proposed in his provincial States that industry should be saved from British competition by a return to something like the Continental System:

> France has the same commercial interest as we, and if we could but convince her that this kingdom will cease to be a stapling place against her of British goods, she would to-day renew with us the serviceable ties necessary to the happiness of both peoples.[1]

If, however, Belgians could be convinced that their government was giving and would continue to give a useful degree of protection in the home market to their industry, then their resentment against the French tariff might take the form of a demand for retaliation and even engender loyalty to the Kingdom of the Netherlands. This hope proved not entirely unfounded.[2]

After much discussion and consideration of many memoranda, during which the king showed a clear though tentative personal leaning towards protective duties even for the benefit of purely Dutch industries, the government proposed a tariff which closely followed its original intentions as shown in its Belgian tariff. The Dutch provinces would thus be included behind the duties which protected the Belgian coal, iron and cotton industries. Many Dutch protests were heard, but some of the commercial party were disposed to acquiesce, as a matter of political necessity. The government easily won enough Dutch votes to secure an impressive majority in the States General. This alliance of Belgian and Dutch politicians in support of a compromise which favoured Belgian industry at the expense of Dutch commerce was largely due to the deepening industrial distress. There was felt to be a threat to public order in Belgium

---

[1] *Knuttel* 25100 (Lecocq, 1817).
[2] *L'Observateur*, 5 March, 23 March and 20 April 1815.

and moderates on both sides avoided embarrassment to the government. In the autumn of 1816, when the new tariff came into force, a harvest failure aggravated conditions in the Belgian towns. Disorders occurred in Ghent, when unemployed workers burned British cotton goods from the shops. There were attacks on the farms of suspected grain hoarders. The situation became serious enough to be regarded by foreign diplomats as a test of the government's ability to maintain the Dutch-Belgian union. Thus, Dutch reactions to the tariff of 1816 were deceptively mild. In 1819, when conditions in Belgium were easier, Dutch criticism became stronger; but it was then too late for a Dutch agitation against the tariff to carry conviction as a spontaneous outburst of outraged national feeling, so the commercial party chose a different theme for its campaign.[1]

The system of 1816 departed from Dutch tradition in other ways too. The meat and flour taxes were abolished. They had been familiar in eighteenth-century Belgium, but had always been unpopular. Any attempt to reimpose them after the long period during which the French had abolished them would have been exceedingly unpopular, especially during years of high food prices. Excise was levied at source, with bonding arrangements for foreign trade. The government attempted to include the Dutch taxes on servants and horses, but dropped them in the face of opposition from Belgian landowners. On the other hand, Appelius firmly opposed Belgian proposals for excises on sugar and coffee, recalling that in 1801 it had been decided that such taxes even levied at the point of consumption and without strict control of the First Hand would injure trade, and much more so when levied at source.[2]

Even before Dutch-Belgian fiscal union came into effect on 1 December 1816, it had become clear that Dutch trade was not reviving to the extent hoped for. Exports of coffee, gin and hides, which had expanded encouragingly in 1815, made little progress in 1816. British imports, which had deceptively stimulated Dutch business in 1814–15, shrank by 37% in 1816. Dutch merchants had acquired stocks beyond the needs of their shrunken area of trade.[3] An English traveller reported from Utrecht in 1819:

I was sorry to find here several young merchants with quantities of English manufactured goods. They had been consigned by their owners

---

[1] *Rec. Fin.* pp. 294–6, 611–19; *L'Observateur*, XVII, 19–26; G. K. van Hogendorp, *Brieven*, v, 391–2; W. M. F. Mansvelt, *Geschiedenis van de Nederlandsche Handel-maatschappij* (Haarlem, 1924–6), I, 94, 106, 140.

[2] *Ged.* VIII (2), 19–23 and (3), 64–75.

[3] W. L. D. van den Brink, *Bijdrage*, pp. 46–51, 83; C. Boissevain, *Onze voortrekkers*, p. 171.

to houses at Amsterdam, where no sales could be made. They were compelled to hawk them about to the different provincial cities, at a great expense, and were disposed to sell them at enormous losses, rather than be at the charge and trouble of conveying them back to the capital; and with every disposition to make great sacrifices, they told me they could effect none but very insignificant sales.[1]

The Dutch commercial party inevitably seized on the system of 1816 as an explanation of this distress, and, forgetting their earlier grumbles, imagined that its introduction was marked by a damning turn for the worse. Van Hogendorp naturally took full credit for the prosperity supposed to have coincided with his period of power: 'I saw the happy consequences of Free Trade in 1814–15. Everything revived and flourished. I saw this progress halt in 1816 and wither away in the following years.' All would have been well if the king had kept the promises made in 1813, before the question of union with Belgium arose, that he would continue the traditional Dutch policies. 'Can this be the prince', wrote a pamphleteer, 'whom we called in to save us from the anti-commercial yoke of Napoleon?' More judicious critics of the 'Appelian' system recognized that it could not be blamed for the failure of the Dutch trade revival, the causes of which were plain enough.[2]

The financial results of the system of 1816 were disappointing to the government. The king wished to establish his kingdom in a manner befitting its dignity, and to undertake public improvements. He had confidence in the future prosperity he was striving to promote and was willing to cover deficits by borrowing, but he had counted on the accuracy of the over-optimistic revenue estimates of 1816. In 1818, therefore, Appelius proposed excises on coffee and sugar.

The government had now great difficulty in securing a majority in the States General. The lower chamber, being without organized parties and being elected not by direct suffrage but by the provincial States, contained many members on whom the government could normally rely, but when national feelings were aroused control became more difficult. The government seems not to have attempted to buy votes by direct corruption. Sometimes it diminished the hostile vote by measures such as delays in filling vacancies, but the outcry on such occasions suggests that this was rare. Usually, when the government was defeated in the Chamber, it offered minor concessions in return for which a sufficient number of

---

[1] W. L. Jacob, *View*, p. 47.
[2] A.R.A., Roëll 162 (ii)—report by Roëll, 1 March 1821, pp. 19–20, 31; G. K. van Hogendorp, *Bijdragen*, IV, 166; F. A. van Hall, *Onpartijdige beschouwing*, p. 181; *Ged.* VIII (3), 292–3.

members were persuaded by the President of the Chamber to vote in favour of the amended proposals. In 1819, many Dutch members were opposing the government systematically in protest against the 'Appelian' policy; and many Belgians, although broadly satisfied with that policy, were ready to embarrass the government in every way in order to win political concessions or to show that they were good Belgians. Appelius was angry when his new excises were rejected in 1819 by this unnatural combination, and he advised against any attempt at the usual transaction because he doubted the good faith of the handful of Dutch members who might be won over and feared that they might either humiliate the government by rejecting the excises, even after concessions had been made, or make the whole matter public and so further inflame Dutch resentment.[1] The government nevertheless made concessions and the taxes were voted, in spite of much petitioning and pamphleteering by Dutch merchants.

The Dutch merchants were so furious at this new offence to their traditional principles that they had no patience to examine or try out the bonding arrangements which, Appelius believed, would prevent any injury to foreign trade. They denounced the very idea of an excise on sugar and coffee as so incompatible with civilization and commerce that one would scarcely expect to hear of it in Spain, the Barbary Coast or even Japan. It was bad enough that the Appelian system imposed a humiliating supervision on the honest First Hand in wine and spirits, of which only one-quarter were exported or re-exported; it was intolerable that the system should be extended to sugar and coffee, of which one-half to three-quarters were re-exported. In spite of the damage done by the tariff of 1816 to Dutch trade in general, coffee, sugar and tobacco were still showing promise. If two of these trades were to be involved in all the unpleasantness of excise formalities, then sooner than submit the merchants would allow trade to come to a standstill and live on the comfortable interest obtainable by lending their capital to their own or a foreign government.[2]

The Belgians complained that they were already over-taxed, but most of them approved the sugar and coffee excises as good taxes in themselves. The Dutch therefore regarded these excises as a further example of pro-Belgian policy. Appelius denied this. To taunts that in view of his long experience, he could not as a Dutchman approve in his heart the anti-commercial laws he had introduced, he replied that the whole system was

[1] A.R.A., Staatssec., 5 June 1819, E4.

[2] A.R.A., Staatssec., 12 Feb. 1824, pt. II, 14 April 1820; A.R.A., Roëll 151; *Mem. en cor.* p. 64; *Ged.* VIII (3), 295-7; F. A. van Hall, *Onpartijdige beschouwing*, p. 103.

his own handiwork, based on his intimate convictions. If, he added, in obedience to the king he had had to introduce a system not his own, then he could only have maintained an embarrassed silence about his own convictions.[1] His enemies supposed that his sole objects were administrative convenience and a good revenue to please the king.

The arrangements for the measuring and taxing of existing stocks of coffee and sugar made Appelius very unpopular with the merchants in the summer of 1819. The First Hand complained that the Second Hand would avoid its fair share of the excise. The matter was mentioned to the king by Roëll, a minister without portfolio, who had been dismissed from the Ministry of the Interior in 1817 for unauthorized conversations with foreign diplomats about a fiscal separation between the Dutch and Belgian provinces, on the lines of a Dual Monarchy.[2] Appelius replied that the First Hand was well able to look after its own interests in its bargains with the Second Hand. An acrimonious correspondence followed between Roëll and Appelius, conducted indirectly, through the king's secretary.[3]

The merchants claimed that the introduction of the new excises was immediately followed by loss of trade, and spread rumours that they were the cause of the considerable unemployment in the commercial towns. Certainly, unemployment was growing worse at this time, and in 1820 the British government asked their ambassador for a special report on the depression in Holland. Appelius pointed out that the introduction of the excises had no obvious effect on the imports of coffee and sugar, but Roëll, after visiting Amsterdam in June 1819, had no doubt that the effects on trade were being felt by the humblest porters and tugmen in the shape of a diminished livelihood.

Memories of the eighteenth century led the government to watch the state of opinion in Amsterdam with some anxiety, especially as ill-informed foreigners interpreted all discontents there as signifying a revival of the old opposition to the House of Orange. There were fears of popular discontent during the food shortage in early 1817, but the corn merchants voluntarily agreed to ensure adequate supplies and all remained quiet. In May 1819, however, the chief of police at Amsterdam reported that the discontent which had been seen to be growing for many months past was really dangerous, and he asked for cavalry reinforcements. All classes were united against the new excises in an unprecedented manner, and even old

---

[1] A.R.A., Staatssec., 12 Feb. 1824, pt. 1, 8 Feb. 1820—report from Appelius, 10 Nov. 1819; *Rec. Fin.* pp. 648–52, 654–61.
[2] H. T. Colenbrander, *Willem I, koning der Nederlanden* (Amsterdam, 1931–5), II, 21.   [3] A.R.A., Roëll 151.

Orangist families were showing open discontent. Officials were avoiding public places for fear of hearing the government insulted.[1]

In June 1819, the king sent Roëll to Amsterdam on a mission 'to remove wrong ideas'. Roëll reported:

The lower orders draw conclusions solely from the fluctuations in their own welfare and attribute their unemployment solely to the Customs and Excise, without considering the general state of European trade. Your Majesty will easily perceive that it will be difficult to restore them to that state of mind from which it would have been better for them not to have been drawn. I have reason however to flatter myself that the upper classes are interested enough to play their part in an improvement. At least, I think that I have removed already a great part of the bad impressions with which those I have spoken to were inspired. They assured me that their opposition was not due to any disloyalty to the House of Orange.

If, however, the excise officials proceeded in a French spirit with the verification of the stocks of coffee and sugar declared by the merchants, feelings were likely to be inflamed anew.

Your Majesty will no doubt have observed that now is the time for a real effort to revive our trade by facilities and even, if need be, by momentary connivance. The state of business in Europe is such that probably for a long time there will not be so good a chance to revive a part of our lost commerce by taking advantage of the misfortune of others.

To this hint, the king's secretary replied:

Nothing could be more agreeable to the king than to co-operate in making use of the present circumstances in order to restore a part of our lost commerce. Let commerce itself propose the means, and His Majesty will willingly do all he can, if he judges the proposal sound and suitable.

Roëll's suggestions were not without effect, for in July he was able to report an improvement. Thanks to Appelius' personal intervention, the 'uncooperative spirit' of officials in Amsterdam had been replaced by 'greater facility'. A new Controller had been appointed who understood 'the golden mean between vexatious formality and excessive facility'. Roëll had even invited Appelius to dinner with some merchants, and the evening had passed without unpleasantness.[2]

In August, there was trouble in Rotterdam. Appelius was involved in a brawl outside the Vauxhall, when his son resented the behaviour of 'certain persons to whom the presence of His Excellency seems to have

[1] *Ged.* VIII (2), 451, 457–61.   [2] A.R.A., Roëll 100 and 120.

been unwelcome'. The absence of the police was explained by the fact that they were engaged in watching for disturbances in less fashionable places. The government urged the British ambassador to report that the incident had no political significance.[1] An English visitor to Rotterdam thought otherwise:

The merchants of this city complain that in the assembly of the States, from the superior influence of the landed proprietors of ci-devant Belgium, the interests of manufactures and commerce are made to yield to those of agriculture; and they instance the repeal of the tax on horses, and the increase of those on doors and windows, as proofs that their complaints are not groundless. They attribute to the same influence the increased tax on patents; as we should call them, licences to carry on trade or manufactures, which all must take out, and which are rated, not as under our late income tax according to the net profits, but according to the amount of the business, whether profitable or the contrary.

The enforcement of the ancient navigation law, which prohibited a citizen of Holland from owning a foreign built ship, is a subject of much complaint; and it has been found hitherto of no benefit to their own ship-builders, whose trade was represented to me as in a state of complete stagnation.

Above all the other complaints of the Rotterdam merchants, the loudest is against some new duties on coffee, the passing of which from one dealer to another is placed by the same law under some severe regulations resembling our excise system. Notwithstanding all these complaints, however, they all unite in ascribing to their monarch the best intentions; but are most vehement in their expressions of wrath against the minister Alopeus (*sic*), who is accused of being the author of the extension of the excise laws to coffee, and who was, lately, first insulted and afterwards expelled from the public gardens of this city, by the whole of the company, who were by no means of the lower class of the people. They all confess that this minister possesses talents, and some allow him integrity; but, having been formed in the school of Buonaparte, who was himself ignorant of the interests of commerce, he is accused of having imbibed maxims which, however plausible in theory, are either impracticable, or, if reducible to practice, become highly injurious. Such are the views of the merchants here; perhaps an acquaintance with the landholders of Belgium might lead to very different, if not opposite views on the subject.[2]

A new political crisis occurred in the autumn of 1819. The Constitution required that only fluctuating expenditure should be approved annually by the States General; the rest was to be covered by a decennial budget.

---

[1] *Ged.* VIII (1), 140; (2), 467.   [2] W. L. Jacob, *View*, p. 11.

In order to reduce the States General's powers of obstruction, the king proposed that out of an annual expenditure of 80 million florins, 70 million should be covered by the first decennial budget, presented in October 1819. Once it was passed, changes could only be made by royal initiative. The Dutch commercial party therefore opposed a budget that would make the system of 1816 largely inviolable for ten years. The agitation against the coffee and sugar excises continued and was broadened into a demand for a complete return to the traditional Dutch fiscal system.

In pamphlets and conversation, the commercial party began to speak of a state of war between the government and the Dutch people, and to suggest that the system of 1816 could not be enforced much longer except by bayonets. Would the king use force against his loyal Dutchmen, for the sake of Belgians to whom every concession was a sign of weakness? The Ministers were condemned as time-servers; they were contrasted with Van Hogendorp and Gogel, who had either resisted the French or served them only in order to protect Dutch interests, but who both refused to collaborate with the present government. Even in the States General, Dutch members prophesied that the disunity caused by the system of 1816 would expose the kingdom to collapse at the first gust of wind. The merchants threatened to withhold support in time of crisis, particularly the financial support on which Dutch governments relied in an emergency. These were no idle threats, for there was a general fear at that time that new revolutionary storms were brewing in Europe.[1]

No disorders occurred, but anxiety remained. In March 1820, the Minister of Justice complained that in Holland anyone was free to slander the king and his government to the peril of all ordered society, for the judges and law officers failed in their duty from fear of unpopularity; no one stirred a finger to prosecute seditious writers except after persistent prodding by the Ministry. This was the more regrettable because in Belgium conditions were now much better. In fact, Belgian sedition at this time was confined to Bonapartist veterans. In 1819, a Belgian newspaper argued that Belgium had enjoyed a truer independence as part of a respected nation of 30 million than now, when 'only the stage has shrunk, so that dwarfs can strut about who would not have been noticed before'.[2]

Behind its bluster, the Dutch commercial party was not in the least revolutionary. Its power was purely negative. By joining its votes to

[1] A.R.A., Roëll 162 (ii)—report from Roëll, 1 March 1821; *Knuttel* 25096 (Vrijmoedige gedachten...Amsterdam, 1822); *Knuttel* 24886 (speech by Van Alphen, 24 Dec. 1819); F. A. van Hall, *Onpartijdige beschouwing*, p. 34.
[2] *Ged.* VIII (2), 449–50, 453, 494.

those of the Belgian opposition, it might defeat government measures, but it could never hope to have a majority for its own proposals, unless by the use of the royal influence. Those merchants whose course of action was that advised by Roëll, of seeking to win concessions from the government by loyal co-operation, justified themselves against the reproaches of their brethren by pointing out that nothing could be gained except by the personal intervention of the king. 'Nothing can save us except a firm hand, for which our present Constitution is well suited. This firm hand must shore up our commerce, protect its freedom, reduce public expenditure and properly appraise public opinion.'[1] The aim of the commercial opposition was to show the government that its support was indispensable for the political stability of the kingdom and would not be given gratuitously. Its threats were always accompanied by an appeal to the king to intervene in favour of 'his eldest children'. The merchants hoped for a new compromise with the government and the Belgians, but one more favourable to them than the 'transaction' of 1816.[2] Van Hogendorp was not willing to compromise, but he was more concerned with principles than with practical politics or practical commerce. He desired representative government as well as free trade, and sought to achieve the latter not by the intervention of the king but by educating public opinion.

There was much Belgian opposition in the States General to the decennial budget because it postponed for so long all hope of considerable tax reductions, and would deprive the Belgian deputies of a weapon for obtaining redress of political grievances. They therefore tried to exact a price for their support, especially concessions in regard to the judicial system. The budget was defeated in December 1819.

The king was indignant. He considered that the Belgians had acted in bad faith, since the fiscal system was designed to please them and had incurred Dutch hostility for that very reason. Appelius felt that the political climate was changing. In December he repeated to the Lower Chamber advice he had already given to the king in November:

The purest intentions and the firmest will cannot, in this conflict of opinions, give the man at the head of this difficult Department the assurance that his views are right, nor the king an ultimate conviction that the advice offered is the best for his people. An expert commission, in which neither commerce nor industry should have the majority, can reassure the king and the States General for the future.[3]

[1] B. C. E. Zwart, *De Kamer van Koophandel en Fabrieken te Amsterdam*, p. 111, (speech by J. Huidekoper, 22 Feb. 1820).   [2] *Knuttel* 24886.
[3] A.R.A., Staatssec., 12 Feb. 1824, pt. 1, 8 Feb. 1820—report from Appelius, 10 Nov. 1819; *2de kamer* (1819–20), A 48–9; *Ged.* VIII (2), 234–7.

Such a commission was appointed by a Royal Decree of 23 January 1820. It was understood that if the budget passed, the king would in due course take action to redress as far as possible the grievances of the commercial party. Opinion at Amsterdam grew more moderate and many were said to feel that the only way to get the king to protect Dutch traditions against the Belgians was to give him the means. Supporters of the commercial interest in the States General expressed agreement with the government's argument that a further rejection of the decennial budget would weaken the king in regard to both internal and external security, at a time when strength seemed specially necessary. After 10 million florins had been transferred to the annual budget, the decennial one was passed, mainly by Dutch votes.[1]

The acceptance of the decennial budget showed the weakness of the commercial party; for, whatever the commission decided, the system of 1816 could now only be reformed by royal initiative, and the king had made no promises. The decennial budget had no meaning except in increasing the royal authority, for the king was expected to propose drastic changes at the end of the first year after receiving the commission's report, and many Dutch members declared that they voted for the budget only in the hope of its transformation then into a 'good' one. The budget did not really balance, for it was based on the faulty estimates of 1817, and the commission was instructed to consider how the revenue might actually be made to cover the approved expenditure. The commercial party could have made a good case for insisting that only annual budgets should be voted until the commission had reported.

[1] *Ged.* VIII (3), 298–303; *2de kamer* (1819–20), A 55, 60, 82, 141, 147, 153.

Chapter VII

DUTCH-BELGIAN FISCAL UNION: THE SYSTEM OF 1821

(a) The commission of 1820

The appointment of the commission was a turning point in the political history of the Dutch-Belgian union, but not because there was any hope that it would fulfil its allotted task 'of restoring confidence between the government and the governed, and real unity between the various parts of the kingdom'. The commission, which started work in February 1820, consisted of eight Dutch and eight Belgian members. Roëll was chairman, but with no casting vote. The commission was first to make general recommendations to the king; later, it was to be recalled to draft specific legislation in accordance with the king's final instructions. Since neither side would modify its claims, the proceedings of the commission decided nothing and served merely for the rehearsal of familiar arguments. The representatives of Dutch commerce in the commission were well aware of its futility, but hoped it would prepare the way for the decisions they expected from the king. They made it no secret that if in the second stage of the commission's work they were required merely to prepare minor amendments of the Appelian system they would resign, 'unable to bear the blame of their fellow-citizens for appearing to co-operate in such work'. Not all the Dutch members represented commerce or Holland, but with one exception they supported the commercial demand for the abolition of the coffee and sugar excises, and their replacement by taxes on flour, meat, horses and servants. The member who represented North Brabant, as was to be expected, joined the Belgians in support of the system of 1816. For what it was worth, therefore, the Belgians had a majority in the commission.[1]

The Belgian members consulted separately among themselves about their line in the commission, and one of them even spoke openly of a Belgian mandate. Belgian members who disagreed with this 'mandate' on any particular point usually conformed in the end. The only important exception was that the member from Antwerp persisted in supporting the Dutch proposal to cover the deficit by a tax on flour, provided it was not too strictly enforced in rural areas. It was said to be the unanimous desire of Belgium that the deficit should be abolished by retrenchment, but that

[1] A.R.A., Roëll 162 (iii and vii).

tobacco, tea and rice should be taxed in order to provide relief from the taxes on real property. The most generous concession the Belgian members dared to offer, they said, was to leave things as they were; if they agreed that the coffee and sugar excises should be abolished instead of being increased, they would become objects of public detestation in their own country.

The discussion degenerated into a quarrel as to the relative incidence of taxes in the Dutch and Belgian provinces. The greatest ill-feeling arose over the question of the fuel excises. The Dutch complained that their peat was much more heavily taxed in relation to its calorific value than Belgian coal, and proposed a large increase in the coal excise. The Belgians replied that coal-mines required more capital and labour and were more useful to the state and to the national industries than were peat diggings. The Belgians conceded that the peat duty might be slightly reduced, but this was scornfully rejected by the Dutch, who claimed that they did not wish to avoid reasonable taxation themselves but merely to ensure that the Belgians paid their share. According to the Dutch, the Belgians were under-assessed for direct taxes. Each side accused the other of widespread fraud and evasion.[1]

Only about tariff policy was the commission able to make unanimous recommendations. Both sides admitted that a compromise between free trade and protection was necessary and possible, and Roëll carefully confined discussion to principles and shelved all consideration of particular rates of duty. The following principles were agreed to:

1. 5% to be the maximum duty for purely commercial goods.
2. Higher duties to be admitted when necessary for the protection of industry and agriculture, but not so high as to stimulate smuggling unduly.
3. If various interests conflicted, their relative importance to be taken into account.
4. Prohibitions to be enacted when absolutely necessary.
5. The system of a special transit duty to continue for goods liable to high import or export duties, with appropriate bonding arrangements.

Unanimity was marred, however, by the insistence of the Dutch commercial members on the inclusion in the record of their 'interpretation' of these principles, to the effect that exceptions to the 5% maximum must be rare in order that transit and bonding might not become a normal and obligatory procedure in general trade. The Belgians, in a counter-statement, interpreted the commission's recognition of the principle of

[1] A.R.A., Staatssec., 12 Feb. 1824, no. 67, pt. II, 16–30 May 1820; pt. III, 7–16 June 1820.

protection to mean that industry should not be sacrificed to commerce, as in the old Republic, but should share priority only with agriculture. The experience of commercial peoples, they said, had long borne out the utility of transit and bonding as a means of carrying on foreign trade without injury to home industry, so that Dutch objections could be discounted as mere prejudice. Free trade in Europe was good as an ultimate ideal; but it must be pursued by protection and reprisal, and above all by continued economic resistance against England and by a commercial treaty with France. The final aim might be a European commercial congress which could force England to come to terms. To this, the Dutch commercial members replied again:

We are convinced that manufacturing enterprises in all countries are exaggerated and that half their products cannot be consumed. Nothing can prevent the ruin of most of these factories within a few years. And their public usefulness has in any case been much diminished by the use of machinery.

How, they asked, could the Kingdom of the Netherlands challenge the supremacy of British industry when Hamburg was a willing distributing centre for British goods? How could it be said that commercial experience approved the bonding system, since it had been unknown in Holland, the cradle of commerce?[1]

When the commission had finished its first task and placed the king in possession of the views of the Belgian majority and of the Dutch minority, Roëll privately sent in a separate report urging the king to decide in favour of the minority.

Your Majesty is no doubt mindful that the advantage of union with the South is far to seek, as far as the northern provinces are concerned; so that in comparison with what might otherwise have been they can only regret the European necessity that prevented their separate existence.

In order to reconcile his northern subjects to the union, Roëll advised the king to relieve Dutch trade from a depression worse than had ever been known in time of peace by remedies which would have to be more drastic than those proposed in 1751; it was a great opportunity, for the depression was international and when recovery began 'a general staple market will be established by choice wherever imports are least restricted and where the foreign merchant can be sure of selling his goods and of finding what he needs.' Only through such a general market could the products of the

---

[1] A.R.A., Roëll 162; A.R.A., Staatssec., 12 Feb. 1824, no. 67, pt. II, 16–19 May 1820.

kingdom be exported by sea, for they could never make up complete cargoes. The reform need not ignore legitimate Belgian interests, for according to Roëll the Dutch merchants would agree to the continuance of some protective duties for industry on condition that sugar, coffee and other purely commercial goods had appropriate freedom. Fiscal difficulties could be overcome by taxes on meal and meat, servants and horses. The king's proposals should be sent to the commission, when it was recalled, in very detailed form and discussion of anything else should be forbidden. Otherwise, the majority would again press for taxes on tobacco and so on, which the Dutch believed would be ruinous.

If this is not the feeling of Your Majesty, then no doubt the importance I attach to conducting the proceedings of the commission in the manner described would be needless...but without such instructions from Your Majesty, I tremble to think of the renewal of our deliberations.... Perhaps, however, the principles of freer trade, which are making such headway in many European countries, may alter the ideas of certain members: otherwise I see no likelihood of a good outcome to the second part of the work.[1]

(b) Gogel's proposals

In contrast to the experience of Appelius after 1816, Gogel's system of 1805, in spite of the political and natural disasters that followed its introduction and in spite of obstruction due to national disunity, had always yielded revenue beyond his estimates.[2] The disappointing financial results of the system of 1816 were probably the main reason for the king's decision to try a change. By the end of 1819, it was clear that new revenue could not be found simply by adding new taxes to the existing system; for many Belgian members of the States General would vote against any new taxes except anti-commercial ones intolerable to Holland. The only constitutional means of increasing taxation was by winning the necessary Dutch votes, and for that the abandonment of the Appelian system was necessary. The king therefore consulted Gogel.

Gogel was not a member of the old merchant oligarchy, though he was a supporter of traditional Dutch commercial policy. The son of a German officer in Dutch service, he was one of those ambitious outsiders who had resented their exclusion for social or religious reasons from the public life of the old Republic and had found scope for their enthusiasm in the revolution. The French connexion made his public career possible and he remained loyal to the Napoleonic government as long as it existed, to

[1] A.R.A., Roëll 162 (i).
[2] *Mem. en cor.* p. 129.

the extent even of going into exile in France after the Dutch uprising of 1813. In December 1814, William I, in accordance with his policy of employing for preference the talent trained by the French, invited Gogel to resume his official career, but Gogel preferred an honourable retirement. He did not renew his former attempts to establish himself among the merchants and financiers of Amsterdam, but was content with the ownership and management of a small provincial blue-powder factory.[1]

In France, in the spring of 1814, Gogel wrote out a plan, in the language of a 'Batavian', whereby the Continental allies could free the commerce of Holland from English dictatorship. He described the uprising of 1813 as an intrigue of a few Orangists and English agents who, to forestall any movement for 'genuine independence', had frightened the public by acts of pillage and then brought in the Prince of Orange as guarantor of order. Europe needed Dutch independence, however, in order that Holland might fulfil her old function as 'universal market-place, free of all foreign domination'. Unless such a centre existed, European countries would be unable to obtain or export any goods for which the demand did not justify complete cargoes, their economic life would be handicapped, and the production of wine, for instance, would diminish. In order to guarantee the inviolability of goods entrusted to Dutch trade, Dutch neutrality should be protected by an international treaty, whereby a Dutch Republic should be set up and forbidden to contract foreign alliances or to impose any customs duty higher than 3%.[2] By such a plan, Gogel afterwards considered, Holland might have seized a rare opportunity 'for restoring her commercial glory' while Hamburg had still not recovered from the war.[3]

Gogel was suspicious of the king's intentions when in January 1820 he received the offer of membership of the commission and hints of high office later. He would only agree to give his advice privately, and in order not to blemish his reputation, he insisted that the consultations should take place in an atmosphere of conspiratorial secrecy. Documents and statistics from the royal cabinet were supplied to him. Appelius and most of the Ministers knew nothing of this. Roëll knew, however, and he consulted with Gogel in order that their advice to the king might be in harmony.[4]

Gogel's sympathies were with small enterprise. Great fortunes, he said, were pests in the state. Yet he recommended a bread tax as the chief means

---

[1] J. A. Sillem, *I. J. A. Gogel*; *Ged.* VI (2), 15, 41.
[2] J. A. Sillem, *I. J. A. Gogel*, pp. 116–26.
[3] *Mem. en cor.* p. 63; *Ged.* VIII (2), 223–31.
[4] *Mem. en cor.* pp. 1–8, 181–8; A.R.A., Roëll 162 (v).

of covering the deficit and of replacing all anti-commercial taxes. His reason, he explained, was that no satisfactory way existed of taxing wealth. An income tax of the English type was theoretically attractive, but he rejected it as impracticable. Its enforcement would probably require bayonets, and the higher incomes would anyway escape, for the great ones would complain too much and were too near the government not to be heard. Direct taxes should therefore only be imposed on easily verifiable bases, so that in the main the authorities could rely on self-assessment by the taxpayers. Such taxes could be levied on the ownership of real property, on its use according to rental value, and on servants, horses, hearths, doors and windows, and furniture; but not much extra revenue could be found thus, for many of these taxes existed already, and were too high to give the best results.

Gogel was bitterly opposed to the patents tax, levied on the profits of all industrial and commercial undertakings. Assessment was based on the type of business, the populousness of the district, the nature of the equipment and the number of workers. The tax was believed on average to be about $2\frac{1}{2}\%$ of net profits. Gogel believed that it discouraged enterprise, and complained that the taxpayer had to reveal to officials business secrets which a prudent man would conceal even from his wife. The tax was very unpopular with small men, who said that the rich were spared; he had heard them, in Haarlem, wish that Napoleon were back, because the imperial officials had not been afraid to make the rich pay. Gogel proposed to replace the tax by stamped licences at flat rates.

Gogel believed that the middle classes were the most useful, and that workshops were preferable to factories. The traditional policies of Holland had in his opinion fostered small enterprise, whereas the interfering and protective system of 1816 encouraged only a few unhealthy, privileged interests. If excises were levied only on the traditional objects and not before the Third Hand, and if customs duties were reduced to 3%, then the yield of all taxes would gradually improve with the spread of prosperity among the small men who must always bear the main fiscal burden. He was not actuated by free-trade theory, but expected tangible benefit from a return to tradition, especially as embodied in the system of 1805. Among the innovations he proposed, was an excise on foreign refined sugar to protect Dutch refiners in the home market. Since all excise would be levied from the retailer and bonding would be unnecessary, this would not affect foreign trade.[1]

[1] *Mem. en cor.* pp. 15–25, 37, 129–69, 291–330; A.R.A., Roëll 100—letter from Roëll to the king, 11 Sept. 1820; J. A. Sillem, *I. J. A. Gogel*, pp. 187–99; F. N. Sickenga, *Geschiedenis der Nederlandsche belastingen sedert 1810*, I, 74–95, 137–74.

In August 1820, the king, having considered all the advice he had received, instructed Roëll to try to persuade Gogel of the need to compromise in accordance with political realities, and to secure his acceptance of responsibility for introducing a new system under the king's orders. Gogel's reply was not encouraging, but after being received with Roëll in secret audience by the king, he consented to assist in preparing legislation. The interview lasted four hours, being mostly spent in discussion of the methods by which flour excise could be levied with least offence to rural Belgium. The king indicated his intentions, and invited Roëll and Gogel to embody them in a draft 'general' law which would enact nothing, but would set out the broad lines of a new fiscal system to be implemented later by 'special' laws.[1]

The draft law prepared by Gogel and Roëll included new taxes on servants and horses, flour and meat. The quarrel over the fuel excises was resolved by their abolition, and replacement by a hearth tax. This compromise was suggested by Roëll, who considered Gogel's desire to increase the coal tax to be impolitic. Roëll contended that most of Gogel's wishes in regard to customs and excise administration could be attained in substance in the detailed regulations, without offending Belgian opinion by formal abandonment of the principle of controlling customs at the frontier and excise at the source. The draft law was therefore vague on these points. Excise was to be assessed at the source but paid only at the Third Hand. Control of the First and Second Hands was to be by documentation and inspection, but the full bonding system was to be enforced 'when necessary'. Customs formalities were to be made less annoying for the merchants, and interior controls were consequently to be introduced 'when necessary'. The question of the customs tariff was only vaguely mentioned; Roëll and Gogel pressed hard for decisions in favour of the Dutch tradition, but the king would not commit himself and suggested that it would be as well to postpone further controversy until the flour excise, which would be the most unpopular innovation, had been approved by the States General. The king tried to remove suspicions that once he had secured additional revenue his concessions to the commercial party would cease. He wrote to Roëll:

Would not the following remarks largely remove your present objection to the omission from the first general law of provision for the tariff in all its details? First, in the interest of commerce and in order to meet complaints from that quarter without loss of revenue, two taxes will be laid on the consumer, those on meat and flour, which not only caused opposition before but are quite unknown in many provinces,

[1] *Mem. en cor.* p. 194.

where obstruction may therefore be foreseen. Secondly, the draft law estimates the customs revenue at 5,500,000 fl. instead of 7,400,000 as at present.[1] . . . If nevertheless any doubt can remain about present intentions for the tariff, it will lapse owing to the direction taken by the resumed proceedings of the commission; and your personal opinions are a guarantee that you will not lend your hand to measures not designed to meet the needs of commerce.[2]

The king would not agree to the abolition of both the coffee and the sugar excise. Although the coffee excise was the more unpopular, Gogel considered the sugar excise to be the more corrupting to business morals and so it was the coffee excise that was retained in the draft law. The proceedings of the commission had in fact shown that some Amsterdam refiners had no objection to the sugar excise and that the claim of the merchants who petitioned against it to speak for the whole trade was unfounded. This was due to the drawback or write-off of the excise on imported raw sugar which was granted on the export of refined. The government always intended this to be generous enough to constitute a concealed export subsidy. The practical results were quite arbitrary, for they depended on the extraction ratio, which varied greatly and was a sacrosanct trade secret. The refiners generally do not seem to have had much practical benefit until the scale of drawbacks was made both more generous and more scientific in 1830, but some refiners were making unfair and perhaps illicit gains under the law of 1819. Another unforeseen result of that law was that large refineries were encouraged. Small refiners began to join in partnerships in order to get the maximum benefit from the law. Roëll and Gogel condemned these tendencies. The smaller, more individualistic and more honest refiners, they believed, joined with the First Hand in opposition to the excise and to those refiners who wished it to continue. Under conditions of free and healthy competition from 1813 to 1819, they asserted, the Amsterdam refineries had increased in number from the two that survived the Continental System to sixty; no export subsidy was needed therefore, and certainly not one that distorted natural development and injured small operators, who ought to be encouraged rather on social grounds.[3]

When, after two months of negotiation, the terms of the draft law were decided, Gogel refused finally to accept any public responsibility for intro-

---

[1] The customs revenue actually realized under the system of 1816 was about 6,500,000 fl.: F. N. Sickenga, *Geschiedenis der Nederlandsche belastingen sedert 1810*, II, 128.
[2] A.R.A., Roëll 86 and 100.
[3] A.R.A., Roëll 162 (i); *Mem. en cor.*; J. J. Reesse, *De suikerhandel van Amsterdam 1813–1894* (The Hague, 1911), pp. 5–7; J. C. Westermann, *Kamer van Koophandel en Fabrieken voor Amsterdam* (Amsterdam, 1936), I, 155.

ducing the new system. The main reason he gave was that the draft law allowed for the continuance of too many obnoxious formalities. 'I fear that if the words Free Trade were inscribed on the banners of a neighbouring French or Prussian revolt, many a traditional Netherlander would be tempted to collaborate.' He seems in fact to have felt that he would not be given enough power to achieve the 'decisive act of will' necessary for effective reform. He believed that a coherent fiscal system could be built only by a single, independent architect, and that compromises, negotiations and committees implied botched workmanship. Roëll urged that the draft law promised real benefit to commerce and that its success was still worth working for; but that if the administration of the new system were left to Appelius and his 'paper-sick' clerks much of the advantage would be lost.[1]

The draft law, modified, since Gogel's views need no longer be deferred to, by omission of the coffee and the retention of the sugar excise, was revealed in January 1821 to the two ministers most concerned. Appelius, who was now in charge of all revenue departments, raised no objection to taking the main responsibility for introducing the new system. The Minister of Finance, however, who was responsible for expenditure and borrowing, submitted to the king a long memorandum against it. He thought it unwise to reopen fiscal controversy and so lose the advantage of the decennial budget. The introduction of Gogel's system in 1805 was a warning of the bitterness and obstruction aroused by changes in taxation even when questions of principle were not involved and the country was united on the main lines of policy. The proposal of a flour tax would cause unpleasantness much greater, though from a different quarter, than that attending the introduction of the sugar and coffee excise in 1819, and controversy would continue until all the special laws were enacted. It was even doubtful whether a majority could be secured in the States General, for all the Belgians were likely to vote against and to be joined by some deputies from those Dutch agricultural provinces that by tradition always resisted fiscal changes desired by commerce. Public confidence would be upset and it would become more difficult for the government to borrow. He believed that the deficit would continue, for the unknown author of the draft law had overestimated the yield of the new taxes, having based his calculations on their yield in the Dutch provinces under Gogel and ignored the fact that the Belgians had a different moral standard and a different attitude to taxation. The productiveness of the Dutch flour excise had been almost wholly due to Holland, Zeeland and Friesland, where enforcement was strict; but such enforcement was unlikely to be

[1] A.R.A., Roëll 100; *Mem. en cor.* pp. 227–9.

possible anywhere in Belgium. He asked to be excused from defending the draft law in the States General, on the ground that his own department was not concerned and that he was ignorant of revenue matters; but the king refused, and he resigned.[1]

The commission met in Brussels in January 1821, under an oath of secrecy, to consider the draft law. The Belgian public soon surmised the nature of the king's proposals and the Belgian members of the commission responded to the pressure of opinion by increasing restiveness under the firm chairmanship of Roëll, who ruled that their duty was not to criticize royal decisions but merely to advise on their implementation. Each clause was considered in isolation from the rest and no general discussion was permitted; but Roëll could not prevent the majority from opposing the government on all the main points. The majority was against the flour and meat excises, and for the continuance of the coffee and fuel excises and the system of bonding and levy at source. Two Dutch members voted against the flour excise. On the other hand, the voting on the horses and servants' taxes occurred at an early stage when feelings were less excited, and the majority was content merely to attach to its reluctant consent a request that the proposed rates of tax should be reduced. Approval was also given to some proposals of minor administrative reform. This enabled the government to take up an official attitude that 'it appears to the king that the great majority in the commission have felt compelled to agree with most of the points put before them'. This deception was possible because the proceedings of the commission were not published and its members were under oath of secrecy. In reality, the king had been irritated by the attitude of the Belgian members. When Roëll asked for the formal dissolution of the commission, the king replied that it was unnecessary, as after the course taken by their deliberations the members could hardly expect the fulfilment of the declared intention to consult them again about the special laws.[2]

(c) The system of 1821

The appointment of the commission of 1820 revived in Holland some of the optimism of 1813. Pamphlets were published to show that Dutch commerce could yet be saved if it were freed of fiscal burdens.[3] In the autumn of 1820, however, as there was still no evidence that the king's promise to investigate Dutch grievances was to lead to any action, opinion in Holland grew restive. There were rumours that the influence

[1] A.R.A., Financiën diversen, ZZ 101.
[2] A.R.A., Roëll 120; A.R.A., Financiën diversen, ZZ 101; A.R.A., Staatssec., 12 Feb. 1824, no. 67, pt. IV.   [3] *Knuttel* 24886, 24888–90, 24916.

of Appelius was again predominant, and the merchants again began to petition against him. In the spring of 1821, the chief of police at Amsterdam reported a danger of public disorders:

If we had not our unfortunate financial system, we should have little cause for anxiety; but discontent grows from day to day. I realise that in the present state of Europe we cannot hope for great prosperity, but it is as sure as sure can be that the displacement of our American and Iberian trade to Hamburg and Bremen and the decreasing activity of our sugar refineries are due to that system.[1]

News of the government's intentions, however, was spreading among the leaders of the commercial interest, and those in the know had now high hopes that if the king stood firm traditional Dutch policies might slowly be imposed on the kingdom. They attached no importance to the proceedings of the commission, but began canvassing members of the States General. The results of these inquiries were discouraging. It was clear that the draft law would only pass if 'in one way or another' all Dutch members could be persuaded to drop personal or provincial objections and form a common front against the Belgians. In addition it would be necessary to find a few 'yes brothers' among the Belgians. Even so, concessions might have to be made by reducing the proposed flour excise and especially its incidence in rural areas.[2]

The draft law was submitted to the States General in April 1821. Discussions in the sections of the Lower Chamber went badly for the government. It was believed, reported the central section, that a nominal roll of opinions expressed would have shown that all the southern and most of the northern deputies except those of Holland were against the proposal to relieve commerce of part of its fiscal burden by introducing a flour tax.[3]

The government made concessions, mainly by reducing the proposed rate of duty on rye and by providing for the commutation of the tax by rural communes for a maximum annual payment equal to 1.40 fl. per head of their population, a figure which was based on an average consumption of four bushels of wheat.

Whether as a result of these concessions, or from patriotism, or for other reasons, no hostile criticism of the draft law was heard during the full debate from Dutch members, in spite of challenges by the Belgians to vote and speak as freely as in the sections. The Belgians, quoting

[1] *Ged.* VIII (2), 530; G. K. van Hogendorp, *Bijdragen*, VI, 233; *Gedenkboek der Kamer van Koophandel en Fabrieken te Rotterdam 1803–1928* (Rotterdam, 1928), p. 154.
[2] A.R.A., Roëll 162 (iii and vii); *Mem. en cor.* p. 215.
[3] A.R.A., Staatssec., 12 July 1821, no. 57; *Rec. fin.* p. cxxxvii.

speeches made by Appelius in 1816, claimed that most of the Dutch population was really on their side, but that the commercial interest of Holland, with the help of the government and of servile Dutch deputies, was imposing its will on the whole country. In the old Republic, they added, Holland had purchased the acquiescence of the other provinces in her policies by undertaking the greatest fiscal burden herself; but in the new kingdom, Holland and Amsterdam only paid their fair share and had no right to dictate. The deputies from the Dutch agricultural provinces replied that they would vote with Holland by their own free will, for the prosperity of their provinces depended on the commerce of Holland, and Amsterdam therefore deserved the gratitude of all the North for its loyalty to the old traditions.

Thanks to this Dutch solidarity, the law passed by 57 votes to 53. Every deputy voted. Three Belgians voted for; one Dutchman, from North Brabant, voted against. This unusually complete division between Dutch and Belgians gave rise to dangerous thoughts, for the defeated opposition in the States General represented a considerable majority in the population of the kingdom. Under the existing constitution, Belgian deputies complained, the weaker partner in the kingdom, could, in alliance with the government, permanently impose its 'fratricidal' will; the commercial oligarchy of Holland was now treating Belgium as North Brabant had been treated in the old Republic, and in the same spirit that had secured the closing of the Scheldt and the destruction of the Ostend Company, but before breaking up the compromise of 1816 it would have been prudent to measure the real strength of the two parties.[1]

The solidarity of the Belgians was no less remarkable than that of the Dutch. Representatives of the mining and industrial interests that had always bitterly opposed the coal excise showed no gratitude for its removal, but joined the outcry against the hearth tax that replaced it. In deference to Dutch peat owners, it was said, the government was introducing a tax that discriminated unfairly against the large houses of the Belgian upper classes. There was similar uniformity of argument in the national agitation against the law outside the States General. The Chamber of Commerce and Industry at Liége, for instance, though admitting that the abolition of the coal excise would be a great benefit to the factories, protested that the hearth tax would be unfair to Belgian households and petitioned that the fuel excises should be retained instead, with exemption for coal used in factories.[2]

The general law received the royal assent on 12 July 1821. The preparation of the special laws started at once, but it took longer than had been

[1] *Rec. fin.*   [2] A.R.A., Goldberg 215.

expected, for the government, impressed by the strength of opposition, calculated the balance of forces afresh in deciding each detail. The introduction of the new system was postponed and the draft special law for the flour excise was not debated by the States General until July 1822. It did not differ from the principles of the general law; but it gave the Belgians an excellent opportunity for obstruction, and both sides rallied for a final struggle.

The Belgians argued that there was no longer any hope of restoring Holland's general trade; for, owing to the spread of civilization, all European countries could now provide for themselves by direct trading. In future, only ordinary trade would be needed, and in a country of only five million people such trade must be small. The needs of agriculture and industry must therefore determine government policy. The United Provinces had ruined themselves in the eighteenth century by sacrificing everything to foreign trade. They had not saved their commerce, but had destroyed their industries by low customs duties and high taxes on the necessities of life. The union with Belgium gave the Dutch a thing rare in history, a chance to remedy their mistake; but instead they seemed determined to involve Belgium in the consequences of their folly. The numerous paupers of the cities of Holland were evidence of the results of traditional Dutch policies; only men so accustomed to the sight of this misery as to think it a matter of course could now propose a policy of free trade and a tax on bread. Britain, it was pointed out, was more successful than the Netherlands not only in industry but also, thanks to her bonding system, in commerce; and in spite of her heavy budget she did not tax essential foods, but rather colonial goods imported for home consumption. The effect of the bread tax would be to ruin the Belgian export industries by increased costs, for British competition had already reduced their profit margin to a minimum. The consequent unemployment would be especially dangerous because it would coincide with the completion of the fortifications built as a barrier against France in accordance with treaty obligations. It was absurd to impose such a tax and at the same time abolish the coffee excise, for the coffee trade was a monstrous leech, sucking away specie from the country and discouraging the cultivation of chicory.

The government's supporters claimed that the new system would benefit the poor, for they would be relieved not only of fuel excises, but also of all direct taxation, for under the law of 1821 poll tax was to be abolished and all dwellings of a rental value below 0·60 fl. per week were to be exempt from the taxes on rent, furniture, hearths, doors and windows. Instead of these inconvenient terminal taxes, the poor would only have to pay an excise on rye levied imperceptibly throughout the year. The flour excise was therefore an excellent way of enforcing the necessary and beneficial rule implied by the social contract, that all classes must contribute something to the state; however, if any were too poor even to bear the tax on rye, then they had the remedy in their own hands, for they could eat potatoes instead. The Belgian opposition to the flour excise was said to be a mere feint that concealed the real motive of the Belgian landowners, to escape the new luxury taxes on servants, horses and hearths.

The Belgians replied that the poor had never paid the direct taxes to which they were legally liable. The system of levying had been to decide first the lump sum that could be raised from each tax over the whole country and then to break it down proportionally to each province and commune. The commune was then responsible for raising the sum at which it was assessed. The sum could be divided locally among individuals by rough justice, without excessive regard for the letter of the law. Thus, in practice, the rich, not the poor, had paid. But the Belgian poor could not escape the flour tax, for they were accustomed to eat wheat and rye. Statistics were produced to show that much more corn was consumed per head in the south than in the north of the kingdom. The Dutch merchants were said to be particularly selfish in thus seeking to raise labour costs for Belgian industry, in view of the fact that the workers in Holland were known to eat mainly potatoes. It seemed likely that four-fifths of the burden of the flour excise and other new taxes would be borne by Belgium, but the government sought to conceal this by its deceptively low estimates of the yield from Belgian provinces.

The landowners, said the Belgians, were the true bankers of the poor. They did not hoard their income, like the miserly capitalists and rentiers of the north, but employed servants and bought the luxury goods produced by industry. They would suffer both by the new taxes on luxury and by the rise in wages and prices due to the bread tax. The new proposals were unjust to them; but the exemption of those who lived in poor houses would create a new privileged class, like the former feudal aristocracy, and was contrary to the Constitution, which abolished all tax privileges. The old system had enabled the communes to make the capitalists pay their share, but they could never be caught by Gogel's system of relying on self-assessment and on tax-collectors bound by rigid regulations. For in the country many rich but miserly rentiers lived in premises with a rental value lower than 0·60 fl. per week, although a worker in the industrial towns could not get such cheap living-quarters and so would incur direct taxes as well as the bread tax under the new system.

Van Hogendorp, who was suffering from gout, gathered his strength for a special effort on this occasion. In the latter days of the system of 1816, he had drawn near to tactical co-operation with the Belgian liberals, whose concept of constitutional monarchy was like his own. The law of 1821 rallied him to the defence of the government, but the hesitations of 1822 made him suspicious of its sincerity. So he attempted to revive the true spirit of the law of 1821 by delivering in the Lower Chamber one of his long lectures about Dutch history and political economy. The law of 1821, he said, promised a return to Dutch tradition:

Trade will be encouraged and recaptured by low duties and a correspondingly mild customs administration; young industries will be fostered by subsidies, but not by high import duties; consumption within the country, which will increase with restored prosperity, will be more heavily taxed in order to make up the necessary revenue; new personal taxes will serve to spread taxation fairly between rich and poor.

The flour excise was justified only in order that enterprise might be free, and must be accompanied by a real effort to restore Holland's general commerce by measures of free trade. England also wished to be the central market of the world, but she was so trammelled by the prohibitive legislation of centuries that bold action in the Netherlands could forestall her in the race for free trade. Then the old Dutch commerce would spread prosperity throughout the kingdom, and the north and south would be reconciled.

The government was defeated by 56 to 54 votes. It then made the minor concession of allowing communes that commuted the tax for a fixed payment to deduct the costs of raising the money. The draft law was quickly resubmitted, and passed by 59 to 50 votes.[1]

Enforcement of the flour excise began in January 1823. The results in Belgium were watched with interest, especially by French diplomats looking for signs of a disintegration of the kingdom. Thanks to the government's military precautions and perhaps to some relaxation of the law, only minor disturbances occurred; and when the king travelled through Belgium in May, the authorities were able to arrange seemly welcomes. The yield of the tax, however, was disappointing, and its collection remained troublesome. In spite of the confidence of Dutch deputies that experience would prove it a most satisfactory form of tax for all concerned, almost all rural communes except in Holland and Friesland had contracted out of it by 1825.[2]

---

[1] *Rec. fin.*; *2de kamer* (1821–2); *Knuttel* 25097 (Van Boetzelaar, 1822); G. K. van Hogendorp, *Bijdragen*, VI, 332–50, 362.

[2] *Ged.* VIII (I), 288–90; F. N. Sickenga, *Geschiedenis der Nederlandsche belastingen sedert 1810*, II, 22–3.

Chapter VIII

THE PROTECTION OF INDUSTRY AND THE TARIFF OF 1822

(a) The industrial problem

The Dutch merchants asked in their petitions not for a purely negative fiscal policy, but for one that would 'protect commerce, industry and agriculture'. The word 'protection' was thus used in a good sense by all parties; but measures termed 'protective' by the Belgians were denounced as 'prohibitive' by the merchants, who nevertheless supported several total prohibitions included in the Placaat of 1725.

Though all agreed that industry should be protected, many doubted whether it was desirable to encourage imitation of English methods. British industrial progress was deplored by the majority both of Dutch and Belgians, who wanted only to carry on as they had been accustomed. British production, it was said, had been unnaturally increased by machines. For fear of unrest, the British government gave subsidies to keep the machines working even when there was no demand for the product; but each mechanical improvement made British industry more dependent on foreign markets, and more liable to vicissitudes.[1] In order to provide markets, the British government tricked foreign powers into unequal commercial agreements, such as the Eden Treaty of 1786. Court intrigue made this easier, so they opposed the growth of independent, constitutional governments.[2] Foreseeing that the European market would become saturated or be reconquered in the end by European industry, the British government had subjected sixty millions in India by wars of doubtful morality, in order to destroy native industry for the benefit of their own. Dutchmen who desired protection for their shipping and preferences for their colonial trade joined with Belgian supporters of industrial protection in decrying the liberalism of Huskisson. It was said to be as selfish and hypocritical as the philanthropy by which Britain justified the stopping of the slave trade at a time when Dutch and other colonies were depleted of slaves and her own were well stocked.[3] England, said the Belgians, would be ruined if other nations defended themselves by following her own principles of protectionism; so she tried to dupe

---

[1] *Knuttel* 24916 (Van Alphen, 1819), 1–18.
[2] A.R.A., Van Hogendorp 44, 2a (Pirson of Namur, 20 Jan. 1822).
[3] J. van Ouwerkerk de Vries, *Verhandeling*, pp. 79–88, 127.

them by preaching the doctrines of Adam Smith, which she herself was careful not to practise.[1]

Though British industrial successes caused much dislike and fear, they were quoted in support of all opinions about fiscal policy. The merchants explained the expansion of English industry by the market provided by foreign trade; but the industrialists said that the English merchants owed everything to industries which used imported materials and yielded a surplus for export. On the first view, general commerce was the source of all wealth; on the second, only ordinary commerce was useful, and only as handmaid to industry. The protectionists said that English industry was created by the Elizabethan protective policy.[2] Merchants who wished for shipping preferences pointed to the Navigation Acts. Doctrinaire free-traders such as Van Hogendorp quoted Adam Smith to show that England had prospered in spite of, not because of, restrictions on foreign trade, and pointed to the growing English free-trade movement.[3] Industrialists who wanted subsidies for re-equipment ascribed everything to superior English mechanization and capital; but those who wanted protection in order to avoid changes in method pointed to English machines as an unfair advantage, which they themselves, in order to provide more employment, patriotically refused to instal, and which owed their success to the folly of countries that did not defend their industries from British imports.[4] Dutchmen who hoped to satisfy the manufacturers 'by protecting commerce with low duties and protecting industry by subsidies', claimed that English industrial development was due to subsidies. Some believed that low English wages were the cause, and argued either that protection must be increased, or that it would be rash to encourage Belgian industry until the distress of the British workers was relieved.[5] Critics of old-fashioned Dutch trading methods pointed to English efforts to find markets and to reduce the costs of distribution.[6]

It was agreed that industries in a small state were necessarily at a disadvantage.

The French and English manufacturers have long had a much bigger market than we, and have consequently been able to develop their

[1] *Knuttel* 25099 (*De la nécessité d'un tarif national...en Belgique*, 1822).
[2] P. Vreede, *Proeve over de vrijheid des zeehandels* (The Hague, 1803), I, 67.
[3] *Bijdragen*, III, 196.
[4] R. Demoulin, *Guillaume 1er et la transformation économique des provinces belges (1815–1830)* (Liége, 1938), App. VII; A.R.A., Van Hogendorp 44, 2a (Pirson of Namur 20 Jan. 1822).
[5] A.R.A., Goldberg 215—memo. from Liége Chamber of Commerce, 12 May 1821; *Post. Doc.* II, 68.
[6] P. Vreede, *Proeve*, I, 133.

establishments on a much larger scale. Since the price of manufactures is always to a certain extent proportional to the quantity produced, our competitors have thus a notorious advantage. The English have also a considerable advantage in the drawback at exportation of the import duty on their raw materials. This drawback is so calculated as to constitute a veritable export subsidy.[1]

It was generally believed, with some truth in the case of sugar,[2] that British exports were subsidized, and Dutchmen argued that so long as this continued, no fiscal measures within the power of the Netherlands could preserve the Belgian industries which had grown up under the Continental System. No less than Belgian manufacturers, Dutch merchants disliked the vigour of the British export trade, but they were content to wait passively for better times.[3] Amazed by low British prices, they assumed that such trade must show a loss, and therefore would be checked in due course, since there must be a limit to subsidies.[4]

Van Hogendorp attributed English successes to various causes; to the internal order and security which encouraged investment in productive enterprises all over the country; to the early liberation of industry from gilds and all kinds of official regulation; and to a commerce which, swelled by colonial goods, made England a world market-place. Everything he disliked in England, he attributed to protectionist policies. Protection of industry made industrial goods expensive, so the agricultural interest demanded and obtained protection to bring their prices to an equivalent level. Labour costs rose accordingly, and the industrialists only saved themselves by the invention and use of machinery. The result was continually increasing unemployment and distress, which had brutalized the poor and, through concubinage and early marriages, had prodigiously increased the population.[5] He believed, however, that England was finding her own way of avoiding the imminent disaster. 'Civilization is considered a powerful way to expand trade and industry.' Just as England had benefited by the trade expansion that followed the independence of the United States, so she would in future benefit by the free-trade economy that she was now deliberately fostering, especially in South America and the East. Education, Christian missions and improved

---

[1] *2de kamer*, 1827–8, A, Barthélemy, 27 March 1828.
[2] J. H. Clapham, *An Economic History of Modern Britain*, vol. I, 2nd ed. (Cambridge, 1941), pp. 324, 327.
[3] C. Boissevain, *Onze voortrekkers*, p. 206; *Willem de Clercq—naar zijn dagboek* (Haarlem, 1888), I, 165.
[4] *Knuttel* 24916; *Ged.* VIII (3), 298. There had indeed been a limit. The export bounty on printed cottons (23 Geo. III, c. 21) was allowed to lapse in 1812 (52 Geo. III, c. 96) because increased exports had made it too costly.
[5] *Bijdragen*, VI, 237–8; *Lettres sur la prospérité*, p. 117.

colonial cultivation all helped her purpose. Meanwhile, thousands of English, unemployed because of the machines, were being shipped to Canada and elsewhere for productive work.[1]

Van Hogendorp had a solution for Belgium too. He pointed out that Belgian manufacturers themselves, when asking for favours or trying to persuade Dutch merchants to find export markets for them, were accustomed to urge the advantages of their low labour costs, and certainly Belgian wages were no higher than English; so that only mechanization was needed to make Belgian industry fully competitive. Belgian manufacturers ought easily to be able to command the Netherlands markets, with the help of their advantage in transport costs over foreigners; but perhaps they ought to be protected by import duties just sufficient to offset the high Netherlands taxation, in order to be able to compete against foreigners on equal terms. Instead, the Belgian manufacturers relied on a much higher protection and sought to repeat on a smaller scale the conditions of the Continental System; and consequently, even when they employed English machines and skilled workmen, they failed to import the English spirit of enterprise and secured only disappointing results. They tacitly combined to keep home prices as high as the import duties permitted; and so did the coal producers, thus increasing costs for many industries. Protection, especially in the form of export duties, kept production low and reduced the national wealth. Competition would force manufacturers to bring themselves up to date; even the clothiers of North Brabant, who boasted that they kept to old-fashioned methods in order to give more employment. This, however, would need time; fifty years and the coming of a less prejudiced generation could alone bring the Belgian iron industry up to the technical level of the English. Meanwhile, the government must assist and stimulate industry by subsidies that would be diminished according to an announced programme.

Van Hogendorp did not welcome mechanization, but examined its consequences with impartial curiosity.

After the invention of gun-powder, armies continued to become ever more numerous; and similarly after the introduction of steam power, population has increased each year....It is a comforting truth that the work-people in factories stand, or sit, in roomier and better ventilated premises than others, have less heavy work to do, and remain healthier.

He noted with distress the pale faces, emaciated bodies, ruined morals and bad housing conditions that often seemed the inevitable result of English

---

[1] G. K. van Hogendorp, *Advijs over de verhandeling van J. van Ouwerkerk de Vries over de oorzaken van het verval des Nederlandschen handels* (Haarlem, 1828), pp. 27–37.

methods. In any case, since mechanization reduced employment, there could be no reasons of state for hastening it artificially. The government should simply permit inevitable adjustments to occur without interference and confine itself to 'removing the rubbish from the fallen house'. It was urgent to direct surplus industrial labour to more natural work, preferably the reclamation of waste land. Not much, perhaps, could be done for the adults, but the children and young people should be brought into agriculture, shipping or the army. Yet when schemes were introduced for settling some thousands of paupers from Dutch towns on waste land in Drenthe, Van Hogendorp lamented; for, he said, this was a consequence of policies hostile to commerce, but for which these men could be employed in traditional occupations, useful to the nation as consumers and producers in the market instead of being merely subsistence farmers.

In fact, Van Hogendorp believed, Holland need be little affected by the problems of England and Belgium, since her economy remained closer to nature. She had shared with England the problem of high labour costs, but thanks to her commercial system she had solved it without the drastic remedy of mechanization. The Dutch commercial industries, the refineries, distilleries and so on, were not subject to mechanization; or in cases where machines would be needed, such as steam saws for the timber yards, their introduction would be slow and smooth as in the past, and not like the forced mechanization of English industry, whereby two million had lost their livelihood and whereby similar changes had been made inevitable in Belgium. The Dutch commercial industries, not being hot-house plants, did not ask for protection that would hamper trade. Indeed, he pointed out, the Dutch calico printers, who used Indian fabric as their raw material, were among the strongest opponents of the 'prohibitive' duties demanded by the Belgian cotton industry. Yet, he believed, these Dutch industries, without any privilege at the expense of the rest of the community and, perhaps for that very reason, were able to export about as much in value as the Belgian industries.[1]

The modern capitalist spirit was as yet by no means prevalent even in Belgium; but, despite lack of knowledge and interest about technical improvement, self-interest made Belgian manufacturers desire industrial expansion, if only within a protected economy, within 'that interior commerce which is universally recognised to be the most advantageous of all'. It was admitted that England had gone to excess, and was in great danger because her industrial expansion was causing her population to rise beyond her food production; but the Netherlands need have no fears, for her agricultural capacity was adequate to support a larger population,

---

[1] *Bijdragen*, I and III; *Lettres sur la prospérité.*

which was therefore desirable in itself. Even a Belgian who abhorred English techniques urged the government to assist deep coal-mining because 'this kingdom, created in the interests of the European balance of power and consequently assured of a long existence, ought to realize all the resources of its territory'. The Belgians argued that all industry, whether machines were used or not, provided employment for the poor and should be encouraged, and invited the Dutch capitalists to observe that funds employed in commerce were much less beneficial to the community.[1] The Dutch replied that modern factories, especially cotton factories, were nurseries of pauperism, taking healthy men, wearing them out at a miserable wage and then leaving them to charity.[2] 'There hardly exists in England any branch of manufacturing industry which can permanently maintain its workers without the help of the Poor Rate.'[3] The use of charitable funds to provide industrial employment was traditional in Dutch commercial towns—Van Hogendorp claimed that it had achieved very creditable results in stimulating industry without injury to trade[4]—but it was said that cotton factories were a cause and not a remedy of misery and that no conscientious Dutch capitalist would consider such an investment. Learned discussions took place in Holland about the possibility of discouraging the factory system by a tax on machines and of using the proceeds to subsidize handicrafts.[5] The Rotterdam Chamber of Commerce and Industry advised against any encouragement of research into mechanical flax-spinning; no doubt machines were useful when labour was scarce, and no doubt they had profited England, but if they were now adopted everywhere else the only consequence would be disastrous overproduction, unemployment and civil disturbances.[6]

Van Alphen, a prominent representative of Dutch commercial opinion in the States General, identified the cause of commerce with that of handicraft:

Commerce is the agent of labour.... It creates great central market places for the whole trading world, spying out the needs of all peoples and fixing the proper prices.... It determines the work by which each town, individual and people can obtain livelihood and advantage.... Free trade is the one restraint on those unlimited projects of profit-seeking

---

[1] A.R.A., Van Hogendorp, 44, 2a; *2de kamer* (1819–20) A, 142.

[2] A.R.A., Goldberg 221 (i); F. A. van Hall, *Onpartijdige beschouwing*, p. 26.

[3] *2de kamer*, 1827–8, A, Van Alphen, 27 May 1828.

[4] G. K. van Hogendorp, *Gedagten*, p. 44.

[5] I. J. Brugmans, *De arbeidende klasse*, pp. 200–1.

[6] Z. W. Sneller, in *Bijdragen voor Vaderlandsche Geschiedenis en Oudheidkunde* (1926), p. 160.

which arbitrarily subject labour to their will and force the governments
to those measures of interference...which lead the producer to invest
large capital and to introduce an all too great and all too rapid simplification of labour processes....Under free trade, the spirit of enterprise
and profit could never be spurred to such colossal undertakings; for the
advantage of locality would always ensure a small local market for small
enterprise...so that the worker could bargain fairly with the employer.
But when the workers are at the mercy of big undertakings, then workers'
combinations occur, as already in England, with danger to property....
The source of the evil is the principle on which at present nearly all manufacturing is based; the system of producing without an assured market....
Demand ought to precede production, the producer ought never to be
a merchant and never to work except for definite orders....The ruin of
the great central market-places is therefore a calamity not only for the
land itself but for the whole of Europe....Under free trade, the struggle
between machines and hand-labour would not be so much to the disadvantage of the latter...but instead of encouraging hand-labour, the
governments tax it in order to contribute subsidies for machines....The
present war against labour in Europe makes labour dependent on the
owners of capital, who produce as though for an unlimited market. But
God will not create new worlds for them.

Apart from free trade, his remedies included the encouragement of land-
reclamation, because agriculture was not liable to mechanization; a tax
system that would encourage small enterprise rather than large; and the
re-establishment of gilds, in a modified form, to regulate labour and
restrict production.[1]

The idea that free trade would prevent the growth of factories was based
on the past experience of Holland. In the golden age of the Republic,
Dutch maritime trade had indeed been free, but traffic by land had been
slow and expensive and even within the United Provinces had been subject
to fiscal impediments. Most production had accordingly been for a purely
local market; and only while this remained so could Amsterdam remain
an indispensable central market for those goods that entered international
trade. Improved conditions for the movement of goods in Europe not
only made it possible to supersede the central market by direct trading,
but also to increase the division of labour and the scale of industrial production. The appearance of commercial travellers in provincial areas of
western Europe in the second half of the eighteenth century heralded
these changes, and the principle established by the French Revolution
of banishing customs' barriers to the frontiers hastened the growth of
industries producing for more than a local market. The expansion of

[1] *Knuttel* 24916.

industry in Belgium under the Continental System was therefore not purely artificial, and even though the actual unit of production often remained small there could be no return there to eighteenth-century conditions. On the other hand much Dutch industry still worked for a local market, or for Dutch commerce, rather than for a national home market. The Dutch therefore continued to desire maritime free trade and, in order that the merchant should be free from annoyance, were willing to impede internal traffic not only by municipal excises but also by national customs and excise controls; while the Belgians insisted on the levy of excise at the source and the banishing of customs formalities to the frontier.

(b) *Alternatives to Tariff Protection*

Having decided to reduce customs duties, the government naturally took up again the plans of earlier governments to compensate industry by other means. Before the union with Belgium, the Dutch woollen industry had been the main object of solicitude, and on the king's instructions a scheme was drawn up for its benefit in 1820. The preparatory investigations of the Minister of Commerce concerned only the Dutch industry, for he believed that the Belgian clothiers needed no assistance. He reported that national markings and patriotic exhortations were unlikely to achieve much unless the prices of Dutch cloth were reduced. In future, he proposed, government departments should buy only national cloth and should pay a price above the competitive level, so that in effect a subsidy would be granted. Those who worked for government contracts should be closely supervised by inspectors, in order to ensure that they really used this subsidy to reduce their prices in the open market and to improve their methods of production, not merely to increase their immediate profits. In order to force the manufacturers to improve, the government should gradually reduce its prices. Strict precautions against fraud would be necessary, for the government departments were already trying to give contracts by preference to Dutch manufacturers, and found it very difficult to avoid being deceived by English imitations. English cloth was believed to wear less well than Dutch, but the lower quality was hard to detect at the time of purchase. English producers took advantage of this by weaving into their material the markings of a Dutch firm in order to sell it to the authorities as Dutch cloth by the collusion of a Dutch trader or bogus manufacturer. The English supplied the goods to the Dutch swindler on credit of three months or longer, so he could profit handsomely without needing any capital.[1]

---

[1] A.R.A., Goldberg 221 (ii and iii).

After further consultation, the king took action by a royal decree in June 1820. Only cloth bearing the national mark was to be used by the royal household, the public services and armed forces, the prisons, and the charitable institutions that enjoyed official support. Government officials and their families were requested to conform. Government supervision of the industry was not to extend beyond the granting and verification of the national mark; but it was hoped that the measure, adjusted according to experience, would suffice to restore the vitality of the Dutch industry even if the import duties were reduced.[1]

The extension of subsidies to Belgian and Dutch industry as compensation for a reduction in import duties was suggested by several leaders of Dutch commercial opinion and was particularly acceptable to the king. He believed in the usefulness of protective duties for young or improving industries, but he did not desire that unprogressive industries should be sheltered from the stimulus of competition. He regarded the details of the tariff as a matter for trial and error and for bargaining between affected interests; he made suggestions himself, but left most decisions to his expert advisers. On the other hand, he had many schemes of his own devising for the direct stimulation of industrial improvement and investment, which he believed to be the only means of reviving Dutch industry and of enabling Belgian industrial development to continue without the easy profits of the Continental System. Thus he sought to fulfil the task suggested to him by an adviser in 1814:

The present position of the Belgian factories cannot be regarded as natural and permanent, because it has arisen largely from circumstances which have now ceased. . . . It is the task of the government to lead and modify the approaching changes to the advantage of the country and of its inhabitants, and especially to find out which factories are natural to Belgium and thus cannot be created or destroyed by circumstances but can indeed be promoted or hindered.[2]

He wished to persuade industrial entrepreneurs to imitate English techniques, and Dutch capitalists and Belgian landowners to invest in industry. This double educational task could be accomplished only by showing that good profits could be made. He set the example by investing in progressive enterprises part of the considerable private fortune which he accumulated in the first years of his reign, apparently by fortunate speculations. If the resources of the state could be used in the same way, he believed, the expansion of national industry could be

---

[1] A.R.A., Goldberg 214 (ii); N. W. Posthumus, *Recueil de documents internationaux relatifs à l'histoire économique 1814–1924* (Amsterdam, 1925), p. 168.

[2] Koninklijk Huisarchief (The Hague), Willem I, xviii, 112.

hastened, and the profits could be used to pay off the national debt. It was not easy to convince his ministers or the States General of the soundness of such schemes, but he obstinately put them forward at every opportunity. In November 1820, he proposed that the law which Gogel and Roëll were preparing should provide for a fund, to be charged against the customs revenue, for loans and subsidies to industry, agriculture, fishing and shipping. Gogel objected that the government was not competent to judge the merits of entrepreneurs and that intriguers would always get most; it would be fairer simply to reduce the patents tax for industries in difficulty. Roëll, however, agreed to the king's proposal, and the law of 1821 provided for an annual sum of 1,300,000 fl. for the assistance of any enterprise that required protection beyond what the interests of commerce or the activities of smugglers permitted by way of customs duties. The king took care that he should have complete control of this fund and should not be accountable for it to the States General. He hoped that the money could be lent at interest or invested in shares of promising enterprises. Thus the fund would yield a profit for its own expansion, and eventually, for the repayment of the national debt.[1] Belgian opponents of the system of 1821 were not appeased by the promise of subsidies. They said that if the government would maintain existing tariff protection and continue to levy excise at source, they would gladly vote the money to build large 'entrepôt' docks in Holland, in which there could be no possible justification for the Dutch prejudice against the bonding system; otherwise, like several Dutch deputies, they would prefer that it should be used for a general reduction in patents tax.[2]

The iron industry was a case in which the king decided that direct stimulation by the government would be more useful than tariff protection. It was one of the most highly protected industries under the system of 1816, but it remained stagnant and depressed.[3] The import duties, so the king considered in 1821, were merely enabling entrepreneurs to avoid necessary improvements. The industry was agitating for still higher duties but making no effort for self-help. In April 1821, therefore, the government began to investigate the means of teaching the ironmasters their job. Roentgen, a young naval officer whose advice the government took in matters concerning steam-engines and the production and use of iron, was sent on a tour of inquiry, and his report was required in time for decisions to be taken before the new tariff was drawn up.

[1] A.R.A., Roëll 86; *Mem. en cor.* pp. 458–77; R. Demoulin, *Guillaume Ier*, ch. viii.
[2] *Rec. fin.* pp. 1 and 60–5 A.R.A., Staatssec., 12 July 1821, no. 57 (1st and 5th sect.).
[3] H. van Houtte, *Esquisse d'une histoire économique de la Belgique* (Louvain ,1943), p. 158.

Roentgen's report confirmed that the ironmasters were shirking experiment and capital investment in the hope of further protection and of a commercial treaty with France. They refused to see that France was unlikely to relax her tariff, and that if they did not keep up with the times, protection would become so injurious to the consumer that 'in course of time, owing to political changes, foreign iron would be introduced into the home market'. Most of the ironmasters were not even aware of their own technical ignorance; they had had a purely literary education and were interested in everything except their business. Their dependence on inadequate water-power put them at the mercy of the weather. Instead of specializing and engaging in continuous production, they awaited orders and often undertook jobs for which their equipment was unsuitable. The lack of enterprise was especially noticeable in public works. In England, such works were put out to private contractors who arranged everything for themselves and took a real interest in the job; but in the Netherlands, the administration, perhaps of necessity, enforced such close regulation and routine that the introduction of improved methods was unlikely. One or two Belgian ironmasters had tried English methods of smelting, but in such a dilettante manner that they succeeded only in becoming the victims of mountebank English 'experts'. Only J. Cockerill understood what he was about and was succeeding, in so far as his lack of capital permitted.

The government, Roentgen recommended, could best stimulate improvement by sponsoring a model establishment that would perform all the processes to produce steam-engines out of its own coal and iron mine. In order to get quick results and to retain the advantages of private enterprise, the government should not start a state establishment but should enter an agreement with a private operator who already had some of the needed equipment. For a loan of 500,000 fl., Cockerill would carry out the work proposed, under contract to allow everything to be freely inspected by his Belgian competitors. In order to force them to follow his example, the protective duties should be reduced a little every year.[1]

Cockerill had received official encouragement in regard to the purchase of premises for a factory from the public domain in 1817, when he started the production of steam-engines in Belgium. The king had an interest in the enterprise. The Fund of 1821 was used to provide the loan recommended by Roentgen; the loan was made in 1823 and in 1825 was converted by a new agreement into a half share in the great engineering works at Seraing. Loans were also made, in 1825 and after, to Roentgen to assist him in creating an enterprise at Rotterdam for building steam

[1] G. M. Roentgen, 'Twee memoriën', in *Econ. Hist. Jaarboek* 1923, II, 106–46.

tugs and other vessels. The Fund thus made possible the birth of modern heavy industry in both Belgium and Holland. However, it provoked discontent among those manufacturers who were denied its favours, and many Belgians suspected that it was used more for political than for economic purposes.[1]

The lack of capital for industrial investment was widely recognized as a major problem, and was often quoted as a reason for protection. One Belgian deputy remarked: 'The important thing is that we retain our specie, for it is one of the indispensable agents of production, which must be protected by all possible means.'[2] One remedy attempted by the government was to discourage investment in foreign securities by legal regulations and discriminatory taxes.[3] A more promising possibility was the creation of credit institutions. When Vreede urged in a petition that Dutch industry needed protection because it was carried on by enterprises too small to find the capital for mechanization, the Minister of Commerce remarked in the margin that English banking enabled many small producers to mechanize and expand, and that the Dutch could do so too.[4]

The king accordingly followed up the establishment of the Fund of 1821 by proposing in 1822 the creation of a great bank at Brussels, which would be endowed with national domain for alienation. In addition to acting as a banker for the state, it was to be a bank of issue and to introduce modern credit arrangements to Belgian industry. The scheme was rejected by the States General for fear that it would renew the painful experience of assignats, but the king proceeded with it on his own responsibility. Much of the capital of the new bank, the Société Générale, was provided by the king either in liquid form or in public domain which he took from the state for the purpose in return for a permanent reduction in his official income. In order to persuade private investors to purchase the remaining shares, he gave a personal guarantee of an annual dividend of 5%. The government press in Belgium expounded the king's intention.[5]

[1] A. R. Falck, *Ambtsbrieven*, pp. 88–93; M. G. de Boer, *Leven en bedrijf van G. M. Roentgen* (Rotterdam, 1923); E. Mahaim, in *Vierteljahrschrift für Sozial- und Wirtschaftsgeschichte* (1905).

[2] *2de kamer*, 1825–6, A 320.

[3] R. V. Heyliger, *De Nederlandsche wetgeving op de vreemde geldligtingen* (Leiden, 1854).

[4] A.R.A., Goldberg 221 (i).

[5] A.R.A., Van Hogendorp 44 (2k); *Ged.* VIII (2), 293–316; A. R. Falck, *Gedenkschriften*, pp. 436–9.

(c) The tariff of 1822

The Dutch merchants argued that tariff protection for industry was impossible because the geography of the kingdom was so favourable to smugglers. The best way of abolishing both smuggling and tiresome customs formalities would be to reduce the duties below the smugglers' premium. In September 1820, Gogel understood the king to agree with this argument, and he at once followed up this success by submitting a draft tariff based on the principle that 'smuggling begins at 3%'. He proposed, as exceptions, a few total prohibitions, in accordance with Dutch tradition; but the draft appears to have been prepared before 1815, for it took no account of the union with Belgium.[1] The effect of this unrealistic document on the king was not as intended; for the whole tariff question was postponed. The law of 1821 settled nothing. It laid down a maximum for import and for export duties, at 3% for purely commercial goods and 6% for goods affecting home industry. Higher duties were to be imposed when necessary. Industry was to be protected, and trade was to be free.

Although the vague provisions of the law of 1821 were intended to postpone tariff controversy until after the flour excise had been dealt with, the explanatory memorandum with which the government introduced the law in the States General contained language that could not fail to provoke the protectionists. The memorandum was written by Roëll, and, with the intention no doubt of committing the government more firmly to its new course, he inserted into it some of the slogans of the Dutch commercial party. The manufacturers were advised that if they could not compete successfully in the home market under the protection of a 6% import duty in addition to the costs of transport from a foreign country, then their factories had in most cases no right to exist from the standpoint of political economy and the national interest, and they should seek some other investment for their capital.[2]

After this, every interest began to agitate in the hope of influencing the new tariff. Most Belgian industries ignored the provisions of the law of 1821 altogether and asked for existing duties to be increased. The iron-masters explained that the recent rise in the price of their products was a sign not of prosperity but of distress, for two successive dry summers had reduced their water-power and brought production to a standstill. The potters said that the existing 12% import duty was useless; were it not for English imports aimed deliberately at their ruin, they could easily

[1] *Mem. en cor.* pp. 194, 327–61.
[2] *Rec. fin.* p. xiv.

supply the whole home market, but as it was they made no profit and continued to produce only for the sake of their workers. The government did not take this last complaint very seriously, for one of the potters who claimed to be remaining in business only out of philanthropy had recently applied to the king for a loan for re-equipment and had then said that he was sure of a ready market for all he could produce.[1]

In 1820, the clothiers of Verviers and the armourers of Liége had continued to support free trade, though with less confidence than before. Belgians, the Chamber of Commerce and Industry at Verviers explained, could compete against subsidized British exports only by quicker delivery, and could have the advantage only in European markets accessible by land. The French tariff blocked them to the south, so they could export only through the Rhineland and suffered exceedingly from the Prussian transit duties. The Netherlands transit duty equally impeded the cutlery and ironmongery of Cleves, which was exported to France. There seemed a good chance of a reciprocal arrangement with Prussia for free transit, and the support of Dutch free-traders was invoked for the proposal. The clothiers, the Chamber continued, did not ask tariff protection for themselves, although they were continually seeing foreign markets closed to them. They wished for general free trade and hoped that the Netherlands would set an example.[2] The Liége Chamber expressed full agreement with Verviers. It added that protection was a geographical impossibility in the Netherlands, for the Customs Department could never hope to raise the smugglers' premium above 7%. 'We know that free trade is opposed in certain districts where the Continental System created cotton factories which owed their market wholly to prohibitions and must now necessarily collapse.' The Liége Chamber especially desired free trade because the arms-makers required Swedish and Russian iron, although it was sure that most would always patriotically use Belgian for all purposes for which it was suitable. On the other hand, the Limburg Chamber, which represented a woollen-manufacturing district and had previously followed Vervier's lead, in 1820 reported that cloth exports were becoming impossible and asked that the home market should be protected by duties as high as those of other countries. In order to prevent smuggling, legal imports should be marked and all cloth that had neither this nor the national mark should be liable to seizure everywhere in the kingdom.[3] On second thoughts, Verviers asked for retaliatory duties against French wine

[1] A.R.A., Goldberg 215; A.R.A., Staatssec., 12 Feb. 1824, no. 67, pt. I, B 12–13 and pt. II, 2 May 1820.
[2] A.R.A., Staatssec., 12 Feb. 1824, no. 67, pt. I, B 5.
[3] A.R.A., Staatssec., 12 Feb. 1824, no. 67, pt. II, 2–5 May 1820.

and other agricultural goods, for the benefit of countries that consumed Belgian cloth; but otherwise repeated its wish for free trade.[1] In 1822, however, it completely reversed its attitude. The Netherlands, it said, could not afford to open her markets any longer to foreign dumping, unless other countries would be more liberal. The woollen industry was now in such a condition that any mistake would be fatal. It was true that the export statistics seemed to indicate a recent improvement, but those exports had been undertaken speculatively by manufacturers on their own account as a last, desperate effort. They had been impelled by the fear of a new increase in the Russian import duty, and by the hope of pacification and the opening of new markets in South America; and most of the goods were still unsold, in bond in foreign ports. Such an effort ought not to have been needed and could never be repeated. Only security in the home market could now keep the remaining looms in production. Verviers therefore endorsed the proposals made by Limburg two years before. In view of the abolition of the coffee excise, it hoped that commerce would gladly assent to an increase in the cloth duties above the 1816 level.[2]

Many of the Dutch commercial party were willing to give a reasonable tariff protection above 6% to Dutch industries, in cases where no significant damage to foreign trade would result; and they even agreed that the duty on imports of finished woollen cloths might exceed 6%. But they maintained that protection of the Belgian cotton industry was useless and harmful, for it could not keep English goods from the Netherland consumer and did divert trade.[3] However, Appelius, who had the main responsibility for preparing a new tariff to comply with the law of 1821, decided that the industries needing exceptional protection were mostly Belgian, and recommended in particular that the import duties on cotton goods and iron should remain at the 1816 level of 20–30%. The prominent Dutch merchants who were privately consulted admitted that it was not practical politics to bring these duties down at once to 6%, but asked that a beginning should be made.

Before submission to the States General, the tariff had to be considered by the Council of State, a predominantly Dutch body. It singled the iron duties for attack, on the ground that they gave the ironmasters undiminished protection, although they would probably benefit most from the Fund, which had been created solely as compensation for reduced duties. But for the tariff, Swedish, Russian and German iron might once again be

[1] *Ibid.* pt. I, B15.
[2] A.R.A., Goldberg 217.
[3] A.R.A., Roëll 162 (vii).

important in Dutch general commerce, especially for South America; and imported iron was needed in Holland for shipbuilding and hydraulic purposes for which Belgian iron was too brittle. Appelius replied by making a virtue of his resistance to Belgian pressure for still higher import duties on iron; he considered that at the moment a reduction would be ruinous but that an increase would remove the incentive for improvement. The cotton duties, he said, must remain unchanged, for the recent recovery of the industry, which would soon lead to mastery of the home market, was entirely due to them; it had been achieved by patriotic manufacturers who remained in production, despite losses, in confidence that they would be adequately protected, so that a reduction would be a breach of faith. The Council nevertheless asked for a reduction; because the cotton industry was artificial, because it injured the natural linen industry and because a reduction would show whether the cotton industry could ever become natural to Belgium. These remarks were, however, deleted from the record after remonstrance by Appelius. Instead, the Council contented itself with a mild request that the government should consider reductions in the import duties on coal, cotton yarn and pig-iron, since these were raw materials for important industries; and should remember, when the time came to amend the new tariff, that lower customs duties would not only themselves yield more but would improve the yield of the excises, since a revival of commerce would spread wealth among all classes, whereas tariff protection concentrated it only in a few hands.[1]

The Dutch and Belgian clothiers were now united in demanding import duties on woollen cloth of at least 15%. Appelius decided that any big increases in duty would be contrary to the spirit of the law of 1821, and since the existing 8% duty on imported cloth was admittedly ineffective, he saw no case for maintaining it as an exception and so proposed to reduce it to 6%. He admitted that the results of the royal decree of 1820 had been disappointing, but tried to comfort the industry with the hope of subsidies and of the introduction, later, of special retaliatory duties on the cloth of countries that refused to follow the Netherlands on the road to free trade. The Council applauded this, and said that the attitude of the Belgian clothiers in 1815–16 had been wiser than their present one. It quoted the 'horrors of enforcement' proposed by the Chambers of Commerce at Limburg and Verviers as proof that satisfactory tariff protection was impossible in the Netherlands.

As a concession to Belgian opinion and as a precaution against fraud, the government in the law of 1821 had adopted the principle that customs duties should as far as possible be levied by weight instead of *ad valorem*.

[1] A.R.A., Goldberg 215, 217.

The Dutch merchants objected to this as a trick for securing concealed increases in duty and a stricter enforcement. Owing to the fall in prices, they said, the existing cotton duties, which were levied by weight, had become more highly protective than had been intended in 1816. In most cases, Appelius complied with the Belgian wish, but he proposed to keep the cloth duties *ad valorem*, owing to the difficulty of fixing suitable categories for levy by weight. However, in the hope of appeasing the Belgian protectionists in the States General, the government at the last moment replaced the 6% import duty on cloth in the draft by a scale of duties by weight calculated to be equal to 8%. The classification turned out to be so unscientific that the rate on coarse cloth was really much more, and that on fine cloth much less.[1]

The full debate in the Lower Chamber took place in the summer of 1822, at the very end of the session, when all but a dozen of the Belgian deputies had gone home. Everyone seemed tired of the long controversy and the occasion was surprisingly amicable. The Dutch commercial deputies accepted the tariff as a slight improvement on the existing one, hoped that in later amendments the government would advance more boldly to free trade, and even complimented Appelius on his declaration of personal belief in free trade as an ultimate, though rather distant, objective. They acquiesced in the undiminished protection of the Belgian coal mines, but regretted that the ironmasters were not abandoned to the natural laws of economic life, in order that Dutch shipping and commerce might get cheap iron. They seemed to regard the exclusion of British coal merely as a sacrifice of the Dutch domestic consumer and so as a useful debating point in the endless argument as to which side was getting the best of the Dutch-Belgian bargain. If the leaders of Dutch opinion had been more interested in industrial progress, their view of the disadvantage of the coal duty to Holland would have been different.

Only Van Hogendorp strenuously opposed the new tariff, which, he said, proved all his sacrifices in support of the imperfect law of 1821 to have been vain. He would resume his opposition, in order that foreign nations might not altogether give up hope of being served again some day by a Dutch staple market. No doubt, in his own lifetime, his efforts would not have practical results. He was not surprised, therefore, that the commercial interest as a whole acquiesced in the government's policy or that 'a rumour was spread among us, and came to me from several colleagues, that commerce was weary of the long uncertainty and, as no further improvements were to be expected, desired the acceptance of the

[1] A.R.A., Goldberg 217; *2de kamer*, 1821–2, B1011; *Gedenkboek der Kamer van Koophandel en Fabrieken te Rotterdam*, p. 159.

tariff proposed'. The Belgian deputies, thanks, it was believed, to Van Hogendorp's speech, accepted the government's proposals. They mildly regretted the reduced duties: but hoped that good use would be made of the Fund, though some of them feared that it would merely stimulate over-production without providing any real defence against English competition. Only Van Hogendorp voted against the tariff.[1]

Table XII. *British manufactured goods exported to the Netherlands*
1815–32*

Official value (£000)

	Woollens	Woollen yarns, etc.	Cotton goods	Cotton yarns	Silks	Cutlery and hard-ware	Other manu-factures	Total
1815	288	—	1,680	110	2	19	552	2,651
1816	278	—	1,317	133	2	14	604	2,348
1817	237	—	892	13	2	12	655	1,810
1818	295	—	1,024	20	2	10	403	1,754
1819	233	—	1,227	18	2	10	311	1,801
1820	229	—	1,261	21	2	8	382	1,903
1821	226	—	1,304	25	1	11	364	1,932
1822	294	—	1,562	29	3	13	315	2,217
1823	296	—	1,708	332	2	14	396	2,750
1824	316	—	1,486	375	2	15	306	2,501
1825	344	1	1,652	429	2	14	290	2,732
1826	293	2	1,498	462	2	15	360	2,632
1827	407	2	1,533	562	9	16	305	2,835
1828	415	3	1,445	630	4	20	358	2,876
1829	410	7	1,301	703	12	23	399	2,855
1830	380	12	1,330	646	14	21	491	2,896
1831	261	13	1,517	811	4	13	560	3,179
1832								
North	365	19	1,693	920	5	12	527	3,541
South	188	4	567	2	21	4	184	970

Steam engines†

	Official value (£)
1822	1,617
1823	6,904
1824	6,994
1825	11,325
1826	36,331

[1] A.R.A., Van Hogendorp 130 (6), 3; *2de kamer*, 1821–2, A 520–6; G. K. Van Hogendorp, *Bijdragen*, VI, 362–9, 384–7; *Knuttel* 25100.

* *Parl. Papers*, 1839, XVI, 501; 1841, XVIII, 538–44.

† *Parl. Papers*, 1826–7, XVIII, 162–3.

Chapter IX

THE FREE-TRADE MOVEMENT AND
THE PROTECTION OF COMMERCE

(a) Trade

The Dutch commercial interest retained an oligarchic character, for the First Hand merchants claimed an exclusive right to speak for the commercial cities, and even for the whole Dutch people, about economic matters. This was illustrated by the behaviour of the Amsterdam merchants when the government attempted in 1816 to make the Chambers of Commerce and Industry larger and more representative. The existing Chamber at Amsterdam, which had been appointed by the French authorities, consisted predominantly of highly respected First Hand merchants, with only two of the Second Hand and no industrialists. It resisted the government's proposal on the ground that the opinion of Second Hand merchants, sugar-refiners, brewers and so on was only valuable on matters about which they had specialized knowledge; only the First Hand understood the needs of commerce as a whole. In the proposed Chamber, special interests might prevail over general ones; but that could never happen in a Chamber recruited from the First Hand, with only a few leading Second Hand merchants as colleagues but with power to co-opt outsiders to temporary sub-committees when special knowledge was needed. When the government persisted with its plan, most Amsterdam merchants boycotted the new Chamber.[1]

The leadership of the Amsterdam First Hand merchants was sometimes challenged by the humbler traders of other ports. In evidence before the commission of 1820, Appelius agreed with the merchants of Amsterdam and Rotterdam that customs officers must not insist on weighing all merchandise piece by piece when congestion would be caused. A member from Middelburg then denounced this complacency as a return to the 'spirit of the Placaat of 1725'. Like causes, he said, would lead to like results. If assessments were made by mere sampling, collusion would follow. The big ports, under the pretext of congestion, would get all the advantage, and the ruin of the small ports would be completed.[2]

---

[1] F. A. van Hall, *Onpartijdige beschouwing*, p. 21; B. C. E. Zwart, *De Kamer van Koophandel en Fabrieken te Amsterdam*, pp. 82–5, 105–7; J. C. Westermann, *Kamer van Koophandel en Fabrieken voor Amsterdam*, pp. 123–31.

[2] A.R.A., Staatssec., 12 Feb. 1824, no. 67, pt. II, 7 June 1820.

The proceedings of the commission of 1820 also showed that the Rotterdam wine merchants did not support Amsterdam's attack on the Appelian excise system; in fact, they preferred it to that of Gogel, though as a counsel of perfection they asked a return to the easy-going methods of the eighteenth century. In his report to the king, Roëll explained away this disunity in the commercial ranks. Levy at source, he argued, made possible certain concealed profits, at the expense of the consumers, when wine was matured in store, after payment of the excise. This would be the work of the Second Hand, whose voice was seldom heard by the government; but the wine trade, except at Amsterdam, was carried on by merchants who combined the First and Second Hand. At Amsterdam, significantly, the opinion voiced by the wine trade was against the Appelian system. The king, Roëll advised, should therefore not assume, as had the anti-commercial majority of the commission, that the incident showed Amsterdam's agitation against levy at source to be inspired by an obstinate vanity which blinded the merchants to their own interests. Rather, he should conclude that 'regulations that are effective and suitable in Amsterdam cannot be harmful elsewhere, but regulations suitable for all other places may be disastrous in the chief city'. For the main aim should be the revival of that peculiar general commerce of Holland to which Amsterdam was wholly devoted.[1] In fact, it would seem, the economic policy of the Kingdom of the Netherlands was to be determined by the wishes of the First Hand merchants of Amsterdam.

One of the most frequently repeated arguments of the commercial party was that the Appelian system was to blame for the decay of the Second Hand; but the interests of the First Hand were considered to be the most important, for it was said to be the source of all prosperity in that its activity determined the actual volume of goods passing through the Dutch staple market. Often, regulations that injured the Second Hand were condemned most of all for their repercussions on the First, which was said ultimately to bear all the administrative charges and clerical costs of the bonding system, and to pay all the customs and excise on imported goods. For the First Hand was said to be at the mercy of the Second in fixing prices. The First Hand was compelled to sell imported goods quickly, but the Second Hand could afford to wait for a favourable time to buy. Even if, as was doubted, the Second and Third Hands could recover the duties paid by raising the price to the home consumer, they would never admit this when bargaining with the First Hand; but would beat down prices in order to profit by recovering the tax twice. The Dutch general commerce would thus not merely suffer by the costs and delays

[1] A.R.A., Roëll 162 (i); A.R.A., Staatssec., 12 Feb. 1824, no. 67, pt. II, 19 May 1820·

of the system of transit-in-bond, but by the fall in the price of any imports highly taxed for home consumption. This would deter foreigners from sending goods to be sold for them by Dutch commission agents. Since the Dutch staple market had always owed much of its strength to the availability of all kinds of goods, so that mixed consignments could easily be assembled and a wide variety of business could be quickly transacted, an interruption, due to an unwise tax, of the supply of any one commodity might well reduce the number of buyers in quite unrelated trades and damage the whole staple market.[1]

The freedom and protection desired by the Dutch commercial interest had been embodied in Gogel's system of 1805. Excise had been levied, not at source, but in such a way as to ensure that only the consumer ultimately paid. Excise, having always been purely fiscal in purpose, could be strictly administered without objection from the merchants, provided the method was such as to avoid hindrance to foreign trade; in this case, therefore, Gogel swept away the old inefficiency and corruption. Customs duties, on the other hand, were not regarded as purely fiscal, but were intended, in the words of the Placaat of 1725, to protect Dutch commerce. Gogel was therefore most careful that they should be levied in a different spirit from the excise and that the two services should be kept separate. Later, the new administrative spirit spread, under French influence, to the customs; but even the French respected the tradition of separate administration, leaving it to William I to complete their 'anti-commercial' work. First, in 1816, came the monstrous attempt to combine French and Dutch principles of customs legislation, which was attributed to the fact that in the preceding two years the old Dutch tariff had been administered in the French spirit, as though its purpose were purely fiscal, while in Belgium Dutch officials had been employed to execute legislation inspired by French principles. High duties had made necessary an increased customs service to combat smuggling, and this was attacked as being part of a new bureaucracy inspired by a narrow professional spirit, which prided itself on its impartiality and preciseness and on an efficiency measured entirely by fiscal results. Everything, it was said, now had to be referred up through the proper channels to the minister, if it could not be dealt with by rigid application of the regulations. Since the minister could not attend to everything, this meant rule by clerks, who looked after their own kind and saw to it that any subordinates who tried to simplify procedures were duly reprimanded. The new itch to collect statistics was contrary to the wisdom of the forefathers, who knew the value of secrecy in trade matters; the information was always useless and often provided by

[1] A.R.A., Roëll 151—notes on the sugar and coffee excises, 1818.

guesswork; but it served its purpose by making the offices seem busy. Such a spectacle, however, could not win the confidence of those respectable merchants who ought to be the pillars of constitutional government. 'Why is trade being sacrificed?', asked one merchant, 'In order to sustain the new bureaucracy? to increase the number of those gratified with offices and to dispense pensions with a generous hand?'[1] The final stage came in 1819, when the customs and excise services were combined in a single organization under Appelius. The difference between customs levied in the French spirit and excise levied at source being slight, the Dutch were not surprised that Antwerp merchants, having no experience of the Placaat of 1725, should welcome the simplification by which both were to be levied by the same officials; but in Amsterdam it seemed a symbol of the abandonment of correct principles. Under the Placaat, the respectable merchant had been protected from the smuggler, but now he was treated like a smuggler himself. Formerly, an incoming ship could begin to unload as soon as its manifest had been handed in at the customs office; now it had to wait while documents were filled in and until the official arrived who had been detailed to supervise. Excise formalities, instead of being spread fairly over the community, were now concentrated on the merchants alone.[2]

Even in the eighteenth century, there had been complaints that trade suffered by the incompetence and vanity of officials of the Regent class. This older antagonism was still not quite dead. Gogel, for instance, in 1820 criticized the Amsterdam municipal authorities for keeping up an anti-commercial local excise system which needed complicated administration and therefore multiplied the opportunities of patronage. The merchants felt, however, that the Regents had respected essential commercial interests. They had no such confidence in the ministers of William I, who had had their training under alien or revolutionary governments. The merchants were indignant when such persons claimed even to understand matters that affected commerce.[3]

In the law of 1821, and in official interpretations of it, the government promised that formalities and administrative charges would be diminished as far as possible, and that customs and excise controls over the First and

---

[1] *Knuttel* 25096 ('Vrijmoedige gedachten', 1822), pp. 23–34; A.R.A., Roëll 162 (iii)—letter from a merchant, 26 Jan. 1820; B. C. E. Zwart, *De Kamer van Koophandel en Fabrieken te Amsterdam*, p. 106.

[2] A.R.A., Staatssec., 12 Feb. 1824, no. 67, pt. 1, 8 Feb. 1820; A.R.A., Roëll 162 (vi)—letter from J. A. Saxe, 8 April 1820; *Knuttel* 24295, p. 40; F. A. van Hall, *Onpartijdige beschouwing*, pp. 97–110.

[3] *Knuttel* 24295, pp. 28–9; *Mem. en cor.* pp. 84–5; C. Boissevain, *Onze voortrekkers*, p. 169.

Second Hand would be reduced, and replaced where necessary by controls over internal traffic. Appelius, however, drafted the special law to regulate the methods of levying customs and excise with different intentions from those of the authors of the law of 1821. The system of 1816, he explained to the king, had rightly banished the customs and excise controls on imported goods to the frontier and the ports, in accordance with the spirit of the age and the changed composition of the state; but it had not been entirely successful against smuggling, because the administration had hesitated to act drastically enough and the States General had been unwilling to grant adequate powers, for fear of arbitrary practices like those of the French time. The law of 1821 would give more elbow room, by enabling the administration to extend its control to the interior whenever the protection of the revenue and of the national economy might demand it.[1]

The legislation of 1822 accordingly provided for no very great reduction of formalities, and it retained a number of fees to be paid by merchants to officials. Appelius considered that these fees were valuable as incentives for proper compliance with formalities and also for courtesy and promptitude. The merchants denounced them as a very unnecessary incentive to vexatiousness. Furthermore, Roëll remarked, such fees made the foreigner suspicious and perhaps repelled more from the Dutch staple market than the customs tariff itself: 'for the foreigner can calculate the duties accurately and be sure that his commission agent is not cheating him, but he is in the dark about the administrative charges and cannot check his accounts'.[2]

The commercial party attached great importance to the making of separate laws to deal with the levying of customs and excise. This was not due to any practical considerations but to a desire to proclaim that the customs should be administered in a different spirit from the excise, and to a hope that separate laws might lead to separate services; for administrative organization was a matter of royal prerogative and not a subject for legislation. When a single law was proposed by Appelius on the plea of legislative convenience, the fact convinced Van Hogendorp that 'the cause of commerce has again been abandoned by the government' and that the forthcoming tariff proposals would bear further marks of the betrayal. No member, however, actually voted against the combined law.[3]

---

[1] A.R.A., Goldberg 214 (i)—memo. by Appelius, 29 Aug. 1821.
  A.R.A., Goldberg 215; A.R.A., Roëll 163 (d).
[3] A.R.A., Van Hogendorp 130 (6), 10 (x); *2de kamer*, 1821–2, A 480–5; G. K. van Hogendorp, *Bijdragen*, VI, 362–3.

In the excitement of the political struggle of the early 1820's, the commercial party much exaggerated the significance of a separate customs service, for the more responsible leaders had come to realize that the 'spirit of the Placaat of 1725' could never be revived. Roëll advised the king that the free trade needed by Dutch merchants must be attained by low customs duties and a convenient excise system, but not, at least as a permanent policy, by 'the old unequal liberality and arbitrary connivance'; for a return to the 'spirit of the Placaat' would lead, as before, to inequality and quarrels between ports, which would have a new danger when combined with the rivalry between Holland and Belgium, Antwerp and Amsterdam. In Rotterdam especially the old ideas were being abandoned. In 1814, the resident English merchants and the Dutch agents of English houses petitioned against the method of levying weighage. This tax was originally intended to ensure honest weights in commerce, but had come to have a very different effect; for 'various secret deductions' were allowed, which placed the merchants at the mercy of officials, and some Dutch merchants enjoyed the privilege of making a composition. Progressive opinion in Rotterdam welcomed the gradual abolition of these compositions by the government, but Gogel complained that the position of established Dutch houses, and especially of the Second Hand, was thereby being undermined.[1]

If Dutch commerce could no longer be protected by the 'spirit of the Placaat', the problem of the transit trade gained in significance. The Dutch merchants' dislike of this trade was shared by the king, and by Belgian industrialists, who denounced it as a help to smugglers. The Belgian iron-masters disliked the fact that English iron could pass through the kingdom and, after paying transit duty, still undersell their product in the adjacent areas of France. Only the Belgian commercial interests desired to retain their 1% transit duty, so the government had no difficulty in 1816 in establishing a 3% duty for the whole kingdom, and 4% for articles which it desired specially to impede. Thus the Dutch merchants gained a measure of protection against the competition of the more modern methods of Antwerp.[2]

The government hoped in 1816 that the 3% transit duty would not be so high as to drive trade to Hamburg, but high enough to give some discouragement to direct trade between foreigners over Dutch territory. At the same time, it was intended to offer in the transit and bonding systems

---

[1] A.R.A., Goldberg 130; A.R.A., Roëll 162 (i), pp. 133-4; *Mem. en cor.* p. 75.
[2] P. Vreede, *Proeve*, I, 115; *2de kamer*, 1827-8, A, Fallou, 27 March 1828; T. P. van der Kooy, *Hollands stapelmarkt*, pp. 112-13; W. L. Groeneveld Meyer, *De tariefwetgeving*, p. 72.

a means for the Dutch merchants to avoid the higher duties of 1816 in their foreign trade. If he did not wish to pay the import duty, a merchant had normally the choice between placing his goods in 'real bond', that is in a government warehouse, or in 'personal bond', in which case they were locked in his own store by the customs authorities and his access to them was officially controlled. For some categories of goods, he might be allowed the special favour of 'fictitious bonding', provided that he was considered worthy and could give satisfactory security for the whole duty. In due course, the goods became liable either to import or transit duty, according to their final disposal.[1]

The merchants of Belgium, Britain and France seemed quite content to conduct their general trade under bond. To supporters of the Appelian system, therefore, it seemed mere obstinacy in the Dutch merchants to reject transit-in-bond as Pandora's Box, or as 'a French bastard in our family, the ruin of our trade and marketplace, giving away the use of our land, which God and nature intended us to enjoy as middlemen in trade'. The Dutch merchants said they could understand that their brothers in Antwerp, who were children in these matters, should welcome the system; for they had little capital and no traditions and gladly stooped to the degrading work of dispatch agents, which enabled them to entice trade from Amsterdam.[2] But Dutch trade was different, indeed unique; and incompatible with bonding. Roëll explained:

I can easily understand that those who are familiar with trade elsewhere, but not in Amsterdam or our other northern cities, must be surprised at this persistent agitation against bonding. Elsewhere, trade consists merely of buying and selling, but in Holland it consists of sorting; the so-called commerce of detail conducted by the Second Hand which is still established here, could easily be displaced to Cologne, as could our tobacco industry.[3]

Such trade could not follow the English method, whereby goods were left untouched in bond until their destination was fixed and meanwhile all transactions were by transfer of dock-warrants.[4]

Bonding was especially disliked because it facilitated the competitive methods of English exporters. Samples from the bonded warehouse could be canvassed in the Netherlands and in the hinterland. It seemed unfair to Dutch merchants, who considered themselves highly taxed, that foreigners should enjoy such facilities. Further, these foreigners would be able to meet any sudden orders from Germany as quickly as the Dutch

[1] A.R.A., Roëll 162 (vii).
[2] A.R.A., Van Hogendorp 130, 6, 3 (iv); *Ged.* VIII (1), 339, and (3), 270.
[3] A.R.A., Roëll 162 (ii), p. 169.   [4] *Mem. en cor.* p. 184.

commission agents of German firms; and would avoid the costs of the Dutch staple market, whereas the Dutch commission agent hardly dared, in certain cases, to dispense with the services of the Second Hand and of the brokers by dealing with the First Hand directly. It was therefore often urged that transit goods should be admitted to bond only for the time necessary to obtain transport. The industrial protectionists fully agreed. Vreede drew the moral that full free trade would ruin the Dutch merchants, for foreign ships would be used as shops, the cargoes would be sold on board, and there would be no more work for the Second Hand, the brokers, or many of the commission agents. The merchants wanted protection for themselves and should not deny it to others.[1]

The exact function of the Second hand, which the commercial party tried so ardently to protect from the bonding system, was something of a mystery. It could not be discussed in public for fear of revealing trade secrets.[2] A Belgian deputy, who went to Amsterdam in order to discover why the bonding of excise goods was so detested by the Second Hand, came back with the report that the mystery was mainly a matter of counterfeit labels.[3] A Dutch merchant gave other reasons why the Second Hand could not transact its business in bond.

In all our commercial towns, each small tradesman, shopkeeper and artisan had a kind of factory, manipulating innumerable articles in his store, cellar, or workshop. Thus the importer could always find a crowd of small but solid buyers, while the exporter was sure of good and cheap supplies, since this class of industrious, bourgeois tradesmen was content with small profits often repeated, in widespread competition and an infinity of small consignments. However much our trade has declined, this kind of industry is not yet lost to us; indeed, none of our rivals has yet the advantage of such a trade. England and France export by mass; but our trade issues in a stream of small parcels, carried for instance to Cologne by barges.[4]

Of course, the growth in the volume of trade and the consequent development of direct trading implied that many processes formerly carried out centrally in the Dutch staple market would seek more economic locations close to the sources of supply or to the consuming markets. Thus timber-cutting was attracted to the Baltic supply ports and tobacco-cutting to the German markets. The fact did not entirely escape notice. Broad-minded Dutch merchants admitted that the work of sorting was

[1] A.R.A., Staatssec., 12 Feb. 1824, no. 67, pt. II, 14 April 1820; A.R.A., Roëll 162 (iii), 28 Jan. 1820; *Knuttel* 25852 (Vreede, 1829).
[2] F. A. van Hall, *Onpartijdige beschouwing*, p. 92.   [3] *Rec. fin.* p. 546.
[4] A.R.A., Roëll 162 (iii) (Van der Hoop, April 1820).

understood now even in the smallest of the world's market places, so that the Germans for instance could mix American and European tobacco for themselves. To such observers, it seemed inevitable that the Dutch Second Hand should decline, and that consequently Holland would have to be content with a type of trade which could well be conducted in bond. If the bonded warehouses remained emptier in Amsterdam than in Rotterdam and Antwerp, this proved not that Amsterdam was keeping the old type of trade alive but that she was being left behind in the development of the new.[1] The trend was illustrated by the yield of the administrative charges for admitting merchants to their goods in bond during the depression of 1819:[2]

	Amsterdam	Rotterdam	Antwerp
1817	20,600 fl.	13,500 fl.	1,300 fl.
1818	15,500	10,000	3,000
1819	5,000	6,000	1,600

In the early 1820's many Dutchmen hoped that the decline in their old type of trade would prove temporary. Gogel, for instance, hoped that in the long run, foreigners would prefer the small consignments and individual services of the Dutch market to the large-scale operations for which alone the British bonding system offered suitable facilities.[3] Many comforted themselves for the stagnation at Amsterdam by the hope that Dutch caution would be rewarded by the ruin of their more adventurous competitors. An Amsterdam merchant wrote to Roëll in 1820 about the commercial activity of foreigners.

There are now more ships than cargoes, more factories than can find consumers, more merchants than business, more capital than can be employed; and in consequence, innumerable staple markets, all overloaded with goods, but too small to be able to wait for customers.

Providence was already at work, eliminating these superfluities by bankruptcy.

All the surplus trading capital, all the surplus merchants, will automatically disappear; the more so, because most of them built up their businesses on the experience of revolution, do not know the normal commerce of peace-time, and, with the usual obstinacy of men, refuse to learn its ways. If we leave the reorganization of trade to nature, she will

[1] *Knuttel* 24811 (1819, 'Oudste en latere zeehandel').
[2] A.R.A., Staatssec., 12 Feb. 1824, no. 67, pt. II, 14 April 1820—report by Appelius.
[3] *Mem. en cor.* pp. 1–8, 63; cp. memo by Gogel in A.R.A., Roëll 162 (v).

soon show that many staple markets cannot be maintained, but that a central staple market is necessary as of old in Holland to regulate the general supply and demand.

Holland had shared least of all in the recent unfortunate commercial speculations; her capital, safely stowed away in the funds of various states, had benefited by the recent rise in their values and would be ready for new opportunities. 'Yes, even our tariff has thus far been of service to our merchants, by restraining them from taking a greater part in dangerous commercial transactions.' If Holland could now return to free trade, she would triumph in the return of normal conditions and become once more 'King of kings, levying a toll on the trade of all nations'.[1] Van Hogendorp, was optimistic for very different reasons. He believed that the expansion of international trade would continue, and would gradually persuade all nations to abandon restrictive policies, because free trade would allow scope enough for all.

Some say that our old trade is lost for ever, since all other nations are trading on their own account, and that we must not pursue a chimera. Such people carefully ignore a fact, which is nevertheless true; namely that the volume of European trade is at least three-fold, probably five-fold that of the seventeenth century....In my own lifetime, we have seen the arrival in Amsterdam of the first sack of Bengal sugar, the first bale of merino wool from Saxony, the first East-Indian indigo. Java coffee, from a low repute, has increased ten-fold and Cheribon coffee is now considered the best of all....Trade expands daily, and even if we now get only a small share of it, that share can still be much superior to what we enjoyed in previous centuries.

He believed that this new era in the economy of the world would give Holland the opportunity to carry on trade substantially in her traditional manner, which was so dear to him. However, if the Dutch merely waited listlessly for the old conditions to return, they would be disappointed; they must win a place for their market in the new conditions by efficient service and by sending agents abroad to canvas for orders. In that case, trade would inevitably be attracted by the Dutch location and reputation for honesty, and Holland would prosper side by side with England. When the English crisis of 1825 produced hardly a ripple in Amsterdam, many Dutchmen boasted of this as further proof of Dutch prudence, which must be rewarded in the end; for such shocks, of which no country could survive many, showed the new economic order to be artificial and impermanent. Van Hogendorp, however, pointed out that all enterprise implied risks and that the prudent stagnation of Amsterdam might be

[1] A.R.A., Roëll 162 (iii).

more injurious than the losses suffered at Hamburg, for instance, as a result of the English crisis. Van Hogendorp was also less cautious than other Dutchmen in his desire for free trade. He became ever more convinced that general free trade would bring an age of plenty, and gradually adopted the view that the Netherlands should set an example by abandoning even traditional restrictions approved by the commercial interest. He disliked the system of transit-in-bond and hoped to make it unnecessary by reducing the import and export duties to negligible levels; but after touring the country in 1818 he became convinced that it was useless meanwhile to discourage the transit trade by fiscal impediments, for the merchants of the European interior could not be compelled to use the traditional Dutch services if they were not persuaded of their advantage, and so the only effect of the 3% transit duty was to divert a good deal of trade to Hamburg and elsewhere.[1]

Men with practical experience in the 1820's could not share Van Hogendorp's belief that Holland's commercial position was so strong as to need only unlimited free trade. Dutch merchants preferred to deal in the facts of their own generation and to avoid prophetic visions which, though optimistic, were none the less disturbing to settled habits; they therefore clung to any form of protection that seemed advantageous to them. For example, the Dutch commercial interest as a whole desired the renewal of 'the traditional sheet-anchor of Dutch navigation', namely a discriminatory and prohibitive duty on English rock salt. The reason for this was that Dutch exports to France, Spain and Portugal were normally bulkier than the return cargoes. The empty space could be filled by carrying back salt, and this could not be done profitably if Dutch refiners were able to get cheap English rock salt. When the British government refused to allow this discrimination in favour of a former enemy, the Dutch commercial party looked for other ways of achieving the same result, without open discrimination.[2] Another protective measure, which dated from 1750 and was continued in the tariff of 1816 with the support of the Dutch merchants, was the prohibition of cut cork both for importation and for transit. Such a prohibition was apparently quite unknown elsewhere in the world, and was embarrassing to foreign ships, for even a small quantity of cut cork in a cargo involved serious and often unexpected difficulties with the Dutch Customs: but it was considered very important to protect the Dutch cork-cutting industry, not

[1] G. K. van Hogendorp, *Bijdragen*, VI, 251–2; *Ged.* IX (2), 867; cp. G. K. van Hogendorp, *Gedachten*, pp. 23–4.

[2] *Post. Doc.* I, 5–27, 326; J. van Ouwerkerk de Vries, *Verhandeling*, p. 128; B. C. E. Zwart, *De Kamer van Koophandel en Fabrieken te Amsterdam*, p. 89; but contrast *Ged.* VIII (3), 267.

merely for its own sake, but in order to provide a demand for uncut cork, which was useful as packing in ship's cargo.[1]

Only hard experience could teach the Dutch merchants not to seek protection by impeding transit. In 1817, the Rotterdam Chamber of Commerce and Industry was approached by the local sugar-refiners who desired that the transit of English refined sugar to Germany should be made more difficult. The Chamber calculated that a 5% transit duty on refined sugar would be safely within the margin of transport advantage, and advised the government accordingly. The government in 1818 gladly increased the duty. A diversion to Hamburg of trade in English sugar was immediately noticed. The Chamber, on investigation, discovered that the new duty, which was by weight, had been fixed at about 9½%, apparently in error. The government later reduced the duty to 6½%, but the trade did not come back. The advice of the Chamber to the commission of 1820 was accordingly much more liberal. Experience, it reported, had now convinced the more reasonable refiners that the Germans could not be forced to take Dutch rather than English sugar. English refined sugar was now essential for the Dutch staple market and many allied trades depended on its availability for mixed consignments to Germany and Switzerland. The import duty should remain high, but the transit duty should be further reduced; for the transit trade in refined sugar was a real help to active Dutch trade, for it kept the Dutch in correspondence with the European interior and thus enabled them to get orders on their own account or on commission, and information about the business situation.[2] This did not prevent a Dutch member of the States General from proposing in 1822 not only that there should be no 'transit' for raw sugar, but that a specially high export duty should be charged for re-exports by land; and that the same principle might be applied to other raw materials.[3]

The transit question was not one on which there were distinctive Dutch and Belgian points of view, yet in 1820–2 discussion about it, as about other fiscal questions, was warped by political passion. However, most members of the commission of 1820 desired that the transit duties should be as high as the relative transport costs permitted, and Belgian members who voiced Antwerp's demand for a duty of 1 or ½% were persuaded to drop the proposal. The law of 1821 provided that a separate transit duty should be fixed for each item in the tariff, up to a maximum of 3%; but

[1] A.R.A., Roëll 162 (vii)—tariff notes by Smeer and Van der Hoop.
[2] A.R.A., Staatssec., 12 Feb. 1824, no. 67, pt. I, B 3 and B 15; pt. II, 14 April 1820; Ged. VIII (3), 384; *Gedenkboek der Kamer van Koophandel en Fabrieken te Rotterdam*, pp. 149–50; A.R.A., Roell 162 (vii).
[3] A.R.A., Van Hogendorp, 130, 6, 3 (iv).

the commission, in its second session, asked that the rate should be higher for any exceptional goods which could bear more. The law, in the form finally adopted, allowed for such exceptions, and also laid down that goods prohibited for import should also be prohibited for transit. Only by legalistic quibbles could this latter provision be reconciled with the government's obligations under the Treaty of Vienna, regarding traffic on the Rhine.[1]

Belgian patriots, in their opposition to the law of 1821, adopted, for debating purposes, an attitude favourable to low transit duties. They derided Van Hogendorp's idea that the Dutch general market could benefit by the future development of international trade. 'Obviously the parts of a constant whole become smaller as the number of participants increases; for world trade may be considered as a single whole.' In future, Netherland merchants would only profit by their location if they were willing to serve the ordinary trade of others, 'as mere dispatch agents'. The Belgians could not understand why this should be considered undignified. The merchants of Bremen and Hamburg, whom the Dutch so feared, prospered by transit, not by active trade. The Belgians offered low transit duties to enable the Dutch to compete against them.[2]

In his draft tariff in 1822, Appelius proposed transit duties for each article varying from 1 to 3% *ad valorem*; but since the duty by weight varied from 0·80 fl. per 100 kg. on woad ash to 5·0 fl. per kg. on ipecacuanha, it was clear that he had been influenced by the corresponding import duties and by the value of the commodity as well as by transport costs. Dutch criticism varied widely. Some merchants argued that when the import duty was high, the transit duty should be very low, in order to leave at least that way open to Dutch traders; but that when the import duty was moderate, the transit duty should be as high as relative transport costs permitted. The import duty on pig-iron being high, they suggested that the transit duty of about 3% proposed by Appelius ought to be considerably reduced. Most Amsterdam merchants, however, considered that the high transport costs of iron gave an opportunity to discourage transit by a heavy duty, well above 3%. Roëll, on expert advice, estimated that in transport costs from the Channel to the German interior, Rotterdam had an advantage of 4 fl. per 100 kg., and Antwerp 3 fl., compared with Hamburg; and suggested a general transit duty of 3 fl. per 100 kg. Since the Belgian merchants wished for a lower rate, he supposed that Dutch commercial opinion would agree as a sacrifice to a general rate of

[1] A.R.A., Staatssec., 12 Feb. 1824, no. 67, pt. I, B3, B4, B6 and B15; pt. IV, 13 Feb. and 1 March 1820; A.R.A., Roëll 162 (ii).

[2] *Rec. fin.* pp. 343, 361, 363, 570–1, 584; A.R.A., Staatssec., 12 July 1821, no. 57.

not less than 2 fl. He thought, however, that Appelius' proposal for an import duty on cotton yarn twenty times greater than the transit duty was so unnatural and so inviting for smugglers as to make necessary a much higher transit duty. The transit duty on cotton yarn proposed by Appelius and enacted in the tariff of 1822 was 2 fl. per 100 kg. and equal to about $1\frac{1}{2}\%$. Some merchants in Rotterdam and Amsterdam asked that it should be halved.[1]

Adherents of the Dutch tradition of free trade were willing to protect Dutch industry when commercial interests were not at stake. They desired an import duty on paper which would force Belgian publishers to draw supplies from Zaandam instead of unpatriotically preferring the product of cheaper labour in France. They desired to protect Dutch oil-mills at the expense of Belgian farmers who used German oil cakes.[2] It was with their support that in the tariff of 1822 imports of clay tobacco-pipes were prohibited, and import duties well above 6% were imposed on paper, rope and white lead. Appelius had proposed only 6% on white lead, but he was persuaded by Van Hogendorp that the Dutch workshops could not at present stand the shock of reduced protection.[3]

However, the commercial party was agreed that less industrial protection could be afforded than in the past. Gogel, for instance, proposed that the import duty on pottery, which under the system of 1816 was from 8 to 15% according to the nature of the goods, should be reduced not to a flat rate of 8% as in the Placaat of 1725 but to $3\frac{1}{2}\%$. He explained that 8% would prevent the existence of a staple market, without preventing imports for home consumption. On the other hand, he asked that the importation and transit of refined sugar and milled dye-woods should be prohibited. Gogel, however, as he readily admitted, had lost touch in his retirement with the course of trade since 1813. Practical Amsterdam merchants agreed that both these commodities were suitable for protective import duties above the general 6% maximum, but said that it was unfortunately necessary to permit transit at a duty within the margin of relative transport costs. The sugar duties actually introduced by the tariff of 1822 were:

	In	Out	Transit
Raw sugar (per 100 kg.)	1·20 fl.	1·50 fl.	1·50 fl.
Refined sugar (per 100 kg.)	36·0 fl.	0·20 fl.	2·0 fl.

[1] A.R.A., Roëll 163 (l); A.R.A., Goldberg 215.
[2] A.R.A., Staatssec., Geheim, 4 Nov. 1827, U 30.
[3] A.R.A., Van Hogendorp 130, 6, 3; G. K. van Hogendorp, *Bijdragen*, VI, 364–9, 384–7; *2de kamer*, 1821–2, A 520–6 and B 1011–14.

Appelius originally proposed an import duty of 20.0 fl. on refined sugar, but Dutch commercial opinion desired undiminished protection for the refineries. The sugar excise was now paid only on raw sugar at rates said to be equal on average to a duty of 16 fl. per 100 kg. on refined.[1]

Rotterdam was especially interested in the madder industry. The merchants who exported the dye also financed its production by small craftsmen. They desired prohibition of the export of the unprocessed roots, and stringent regulations against adulterated or inferior products. In 1819, the government accordingly set up a corporation similar to that for the deep-sea herring fishery. The merchants complained that such control of quality was useless without prohibition of the export of roots, for the Dutch reputation would be damaged if foreigners were allowed to produce an inferior dye from Dutch roots. Some Rotterdam merchants, who were otherwise liberal in their attitude to the transit trade, desired the prohibition of the importation and transit of prepared madder. In 1822, the Rotterdam Chamber of Commerce and Industry demanded that at least the export of undried roots should be prohibited and that of dried roots highly taxed; for England, the largest customer, was trying to attract the industry by admitting the roots without duty and placing a high import duty on the powder. The interested merchants of Antwerp were more realistic; they supported the stringent regulation of quality, but desired only a moderate export duty on roots, since England could get supplies from Avignon or the Levant. In the tariff of 1822, the government prohibited the export and transit of undried roots of the type grown in the Netherlands, placed a high export duty on the dried roots, and fixed the import and transit duties on the best powder at about 10 and 3% respectively. It proved difficult in practice to prevent the fraudulent exportation of Dutch undried roots. In 1822, despite the opposition of both Rotterdam and Antwerp, the government relaxed the regulations for the preparation of madder in favour of a new mechanical process invented in Belgium, which required a higher extraction rate.[2]

The commercial party boasted that most Dutch industrialists were eager to forgo any protection likely to injure the general market. The gunpowder makers, for instance, had formerly thrived on the Dutch East India Company's command of much of the world's supply of saltpetre. The Placaat of 1725 took advantage of this monopoly to impose a high export duty on raw saltpetre. In the changed situation of 1820, however,

[1] A.R.A., Roëll 163 (I); A.R.A., Goldberg 217; *Mem. en cor.*, 353.
[2] A.R.A., Staatssec., 12 Feb. 1824, no. 67, pt. IV, 15 Jan. 1821, no. 17; A.R.A., Goldberg 213 (III); and 217—report of Council of State 1822; *2de kamer*, 1821–2, A 521–5 and 1825–6, B 384.

the owners of the small workshops concerned were persuaded to sign a petition in terms suggested by the interested merchants. They said that Dutch skill was so great as to preclude fears of competition, provided only that cheap raw materials were available. Everything thus depended on the presence at Amsterdam of a market in saltpetre, which could only be maintained by low import and export duties. They asked that even the import duty on gunpowder should be moderate enough to encourage re-exports. Appelius was not convinced, for the industry had asked for protection in 1816. In the tariff of 1822, the import duty for gunpowder remained well above the 6% maximum.[1] The sail-makers, too, pleased the commercial party in 1820 by asking not to be protected. The free import of foreign sail, it seemed, was necessary in order that Dutch might be exported in mixed consignments. The sail-makers also hoped that free trade would help them by increasing navigation.[2] Sometimes, however, the industrialists of the Dutch commercial towns, when their opinion was directly asked, contradicted the arguments put forward by the commercial party as though on behalf of a united community. The brewers of Amsterdam and Rotterdam, for instance, desired heavy taxation of coffee and tea.[3]

The merchants wished to help certain commercial industries by small increases in the export duties on their raw materials, on condition that the import duties were correspondingly reduced in order to avoid impeding re-exports. They persuaded Appelius to modify his draft tariff in this sense in 1822 in the case of unrefined borax. They failed to gain any such concession for the tobacco industry; which, they said, was on the verge of displacement, partly because the 2% import duty on leaf tobacco was too high and partly because Prussia had retaliated against the Netherland tariff of 1816 by high import and transit duties, and by enticing Dutch enterprise and skill to Münster. Appelius refused to reduce the import duty, because he did not wish to lose revenue on tobacco consumed in the home market, but he offered to increase the existing 1½% export duty on raw tobacco. Commercial opinion was hostile to any such uncompensated increase, and the duties were not changed.[4] Similarly, Appelius proposed in 1822 to prohibit the export of raw salt, partly in order to facilitate excise administration and partly to protect the refiners; and the

[1] A.R.A., Staatssec., 12 Feb. 1824, no. 67, pt. I, B13; A.R.A., Goldberg 215; A.R.A., Roëll 163 (l); Z. W. Sneller, in *Bijdragen voor Vaderlandsche Geschiedenis en Oudheidkunde* (1926), p, 155.

[2] A.R.A., Staatssec., 12 Feb. 1824, no. 67, pt. I, B12.

[3] Z. W. Sneller, in *Bijdragen voor Vaderlandsche Geschiedenis en Oudheidkunde* (1926), p. 155.

[4] A.R.A., Staatssec., 12 Feb. 1824, no. 67, pt. I, B8.

First Hand complained bitterly. The refiners, they said, would probably agree among themselves to force prices down, and the merchants would be helpless in the face of this monopoly. It would be best for the refiners themselves that the First Hand should re-export its raw salt when Dutch prices were too low, in order that the market in salt might be preserved. In this matter, Appelius gave way. He refused, however, to reduce the high export duty on rabbit fur, which had been introduced in 1816 to protect Dutch and Belgian hatters. The Dutch had been accustomed to export fur after it had been prepared for felting from imported rabbit skins. The merchants declared that it was impossible to export it in a more finished state; consequently, the duty had reduced the average annual import from 500,000 to 50,000 skins, caused the skilled workers to emigrate and carry the Second Hand secrets to foreign countries, and perhaps sacrificed for ever the superiority of Dutch fur.[1]

Appelius boasted that his concessions to the Dutch merchants made the tariff of 1822 the lowest in Dutch history. In order to help Dutch trade in its increasing difficulty, and because Belgian industry had had time to adjust itself to peace-time conditions, the protective duties on many Belgian products such as glass, cutlery, carpets, pottery, furniture, hardware, haberdashery and crystal were reduced from 10–15 to 6%, though at the last moment the duty on millinery was restored to 10%, in response to Belgian complaints about travelling French salesmen. Duties on purely commercial goods such as cinnamon and cochineal were also reduced. For cochineal, Appelius proposed an import duty of 10 fl. per 100 kg., which, he said, represented $\frac{3}{4}$% *ad valorem*. The merchants complained that only complete freedom from duty could now restore their general trade in cochineal. Appelius scoffed at this, but tried to make the duty less alarming by expressing it as 0·10 fl. per kg.[2]

(b) Navigation

Dutch commercial opinion was much divided over the question of protection for Dutch shipping. The merchant fleet was depleted and decayed after the war, and foreign shipping had to be attracted at first if Amsterdam was to receive the produce even of Dutch colonies. The purchase of foreign ships for Dutch registration was encouraged. Under the tariff of 1816, the ships of reciprocating powers paid no greater tonnage dues than national ships, and most foreign ships were in fact admitted to this privilege.

[1] A.R.A., Staatssec., 12 Feb. 1824, no. 67, pt. II, 2 May 1820.
[2] A.R.A., Staatssec., 12 Feb. 1824, no. 67, pt. I, B 10; A.R.A., Goldberg 215.

Unprotected, Dutch shipping could not revive. The Dutch wondered to see Americans ply trades in which they themselves could find no profit even with foreign-built ships. They knew that ships could not be built and equipped so cheaply now in Holland as in North America or Scandinavia; but Dutch crews were still small and satisfied with 'sober fare', and this had always been supposed to be the greatest advantage of the Dutch in the carrying trade, though in the late eighteenth century some observers noted that it was offset by the slowness of Dutch navigation. Some Dutchmen hoped that the Americans were being deceived by lucky profits into continuing in peace-time trades which their high operating-costs, and losses due to their commercial imprudence, would force them to abandon in the long run.[1] Others exhorted Dutch merchants to imitate the Americans; to give up the idea of a centrally organized trade, put their offices on their ships and sail 'op avontuur' about the world. They might take European goods to Peru, pick up furs in North-west America and exchange them for tea at Canton; or take Belgian guns to Timor and exchange them for sandalwood to sell at Canton.[2] However, to the Dutch of this period such ideas were mere daydreams. They could rarely find profit in oceanic voyages, apart from those to the Dutch West Indies, in which trade, thanks to the attitude and example of Great Britain, their government was able to give real protection.

By 1820, there was a strong demand for the protection of Dutch shipping by a general customs preference. The tariff of 1822 remitted 10% of the customs duties on goods carried in Netherland ships. The commercial party as a whole welcomed this, and asked for 15%. Dutch shipowners and merchants, however, opposed the attempt which the government was now making to protect the shipbuilders by denying Netherland registration to foreign-built ships. The Amsterdam Chamber of Commerce and Industry complained that this would much increase shipping costs, and suggested that the shipbuilders should be given subsidies instead, at least in so far as their high costs were due to taxation.[3]

The smaller Dutch merchants had no wish that either the shipowners or the shipbuilders should be protected. Privileges and preferences, they feared, would discourage the foreign shipping on which any revival of the Dutch staple market must now mainly depend. They favoured any restrictive policies that could bring to Dutch ports an exclusive or specially favoured supply of Dutch colonial produce, but they wished to

---

[1] *Knuttel* 24797, pp. 103–4; D. J. Garat, *Mémoire*, p. 7, 42; Lord Sheffield, *Observations*, p. 50.

[2] *Knuttel* 24811 (Anon. 1819); J. van Ouwerkerk de Vries, *Verhandeling*, p. 198.

[3] *Knuttel* 24797, pp. 107–10; A.R.A., Goldberg 217—report of Council of State, 1822; *2de kamer*, 1821–2, A 520–6; *Ged.* VIII (3), 393–9.

receive imports as cheaply as possible. Van Hogendorp, too, doubted the wisdom of shipping preferences. One of the lessons of the eighteenth century, he believed, had been that as foreigners learned to trade actively, the Dutch must be content with a more passive role; they must leave the carrying to those who could do it at least cost, and encourage foreigners to use the Dutch market in every way. He hoped that, because of the expansion of world trade, the Dutch shipyards, under a policy of complete *laissez-faire*, would have more work than ever before, simply in repairs to visiting foreign ships.[1]

The tea trade was an old subject of controversy. In the eighteenth century, there was a clash of interests between the East India Company, which had a monopoly of the direct trade with Canton, and the merchants who imported tea from elsewhere. The latter argued that free imports and low prices stimulated consumption and encouraged the use of Holland as a base for smuggling into England the tea not only of the Dutch but also of the Swedish and Danish East India Companies. Thanks, however, to the glut of tea in Holland caused by Pitt's Commutation Act of 1784, the Company was able to secure the exclusion of 'foreign' tea from the Republic in 1791. After 1813, no such prohibition could be considered until Dutch ships were available; and the government was undecided as to whether private merchants would venture the large capital needed for expeditions to Canton, or whether a new privileged company was needed. Merchants who were receiving foreign consignments of tea opposed all privileges and asked for unlimited imports, 'in accordance with the undeniable principle that, for a Merchant State, imports can never be too great'. The Second Hand traders hoped that supplies would be restricted to annual sales held by a new company; half-yearly sales would be too frequent, since some retailers and inland traders had acquired enough capital to take in six months' stock at a time and so would dispense with the services of the Second Hand. In 1815, the government decided to create a company:

In spite of our desire to champion free trade in general, some trades, and especially the trade with China, demand exceptions....We have considered the great benefit to commerce and industry, to shipping and shipbuilding, of preserving the trade with China from foreign hands and keeping it exclusively for this nation as an active branch of its domestic and foreign commerce.

No one subscribed except the king himself, a few professional dealers in securities, and some Leiden manufacturers of camlets for the Chinese

[1] G. K. van Hogendorp, *Bijdragen*, VI, 383–6.

market. In view of this failure, and for fear that their members might be asked to subscribe, all the Chambers of Commerce and Industry except that at Leiden declared for a free trade; and the king agreed in 1817 to the winding up of the company.[1]

Amsterdam remained the chief Continental market for tea; owing, it was said, to the large capital needed in the trade, but more probably to the small consumption beyond the immediate vicinity of the Netherlands. In 1817, the government took advantage of this situation to impose a high import duty and to allow for tea brought in Netherland ships a preference equal to about 10% of its value and 70% of the duty. No concession was made for transit, so all re-exported tea was liable for the appropriate import duty. The commercial party on the whole approved these arrangements, and no change was made by the tariff of 1822. Nevertheless, Dutch trade with Canton remained unprofitable, and complaints continued of 'the evil of unlimited importation of an article for which the demand is limited'. The protective duties for the benefit of Dutch shipping did not, it seemed, deter the Americans from continually flooding the Dutch market, for 'we have not here to deal with a people who, like the Hollander, coolly weigh the pros and cons before deciding. The American is not to be outdone in self-confidence; he defies an unfavourable situation and trusts to his stars to make the circumstances change in his favour'. Experts warned the government in 1822 that Hamburg was taking a growing interest in the trade, so that vigilance was needed and early action if a more liberal attitude towards the transit of tea unfortunately became necessary. In fact, the government introduced transit duties for tea in 1827, but little use was made of them, for American imports through Hamburg and Bremen already dominated the German markets.[2]

---

[1] *Memorieboek van de Pakhuis-meesteren van de thee* (Amsterdam, 1918), pp. 39–53, 74–81.

[2] A.R.A., Roëll 163 (i); *Knuttel* 25685 (P. de Haan, 1827); *Parl. Papers* (1849), LII, 322–3.

Table XIII. *Shipping in Netherland ports, 1824–9*

	Netherland		English		Other		Total	
	No. of ships	Tons (thousands)	No. of ships	Tons (thousands)	No. of ships	Tons (thousands)	No. of ships	Tons (thousands)
*Ships entering Netherland ports with cargo**								
1824	2,262	214	491	47	1,908	195	4,661	456
1825	2,397	221	547	49	1,819	184	4,763	454
1826	2,657	251	641	68	2,151	240	5,449	559
1827	2,648	255	750	96	2,415	283	5,813	634
1828	2,841	284	848	101	2,765	339	6,453	725
1829	2,631	268	954	119	2,513	314	6,098	703
*Ships leaving Netherland ports with cargo**								
1824	2,330	256	834	70	1,387	176	4,551	502
1825	2,108	241	1,028	83	1,292	164	4,428	489
1826	1,765	193	965	86	1,267	162	3,997	442
1827	1,726	172	1,335	136	1,383	151	4,444	459
1828	1,807	186	1,448	140	1,373	154	4,628	480
1829	1,717	179	1,214	118	1,293	142	4,224	440

*Average number of ships entering certain ports in 1826–7 annually,†
including those in ballast*

	No. of ships	Tons (thousands)
Amsterdam	2,006	215
Rotterdam	1,134	129
Antwerp	810	114
Ostend	420	38
Harlingen	451	44
Other Beglian ports	210	13
Other Dutch ports	1,573	114
Total	6,604	667

* A.R.A., Staatssec., 31 March 1830, no. 4.
† J. A. Drieling, *Bijdragen*.

Table XIV.　*Sugar, coffee, etc., 1814–25*

Certain American exports, annual average 1821–2*						
					Re-exports	
	Rice (tierces, thousands)	Tobacco (hogshds, thousands)	Whale oil (gals., thousands)	Coffee (lb., thousands)	Sugar, brown (lb., thousands)	Sugar, white (lb., thousands)
To						
The Netherlands	6	19	132	3,150	5,850	1,330
Great Britain	20	25	—	10	120	—
Hanseatic ports	11	11	408	1,150	1,520	380

British exports of sugar to certain countries† (thousand cwt.)								
	1814		1815		1816		1817	
	Raw	Refined	Raw	Refined	Raw	Refined	Raw	Refined
To								
Germany	233	381	183	488	114	425	79	425
Dutch provinces	213	91	236	11	161	8	110	160
Belgian provinces	104	106	94	126	98	115	82	30

	1818		1819		1820			
	Raw	Refined	Raw	Refined	Raw	Refined		
To								
Germany	53	379	101	317	123	546		
Dutch provinces	55	67	24	26	36	19		
Belgian provinces	88	9	16	1	67	1		

* *American State Papers*, 1832, Commerce and Navigation, vols. I and II.
† *Parl. Papers*, 1821, XVII, 206–31.

Table XIV (*continued*).

	Imports of sugar and coffee to certain Netherland ports‡ (million kg.)						
	Sugar				Coffee		
	Amster-dam	Rotter-dam	Antwerp		Amster-dam	Rotter-dam	Antwerp
1817	16·0	7·3	8·0		13·5	5·6	8·1
1818	17·6	8·5	9·7		10·7	3·8	6·0
1819	13·3	7·6	8·6		7·2	6·6	7·4
1820	16·4	6·0	13·7		8·0	1·4	6·4
1821	18·6	10·2	15·4		?	4·3	?
1822	14·5	6·9	18·3		?	4·3	?
1823	12·6	7·1	16·4		8·3	7·9	6·7
1824	14·3	6·8	13·6		9·4	7·0	11·0
1825	11·5	5·4	12·7		8·3	5·6	12·6

Price of refined sugar at Amsterdam§
(florins per 100 kg.)

1815	144	1818	120	1821	98
1816	128	1819	112	1822	87
1817	122	1820	102	1823	103

‡ P. A. A. van Mechelen, *Zeevaart en zeehandel van Rotterdam*, pp. 226–8.
§ N. W. Posthumus, *Nederlandse prijsgeschiedenis*.

Chapter X

THE PROTECTION OF AGRICULTURE

Until 1818, agricultural prices remained high. During the dearth of 1817, there was a strong agitation of Belgian consumers for the traditional remedy, an embargo against corn exports. The Dutch commercial party resisted, in the belief that Holland was still, as foreigners had recognized her to be until 1795, the regulating granary of Europe. The good demand during the dearth for all the corn Holland could export fostered this illusion. The trade had always consisted of building up stocks in time of plenty and exporting in times of dearth, and the idea of an export embargo was contrary to the Dutch tradition. The introduction of an embargo in 1799 was attributed to French influence or to the desire of 'Batavian' demagogues to appease the foolish urban populace; and its results were held to have proved that any interference with corn exports was fatally discouraging to imports. In 1817, William I adopted a compromise favourable to the Dutch commercial party. An embargo was placed on exports across the land frontier, but maritime exports remained free. On this point, indeed, the government could not give way to the Belgians, if it sincerely meant to respect the needs of the Dutch general market. In 1819, Appelius boasted of the incident as proof of this sincerity:

It is encouraging to see how the corn trade has re-established itself in this land, thanks to the king's firmness in 1817; so that even the most prejudiced must see that in this case free trade is the best way to prevent dearth and to preserve, in all unforeseen circumstances, one ready and profitable employment for commercial capital.[1]

In England, on the other hand, it had long been understood that the war might permanently deprive Holland of her general trade in corn, as in other commodities. London was in all seasons more accessible than Amsterdam. Britain could not offer free trade, but her improved bonding system was a good substitute, especially after the creation of the London 'entrepôt' dock in 1803. British re-exports competed after the war in European corn markets. Holland had always been specially interested in the rye trade; but in 1817, she had hardly enough for her own consumption, and imported 23,000 quarters out of British bond.[2]

[1] A.R.A., Staatssec., 12 Feb. 1824, no. 67, pt. I, 8 Feb. 1820; *Ged.* v, 612; J. J. Oddy, *European Commerce* (London, 1805), p. 509.
[2] *Parl. Papers*, 1826–7, no. 333, pp. 37–8, 134; J. J. Oddy, *European Commerce*, pp. 509–14; Anon., *A Letter to a Friend on Commerce, and Free Ports, and the London Docks* (London, 1796).

In December 1818, Van Hogendorp pointed to the high agricultural prices and rents as proof that the re-opening of maritime trade and the free trade in corn were favourable to rural prosperity. The Belgian landed interest was not convinced, but as yet asked only for lower taxes.[1] In 1819, however, prices fell, and the agitation of Belgian consumers against exports of corn was replaced by an agitation of producers against imports. All the king's Dutch advisers upheld the free trade in corn, even those who supported industrial protection.[2]

The government wished to help agriculture without interfering with trade. It proposed in 1820 to set up a corn immobilization fund, which would buy and store corn when prices were low, and sell when they rose again. The provincial States were consulted, and asked to name the prices at which such a fund should operate in their province. The replies were unfavourable, for the provinces feared that they would have to find the money.

Most of the Belgian provinces urged that stabilization should be achieved not by government purchases but by prohibiting imports or exports when prices were too low or too high. Liége, expressing an industrial point of view, said that high prices were worse than low, because the manufacturing areas always had to maintain a number of unemployed and because foreign competition did not allow wages to rise in proportion to high prices. The corn trade should therefore normally be free, but imports or exports should be prohibited when absolutely necessary. West Flanders' opinion reflected commercial influence. The corn trade was that in which governments interfered most, and should least. The government ought, therefore, to conform with the spirit of the century by not interfering with the internal corn trade, but should control prices by means of a sliding scale of import and export duties, without prohibitions. All the Belgian provinces agreed that the general trade in corn could be adequately safeguarded by bonding arrangements, or by free ports.

All the Dutch provinces except North Brabant insisted on unlimited freedom for the foreign as well as the internal trade. The rich landowners who sat in the States of the agricultural provinces evidently felt that their interests were bound up with those of Holland. The corn trade, said Friesland, was the last sheet anchor of the Dutch staple market. The present low prices, said the South Holland Agricultural Committee, were a normal readjustment to peace-time; the farmers' distress would automatically be relieved by non-agricultural prices falling into line with that for corn; or

[1] A.R.A., Van Hogendorp 128c (notes for a speech, 19 Dec. 1818); *L'Observateur*, XVII, 19–26.
[2] *Ged.* VIII (2), 66.

they could find their own remedy by turning to other crops, or to dairying. The corn trade, said the Amsterdam Chamber of Commerce and Industry, employed three-quarters of Dutch shipping; it would dwindle if foreign merchants were discouraged from sending their corn speculatively to Dutch commission agents by the knowledge that the government was holding stocks to keep prices down artificially in time of dearth.

North Brabant considered low corn prices to be more harmful than high ones, because high prices increased the farmers' spending power and so spread prosperity throughout the nation. The government should not ignore the needs of commerce: but to protect agriculture and to make the foreigner contribute to the national revenue, the import duties on grains should be considerably increased.

In 1821, the government suggested a different scheme. Corn could be immobilized by credit societies which would lend money to enable farmers and landowners to store their crops until prices were satisfactory. The replies of the provincial States were again unfavourable. The Belgians said that a system of import and export prohibitions had become even more necessary, since the flour excise would increase bread prices during dearth and the tax burden on agriculture was being increased. In the north, Drenthe now joined North Brabant in asking for a limitation of imports. Friesland asked for temporary tax relief for agriculture. Gelderland suggested that the government should buy more horses for the cavalry and open negotiations to facilitate the export of Dutch-grown tobacco to Germany. The merchants, however, believed that corn prices had reached bottom, and Holland, Zeeland and Utrecht accordingly expressed confidence that the natural course of events would bring more benefits than any government interference.

In 1822, the king submitted the agricultural problem to a commission similar in composition to that of 1820 and again under the presidency of Roëll. Its terms of reference this time carefully excluded everything the Belgian members were likely to propose. It was to consider the proposal for credit societies, and any other possible means of assisting agriculture without depriving it of the benefit of unlimited free trade in corn. The king's purpose, Roëll was privately informed, was partly to have the question thoroughly investigated and partly to forestall any proposal by members of the States General for prohibitive corn laws. Roëll prepared a long agenda from which everything related to the tariff was omitted.

Roëll kept in touch with the merchant who was most active in organizing political agitation in Amsterdam in defence of the free corn trade, and the two tried to co-ordinate their tactics. They agreed that, if necessary, in order to appease the States General, agriculture might be granted tax reliefs or, as a last resort, the prohibition of corn imports by land, which would neither materially affect trade nor much benefit agriculture, but might soothe opinions.

Speeches inside the commission and many petitions from outside showed that the agitation for restrictive corn laws was by this time making considerable headway in the Dutch agricultural provinces. Landowners and farmers in Groningen, Overijssel and Friesland protested their desire for freedom of trade, in so far as the legislation of other countries permitted Dutch merchants to foster the export of Dutch agricultural products; but they asked that when prices were below a certain minimum the importation of foreign grains should be prohibited, except into bond. Even commerce, they believed, would gain by such restriction; for it would enable the agricultural population to buy more from the merchants, who could not be finding much profit in the corn trade after three years of continuously falling prices. The prohibition must continue at least until farmers had completed their adjustment to peacetime by converting to pasture. Petitioners from South Holland and Utrecht said that agriculture no longer hoped for any help from commerce; for Holland was no longer the regulating granary of Europe, but merely a dumping ground for foreign surpluses. Agriculture, not commerce, now had the first claim to consideration. Corn imports should be prohibited. On the other hand, agricultural interests in North Holland, where less corn was grown, still supported free trade.[1]

Van Hogendorp admitted that a great majority of opinion in the kingdom as a whole now appeared to desire prohibitive corn laws. He replied with a pamphlet. The fall in corn prices, which he supposed had nearly reached bottom, would be beneficial in the long run, especially for the workers. It heralded peace and plenty. Only the time lag in the adjustment of rents and taxes made the initial stage of the new cheap time painful to farmers. Since provisions for the armed forces had become cheaper, the government could and should reduce taxes on land. Landowners would in time have to reduce rents and would be fully compensated by lower prices, for all would come down to the agricultural level. Production for export would be stimulated by lower labour costs and would remedy the miserable pauperism left by the war. Prohibitive corn laws, on the other hand, would keep up prices artificially and so discourage all exports; just as would have been the case in England, but for the dangerous expedient of machinery. Holland was still the granary of Europe. The recent influx of cheap corn was quite normal. Dearth

[1] A.R.A., Roëll 150: and 162 (vii)—notes by Smeer and Van der Hoop, 13 Dec. 1820.

would come again, and the foreign demand would be greater than ever; for although world production of corn was increasing, population was keeping pace with it. At any moment, there might be war in southern Europe, and then big orders would be placed in the old, respected market. Free trade ensured that the farmers could always sell their crop, for the merchants were always willing to accumulate stocks when prices were low; but if imports were restricted, the staple market would be displaced from Holland and merchants would no longer speculate in home-grown corn.[1]

Van Hogendorp ignored many of the arguments of the protectionists. Netherland farmers, they said, could not compete with Polish serfs. Exports from the Dutch market would be much less than in the eighteenth century. Improved cultivation had reduced England's need of imports, and temporary shortages would be met by her own merchants from bond. Mediterranean markets would in future be dominated by supplies from the Black Sea, which would no longer merely trickle through from Constantinople, for 'as soon as Russia became mistress of those territories, their natural fertility and the opening of the Dardanelles created the most powerful competition there has ever been in the corn trade'. The activity of English ships at Odessa showed that Holland's commercial competitors would make sure of these supplies reaching at least Spain; some said that the danger of the grain heating if delayed by unfavourable winds at the Straits of Gibraltar would prevent it from coming further, but there might be some way of overcoming this difficulty, by using steam tugs, for instance.[2] The corn merchants themselves felt that Van Hogendorp's description of their trade was unrealistic. W. de Clercq, the secretary of their fraternity at Amsterdam, who was active in the agitation for free trade, wrote to Roëll: 'This idea of a time of cheapness seems to many to be an illusion, in the present troubled state of Europe; and it is so contrary to the immediate interests of many in all branches of trade, that it is not much believed.' He admitted that the weakness of the free trade argument lay in the uncertainty of export opportunities, which he attributed to the prohibitive policies of other nations. Even if a lucky Mediterranean war were to cut off supplies from Odessa, he feared the Baltic exporters might reap most of the advantage by direct trading. As things were, they exported not only to Holland but also, whenever the ports were open, to Portugal and elsewhere, so that not only the stapling place but also the ultimate markets were flooded. It had often been supposed that much

---

[1] G. K. van Hogendorp, *Bijdragen*, VI, 389–407.
[2] *Knuttel* 25853 (Beerenbroek, 1829); A. Moreau de Jonnès, *Le commerce au 19e siècle* (Paris, 1825), I, 304–9.

of the strength of the Dutch corn trade was due to the danger of heating if grain were shipped directly from the Baltic to the Mediterranean, and to Dutch skill in cleaning, drying and stowing for the voyage. In the 1820's, however, cargoes were sent directly from Danzig to Marseilles, and even small-grained Polish wheat was found to heat only rarely, and probably as a result of negligence.[1]

De Clercq's conclusion was that too many merchants were trying to live by the trade, both in Holland and in the Baltic ports, and that its volume must be reduced; meanwhile, Holland must hang on as well as possible.

The power of our reserves of capital and our location still give us the *appearance* of a continued staple trade, and it is the duty of all Netherlanders to conceal from the eye of Europe that we have lost the reality. The foreigner should never know how much of the grain he consigns to us as to a general European market is used solely for the consumption of our seven provinces, often indeed of Holland alone.... The fact is, as the Belgian sees well, that imports this year have already been considerable and his hopes of *export* vain. He knows that only the large consumption of our northern towns conceals the import surplus and he wishes to secure that consumption for *his* corn.

In a manifesto, the Amsterdam corn merchants pointed out that they needed a rise in prices just as urgently as the farmers; but they thought of the future and rejected artificial remedies, for any rise above the international level would destroy the hope of export. It was still quite possible that the Netherlands would again become the granary of southern Europe. The English prohibitory laws prevented English greed from taking away that chance also; but if both countries had to conduct their general corn trade under bond, then the large and well-organized London entrepôt dock would undoubtedly conquer. Prohibitions or high duties would destroy confidence, for corn in bond, cut off from the home market, would have no negotiable value. Trading capital would be withdrawn and probably invested in foreign securities. Still more Baltic merchants would become bankrupt, if they were thus deprived of Dutch credit. The advantage would be to Odessa, and the Dutch corn trade, the mainstay of the whole staple market, might be lost for ever.

In the commission, both free-traders and protectionists considered that the government's immobilization schemes would be unworkable unless accompanied by restriction of imports. A few Dutch and Belgian protectionists supported the immobilization fund as a subsidiary measure,

[1] *Ged.* vi, 1317; A.R.A., Roëll 150; *Knuttel* 24797 (Van Ouwerkerk de Vries, 1819), p. 103; and 25853.

but they feared the credit societies as a new source of assignats. Most of the Belgians believed that exclusion of foreign imports would be a sufficient remedy, and used *laissez-faire* arguments against government interference in the internal corn trade. Members from the Dutch agricultural provinces agreed that foreign imports must be excluded, but wished to allow commerce the privilege of fictitious bonding. Dutch commercial members rejected this compromise. Fictitious bonding would destroy the trade, for everyone would regard it merely as a first step in restrictions and trade was impossible without confidence in the free disposal of stocks for some years ahead.

The protectionists were in a majority in the commission. They considered that bonding facilities would provide adequately for the maintenance of a free corn trade in accordance with the king's instruction, and recommended that the government should prohibit imports to the home market except when prices in it were unduly high.[1]

The proceedings of the commission provided the government with an excuse for keeping the corn question out of the tariff debates of 1822. The tariff of 1822 left the corn duties provisionally unchanged, on the ground that the king was still considering the commission's report. He was in no hurry, for his decision was not announced until his speech from the throne in October 1823. He then declared that no action by the state was necessary or desirable. The landowners of Groningen had, however, decided to form a credit society on the lines of his proposal and he hoped that, if it succeeded, other provinces would imitate and thus prevent future agricultural difficulties.[2] The Groningen Credit Society came into being under a royal decree before the end of 1823. The king refused to grant it exemption from registration duties, on the ground that the constitution forbade fiscal privileges; he explained that the Société Générale, which had been granted such exemption, existed more for the general interest, not only for agriculture or for one province. The Groningen Society granted 142 loans in eighteen years. Its example was not followed in any other province.[3]

Meanwhile, the situation had further deteriorated. Even Britain, in 1822, had a surplus of exports over imports and sent 15,000 quarters of wheat to Holland.[4] In September 1823, a number of Amsterdam commission agents in the corn trade resolved that, owing to lack of exports, to the falling prices and to lack of storage space, imports must be restricted

---

[1] *Verzam. gran.* pp. 1–96, 215–44; A.R.A., Roëll 150; *Knuttel* 25303 (Andringa de Kempenaer, 1824).

[2] *2de kamer* 1823–4, A2.

[3] Koninklijk Huisarchief, Willem I, xviii, 90.

[4] *Parl. Papers* 1826–7, no. 333, p. 134.

'without prejudice to the principle of free trade'. They accordingly bound themselves to take no further consignments until the end of the year.[1] De Clercq wrote to Roëll at this time that the crisis was now as serious for commerce as for agriculture.[2] In October, an address to the king was circulated for signature among commission agents and brokers in Amsterdam. It complained that the governments of Prussia and Denmark were now compelled to receive corn in payment of taxes and were sending it to Amsterdam for sale at any price obtainable. This was ruinous for the owners of corn in store. The consumer naturally preferred fresh supplies to old stocks. Imports must be restricted until existing stocks were disposed of. It was useless for the Netherlands 'to continue to pay the taxes of the Prussian and Danish peasants' merely for fear that restrictions now would prejudice the chances of future revival of the Dutch market; for when conditions improved, foreign merchants would be guided by purely economic motives, not by gratitude.[3] This document was sent to the corn merchants' fraternity, for onward transmission to the king. Roëll, however, advised De Clercq that this would be unseemly, at a time when the king had recently decided, after long inquiries, to comply with the desires expressed by Amsterdam for a free trade. The address was accordingly returned to the signatories.[4] They nevertheless submitted it to the States General, as though in the name of the whole trade: to the great delight of the protectionists. De Clercq assured Roëll that none of the main houses in the trade had supported the address. For his part, he could not agree with all its arguments, but confessed that he now saw more objections against a free trade than he had in the previous year.

In December 1823, De Clercq informed Roëll that a counter-address was being circulated which reproduced the free-trade arguments of 1822 and ignored what had happened since. It had been drawn up by a house that was not directly concerned with the corn trade and few of the corn merchants supported it.

For my part, I have suffered enough by the continuous fall in prices to be entitled to speak, but I can declare on my honour that I do not know what my personal interest would be—it grieves me, however, that there should be this miserable quarrel here in these crucial times.

In February 1824, a prominent leader of the commercial party sent Roëll a German trade report which ascribed the collapse of the European corn

---

[1] *Knuttel* 25303, pp. 45-7.   [2] A.R.A., Roëll 150.
[3] *Knuttel* 25303, pp. 47-51.
[4] B. C. E. Zwart, *De Kamer van Koophandel en Fabrieken te Amsterdam*, pp. 122-3.

trade to the capture of the South American markets by exporters of flour from the United States; with the comment that this placed the problem in a new light, as far as he was concerned. He was not comforted by Roëll's suggestion that if the Dutch could find a way of sending flour to South America in good condition, instead of grain, the competition from the United States might prove not to be invincible.[1]

Agricultural agitation continued in the Dutch provinces. In December 1823, a large number of landowners and farmers of Groningen signed a long address in favour of prohibitive corn laws. The law of 1821, they added, had singled out agriculture for the new and unfair burdens of the meat and meal excises; yet agriculture deserved more protection than did commerce, in accordance with the principle established by political economy that a nation became rich by exporting much and importing little. Similar complaints appeared in the newspapers not only in the inland provinces, but also in Holland.[2]

In early 1824, Roëll remarked to the king in conversation that, if action to appease the agricultural protectionists ever became necessary, it should take the form of increased import duties, but never of prohibition; a moderate increase, whatever some of the merchants might say, would not injure trade. In April, the king was pressed by the governors of Groningen and Zeeland to take some urgent action to relieve discontent in their provinces. The king instructed Roëll to make proposals accordingly. On reflection, Roëll replied that he could not advise any action at all. Anything more than a doubling of the existing duties would certainly injure commerce, but double duties were unlikely to help agriculture or to check the agitation for prohibition. Even the double duties would be equal to 10% and so would be contrary to the law of 1821. Exporting countries might retaliate and in any case the king's effort to lead the nations to free trade would be spoiled. Since the system of 1821 had been proclaimed as an example to the nations, it would be wise to allow it to bear fruit; prohibitive corn laws so soon after its introduction would be an inconsequence. If the price of bread were increased by a restriction of imports as well as by the flour excise, some of those very Belgians who were now agitating for protection would start stirring up 'so-called liberalism' among the workmen, whose wages would not follow prices.[3]

In the autumn of 1824, the government proposed to the States General that the import duties on corn should be trebled. It was to be merely an

[1] A.R.A., Roëll 150; W. F. Roëll, *Aanmerkingen aan den Koning op 24 Juni 1825* (The Hague, 1825), p. 42.
[2] A.R.A., Roëll 150—Groningen request and various press-cuttings; *Knuttel* 25304 (J. Hora Siccama, 1824).
[3] A.R.A., Roëll 150; *Verzam. gran.* pp. 97–197, 244–78.

emergency measure and the king was authorized to reduce the duties again by decree as soon as conditions became normal. A royal decree brought the new duties into immediate effect, subject to repayment if they did not pass into law. The government described them as moderate, unlikely either to encourage smuggling or to incommode the consumer. The free-traders described them as prohibitive, the protectionists as ineffective. Appelius said that they would prevent imports by land, which depressed prices on the country markets, but would permit sea imports, which served almost wholly for the general staple trade.

Some Belgian deputies made this the occasion for a general attack on the system of 1821. The 6% customs maximum, they said, had proved a useless sacrifice, for no other country had followed the example. Bonaparte had shown a clearer insight when he opposed the English by a system of exclusion, though his methods had been too violent and vexatious. Under the system of 1821, the proper functions of customs and excise had been reversed; foreign goods were admitted with excessive liberality but the excises on home products were levied with incredible ferocity. At present prices, the subsistence farmer had to sell one-third of his corn crop in order to pay excise for the right to consume the remainder. The flour excise was so unpopular that it had to be levied by armed force, after eight years of peace. The trebling of the import duties on corn was an inadequate remedy for all these evils, but was acceptable as a first step back to sound principles. The duties would slightly increase the price of bread, but would really benefit even industry; for the land-owners as a class kept industry going by their luxuries and vanities, so that the maintenance of their fortunes was more desirable even than low wages. Over two centuries, Belgian corn prices had been maintained by government policy at a certain level, land values had been fixed accordingly, and so agriculture had a prescriptive right to higher prices than the present ones.

Deputies from the Dutch agricultural provinces argued that the trade in foreign corn no longer deserved the privileges it had rightly enjoyed under the Republic. Economic self-sufficiency was now a safer, more natural and more patriotic objective than the re-establishment of the old staple market. Foreign trade could well be carried on in bond, for the London entrepôt dock contained more corn than the whole of Amsterdam and had recently been re-exporting more than the whole of the Netherlands. The majority of Dutch corn merchants, they claimed, agreed with the protectionists, for only the bankers and the agents of foreign merchants had signed the latest petition for free trade. Foreigners should not be allowed to influence national economic policy. Bankers like Van der

Hoop were little better than foreigners and could be regarded as English or French as much as Dutch: they even advanced money to the Danish and Prussian governments on the corn they were dumping in the Netherlands with such disastrous results. It was these bankers and foreign agents, they added, who in 1821 had instigated the government to introduce the meat and meal excises, to the detriment of the agricultural interest.[1]

The Dutch commercial deputies repeated their old arguments without much conviction. They admitted that the system of 1821 had not had all the results hoped for, partly because the reform had not been radical enough and partly because the disturbance due to the war had been too great to permit rapid recovery. The Dutch staple market would, however, recover in time, provided only that the work of 1821 were not tampered with. If public opinion even in Holland appeared to favour the injurious new corn duties, this was due to panic at the recent trading losses; but wise merchants and legislators thought of the future. Holland had agreed to the union with Belgium; but she had never agreed to sacrifice her commerce, which had found the money for the victories of William III, for the Netherlands' share at Waterloo and in the Anglo-Dutch victory over the pirates at Algiers in 1816, and for the Dutch victory at Palembang in Sumatra in 1821. Even if commerce had not yet gained much by the system of 1821, at least industry had not suffered. Foreign competition was stimulating the linen and cotton industries to new improvements and successes; only the over-protected iron industry was stagnant. The time was at hand when all would admit that industries were strongest where the import of food and raw materials was least obstructed. The new duties would only be temporary, according to the government; but recent experience showed that trade once interrupted was not easily recovered. Holland had still the readiest market for meeting exceptional demands for corn and the advantage should not be thrown away.

Some Dutch deputies who professed loyalty to the commercial tradition nevertheless supported the new corn duties. Roëll attributed their attitude not to any change of principle, but to a desire to appease the Belgians and to a consciousness of the falling away of the corn trade due to competition from the Black Sea. One of them said that he disagreed with the new duties in principle, but felt it right to submit to the will of the government and of nine-tenths of the people. Nevertheless, twenty-three deputies, mainly from Holland, voted against the duties; seventy-two voted for.[2]

---

[1] *2de kamer*, 1823–4, A 177–222 and B 397–402; G. K. van Hogendorp, *Bijdragen*, IX, 186–216; *Knuttel* 25303 (Andringa de Kempenaer, 1824).

[2] A.R.A., Roëll 112 and 150—address by merchants of Rotterdam; *Ged.* VIII (3), 69–70; *2de kamer*, 1824–5, A 127–77 and B 269–76.

Table XV. *Butter, cheese, grain and madder, 1813–30*

	Prices at Amsterdam*			Prices at Rotterdam† in sterling per imp. quarter			
	Butter (Friesland) per 50 kg. Florins	Cheese (Leiden) per 150 kg. Florins	Rye (Prussian) per last Florins	Wheat *s. d.*		Rye *s. d.*	
1813	—	—	—	69	9	48	1
1814	—	—	—	49	1	32	7
1815	—	—	—	48	2	32	5
1816	34·78	41·44	337	65	5	44	4
1817	36·47	41·75	305	104	4	56	10
1818	42·18	49·50	225	70	11	43	10
1819	41·45	45·50	187	48	7	35	5
1820	40·13	38·50	137	43	10	27	6
1821	34·83	35·63	109	41	2	21	9
1822	31·20	30·75	109	34	11	21	1
1823	32·03	26·90	105	32	5	15	9
1824	36·70	28·50	86	26	4	16	11
1825	—	—	109	28	0	—	
1826	—	—	116	—		—	
1827	—	—	—	—		—	
1828	—	—	166	—		—	
1829	38·0	32·45	168	—		—	
1830	46·38	36·88	172	—		—	

Imports to the United Kingdom‡ (thousand cwt.)									
	1819	1820	1821	1822	1823	1824	1825	1826	1827
Butter from the Netherlands	62	66	99	109	102	132	160	137	143
Madder powder from France	?	2	7	23	19	33	30	19	?
Madder powder from the Netherlands	?	59	49	71	63	31	60	20	?
Madder roots from Turkey	?	15	15	10	14	22	22	25	?
Madder roots from France and the Netherlands	?	1	—	—	—	—	—	—	?

* N. W. Posthumus, *Nederlandse prijsgeschiedenis.*
† *Parl. Papers,* 1826–7, no. 27, p. 36.
‡ *Parl. Papers,* 1826–7, XVIII, 2–7, and 392–3.

Chapter XI

RECIPROCITY AND RETALIATION

In 1815, the United States put forward the idea of reciprocal non-discrimination between flags. Dutch statesmen and merchants welcomed this, for their own shipping was then not worth protecting and they were anxious to attract American ships to their ports. They hoped that by subscribing to American slogans they would evoke some action by the United States to make the Netherlands the main stapling place for American trade with Europe and to assure to Dutch shipping, when it revived, a share in transatlantic trade. There were even hopes of privileges that would encourage the import of goods to the United States from the Dutch staple market rather than from the country of origin. In order to facilitate such negotiations, the tariff of 1816 gave power to the king to remit in favour of reciprocating states the extra tonnage duties paid by foreign ships.

Dutch enthusiasm cooled when it was perceived that the American reciprocity proposals were due to confidence in the competitive supremacy of American shipping and to a desire for admission to colonies on equal terms with the colonial powers. Negotiations for a wide agreement broke down in 1817, because the United States insisted that the Dutch West Indies must be included and the Dutch demanded lower duties in the United States on their imports of cheese and gin. Agreement was reached that American ships should pay the lower rate of tonnage in the Netherlands; and that Dutch ships should be entitled to the 10% remission of customs duties which the American tariff of 1815 offered to reciprocating powers as well as to American ships. This concession, however, applied only to goods produced in the Netherlands or in their natural hinterland and shipped from Netherland ports; the Dutch had pressed hard for it to extend to all goods from their staple market.[1]

The tariff of 1822 reflected the change in the Dutch attitude. The 10% customs rebate granted for Netherland ships was not extended to reciprocating powers, and thus it infringed the agreement with the United States. The complaints of the American Ambassador were ignored. He reported that Dutch merchants would not speak patiently of conceding the 10% rebate to American ships. The Netherlands government pointed out that

[1] J. C. Westermann, *The Netherlands and the United States; their Relation in the Beginning of the 19th Century* (The Hague, 1935), pp. 180–94, 243–77, 316.

the benefit expected from the American concession to Netherland ships in 1817 had not been received, for their share in American trade remained negligible; for this, it said, the high American duties on cheese and gin were responsible.[1]

The Dutch aim, in fact, was not to attain equal opportunities in international trade by reciprocity and most-favoured-nation agreements, but to win privileges by bilateral commercial treaties. Belgians and Dutch were agreed on the usefulness of the weapon of retaliation to win concessions of this type. Even Van Hogendorp, the keenest advocate of the idea that the Netherlands should take the lead in the race towards free trade, was willing that other nations should be spurred to follow this example by punitive and discriminatory customs duties. The tariff of 1822 therefore gave the king power to prohibit, or to increase the duties on, imports from countries where Netherlands products or merchandise were subject to unreasonably high duties. The Dutch commercial party did not quite trust the government to make wise use of this power, and would have preferred to reserve it to the States General; but it agreed to the principle.[2]

The Dutch and Belgians were not agreed about the use that should be made of retaliation. It was invoked first in 1823 against France, whose duties on Belgian hops, cloth and other products had recently been further increased. The Dutch were not much in sympathy with Belgian demands for reprisals, and the merchants feared serious loss of trade if their maritime imports of French salt and wine were impeded. Accordingly, the government did not retaliate against French salt, and against French wine only if it came by land. General discriminating duties were imposed on French glass, cloth, hosiery and a few other articles. The government resumed commercial negotiations with France, which it had initiated rather halfheartedly in 1816 in response to Belgian petitions, especially from merchant-manufacturers of the nail industry; it asked for reductions in the import duties on many Dutch, Belgian and Dutch-colonial products. France refused any considerable concessions, explaining that she feared to provoke a demand from Britain for equally favourable treatment; and threatened counter-retaliation in the shape of an increase from 9 to 20% *ad valorem* of her import duty on linens, which she received mainly from Belgium. In that case, the Netherlands threatened retaliation against French salt, but forebore when France raised her linen duty only to 15% *ad valorem*. Thus, the attempt to force France to follow the liberal example of the 1822 tariff failed. The result was popular with those who were attempting to revive

---

[1] P. Hoekstra, *Thirty-seven Years of Holland-American Relations 1803–1840* (Michigan, 1917), pp. 146–52; *Knuttel* 25686.

[2] *2de kamer*, 1821–2, A 520–6; G. K. van Hogendorp, *Bijdragen*, VI, 365.

vine-growing in Belgium, but not with inland Belgian consumers of wine, who thought it a national grievance that they should have to pay more for their wine while it was as cheap as ever in Holland. In 1828, the government abandoned its discrimination against French wine, but granted the Belgian vineyards a mildly protective import duty on all wine that came by land.[1]

The French government produced statistics to show that the Netherlands had a favourable balance of trade with France, but an unfavourable one with Great Britain; and suggested that Britain was the proper subject for retaliation. The Netherlands government replied that they did not trust statistics, for they suspected that much more was smuggled into their country than into France, and pointed out that their unfavourable balance with Britain was due to their re-exports to Germany. They were, however, certainly more cautious in their attempt to hurry Britain towards free trade than in the case of France. On the other hand, the king was sensitive to suggestions that he was subservient to England. Early in 1824, he received a letter from an anonymous Belgian urging him to retaliate against England as well as France, in order to convince Belgium that the Netherlands was really an independent state. The king passed the letter on to his Minister of Commerce with instructions to negotiate for concessions from Great Britain.[2]

The British government meanwhile was asking for concessions from the Netherlands to comply with the Reciprocity Act of 1823. The Netherlands had little to gain by that Act, except the very doubtful possibility that the withdrawal of British discrimination might enable Frisian shipping to recover a share in the export of butter to London. Britain did not offer any change in the Navigation Acts under which a consignment of American turpentine from Amsterdam and a Dutch cargo from Russia had recently been turned back from London. The Netherlands would remain free to prohibit British vessels from bringing American, African or Asiatic products, but the commercial party felt that any such measure would be suicidal, for it would merely divert the cargoes to Hamburg. On the other hand, Dutch shipping would have to forgo privileges in the direct trade with Britain, including the general 10% customs rebate and special rebates on salt and raw sugar. The Dutch attached great importance to the salt preference, since it had been introduced as a partial substitute for the old prohibition of English rock salt. Its abandonment would not only rob Dutch shipping of a monopoly in bringing salt from Liverpool, but

[1] A. R. Falck, *Gedenkschriften*, pp. 428–35; *2de kamer*, 1827–8, A 196; C. Smit, *De handelspolitieke betrekkingen tusschen Nederland en Frankrijk 1815–1914* (Rotterdam, 1923), pp. 4–18.   [2] *Post. Doc.* I, 105.

would further reduce the importation of French and Spanish salt, which was cherished as an essential element in a traditional trade.

William I insisted that negotiations over the navigational question should be linked with those for a commercial treaty dealing with customs duties. The Netherlands had here nothing to offer, for the tariff of 1822 was as liberal as the needs and political influence of Belgian industry would allow. The British government would have been glad of any reduction in the duties on coal, iron, cotton goods and pottery, but the Netherlands could offer none. The Netherland government asked tariff concessions for many goods which it hoped could compete in the British market, if given a fair chance; Belgian industrial goods, such as linen, lace, carpets, furniture and glass, Dutch products such as madder, gin, paper, white lead, glue, butter, cheese and rape seed, and Dutch commercial goods such as tea, tobacco and coffee. The British government, however, was unlikely, for the sake of the Netherlands, to offend the Irish linen and butter industries, the East India Company, and many English landowners and manufacturers, or to upset its arrangements for the excise on spirits. The British negotiators, in fact, did not give much serious consideration to the point of view of the Netherlands government or of the Dutch commercial party. They offered to admit Dutch shipping to their West Indian colonies in return for reciprocity in those of the Dutch; but the Dutch knew that, in that case, they would hardly be able to compete with the British even in their own colonies and could certainly not hope to trade successfully in British ones, for they hardly dared to risk a cargo to independent South America. The British government threatened to retaliate against Dutch shipping preferences by a discriminatory export duty on salt loaded into Dutch vessels, and carried out its threat in 1826; but this measure was not unpleasing to the Netherlands government and to the Dutch commercial party, whose real desire was to exclude British salt altogether, in favour of French and Spanish; nor to the College of Deep-sea Herring Fishery, which asserted that the use of British salt was spoiling the quality of Dutch salt herring, though the salt-refiners and some of the fishermen disputed this.

The Netherlands Foreign Minister desired a commercial agreement with Britain for the sake of diplomatic prestige, and suggested the acceptance of navigational reciprocity on the British terms for a trial period of two years, in order to test British sincerity by finding out whether there would be any practical advantage to the Netherlands. The king, however, refused to consider any agreement that did not include British tariff concessions, and negotiations broke down. The Netherlands did not introduce new retaliatory duties, but merely continued the existing preferences and allowed Britain to retaliate against them. Dutch ministers comforted themselves that the breach would have good political effects in Belgium and that its economic consequences would be less harmful to the Netherlands than Huskisson's reciprocity would have been. On the whole, Dutch commercial opinion approved their government's stand. Van Hogendorp, however, desired the acceptance of the British terms, since he believed that no considerable revival of the Dutch carrying trade was possible but that every extension of free competition would benefit the Dutch staple market. The most influential merchants of Rotterdam also desired an agreement, in view of their close commercial relations with London. But they believed that no possible advantage in the shipping of butter to London could compensate for the abandonment of the salt preference, and they wished for no concession on that point.[1]

The Netherlands government proved to have overestimated its strength. No concessions from any foreign power were obtained by the threat of reprisals under the tariff of 1822. The king believed that this might be because the Netherland tariff was so much lower than that of other countries. He therefore considered in 1826 whether it might not be better to revise the whole system, and to replace the principle of 1822 of a low tariff which could be increased in retaliation against particular countries, by a higher tariff which could be decreased in return for foreign concessions. His advisers dissuaded him from this plan, on the ground that it would revive controversy and bring the government into conflict again with the Dutch commercial party.[2]

[1] *Post. Doc.* I, 85, 108, 138, 143, 166, 194, 207, 214, 244, 280, 292, 326; *Ged.* VIII (3), 319–20; J. Van Ouwerkerk de Vries, *Verhandeling*, p. 217.
[2] *Post. Doc.* I, 300–1.

Table XVI. *Shipping in United States ports, 1821–2. Tonnage (thousand tons)*★

	Nationality of shipping entering United States ports							
	American	British	Nether-land	Han-seatic	French	Spanish	Swedish	Danish
1821	765	55	2	6	2	4	5	4
1822	788	71	2	8	1	7	4	4

	Shipping entering United States ports from certain countries					
	Nether-lands	England	Hanseatic ports	France	Russia	Sweden
1821	27	151	19	26	14	11
1822	19	165	11	30	23	17

★ *American State Papers*, 1832, Commerce and Navigation, vols. I and II.

Chapter XII

FREE TRADE AND MERCANTILISM IN
THE DUTCH EAST INDIES

(a) Reluctant liberalism—1816–24

Dutchmen of the early nineteenth century who attempted to defend their fiscal traditions by appealing to the doctrines of political economy, were sometimes embarrassed by the mercantilist character of the former Dutch East India Company. Most supporters of the commercial interest, however, cared little for theoretical consistency. Van Alphen, in 1826, recalled with approval the Company's arrangements, which, he said, had been the main source of the prosperity and greatness of the Republic.

The system was simple and well co-ordinated: to exclude competition; to establish settlements either for the extension of trade or for the enforcement of the monopoly; to make the natives work as much as possible, and to pay the lowest price for the products of forced cultivation in order to sell them at the highest price; to restrict production from time to time in order to maintain prices; to keep secrecy about the Company's operations and to exclude foreigners from the interior of its colonies. Such were the main features of a commercial system in which everything worked for a single end, the enrichment and well-being of the Company and thereby of the motherland, to which all the interests of the colonies themselves were wholly subordinated.[1]

He justified this system by the argument that because Java was in the infancy of its civilization, because it lacked capital, and because its people were incorrigibly indolent, its balance of trade could not be left to chance but must be regulated in the interest both of the colony and of the motherland. Though he did not advocate precise imitation of the Company's system, he wished for measures to ensure that, in the changed circumstances, Java supplied cheap colonial produce for Dutch trade.

Since the fall of the Company in 1795, there had been a doctrinaire party in Holland, originally inspired largely by political enmity to the Company, proclaiming free trade, free labour and free enterprise to be the means for making the colonies more valuable to the motherland. G. K. van Hogendorp became a convinced adherent of this policy, before the end of the eighteenth century. He did not make clear the conditions on

[1] *2de kamer*, 1825–6, A, Van Alphen, 23 Feb. 1826.

which he would wish to admit foreigners to the colonial trade, but he praised the arrangements in the Dutch West Indies, where planters had long been able to dispose freely of their products, if they were not mortgaged, for export in Dutch ships to Dutch ports in Europe. He asserted that under this system the Dutch West Indies had so prospered in the eighteenth century as to exceed the eastern colonies in importance, but hoped that native peasants and Dutch planters could achieve even better results in the East, since free men work better than slaves. After 1813, his opinions became increasingly liberal. He foresaw a time when the Javans would become civilized and politically independent, and believed that they were already well on the way to economic freedom, as a result of the reforms introduced by Raffles after the British conquest of Java. He believed that the completion of this process would bring greater benefits to Holland than any system of monopoly; just as the political and economic independence of the United States had brought increased trade to Great Britain.[1]

In order that Dutch colonial authority might be re-established, British good will was at first necessary. For this reason, rather than because of the personal opinions of Van Hogendorp, the Kingdom of the Netherlands became firmly committed to liberal policies in the East. An official announcement was made in 1815, before the eastern colonies had actually been reoccupied, that their trade, except for the Moluccas, was to be 'free and open', though with customs preferences for Netherland trade and shipping.

The cultivator is recognized to be entitled, after he has paid his land-rent, to dispose freely of his products, except for any that have to be delivered to the Government under regulations still in force when the colonies are taken over from the English.

Products received by the Government of the Indies as contingents, forced deliveries, or otherwise, and not required for its own use, will be sold in the Indies either by public auction, or on application at fixed prices. If any such products remain unsold which are suitable for the Netherland market, they will be sent to the fatherland for sale, together with the spices, which are reserved for special arrangements.[2]

Raffles, who opposed the restoration of Dutch power in the East, distrusted this change of heart. Java was given back in 1816, and already

---

[1] G. K. van Hogendorp, *Bijdragen*, x, 246; G. K. van Hogendorp, *Advijs*, pp. 27–31; G. K. van Hogendorp, *Verhandelingen over den Oost-Indischen handel* (Amsterdam, 1801), I, 20, 147.

[2] M. L. van Deventer, *Het Nederlandsch gezag over Java en onderhoorigheden sedert 1811* (The Hague, 1891), pp. 53–4.

in 1817 he asserted that prohibitive duties against British shipping there were under consideration in Holland. His fears were premature, but not groundless. Dutch commerce desired protection in the Java trade, but the Chambers of Commerce, 'aware of the possibility of secret diplomatic reasons', did not press for it until the colonial settlement with Britain had been completely carried out. In 1817, however, the Amsterdam Chamber asked for a discriminatory duty of 25% *ad valorem* in Java on all imports or exports carried in foreign ships, 'until the time when it shall appear that Netherland trade and shipping have means enough for the free trade of Java to be reserved exclusively for them'. The Chamber wished that the export of coffee from Java should at once be confined to Netherland ships clearing for Netherland ports.

Is it not of the highest importance to establish here the market for Javan coffee? Is not that product unique in its kind? Is not its exclusive possession a priceless national property? And must not foreigners come to seek it here? Can we not take care to maintain a reasonable price for it? Does not the merchant who is compelled to come to our market for a certain article also make other purchases here, thus giving a double advantage to our trade?[1]

Commercial opinion was divided as to whether a new privileged company should be set up in place of the old East India Company. The system by which the produce of the eastern colonies was made available to Europe solely through the Company's annual sales, suited admirably the Second Hand merchants and commission agents who dealt in colonial goods in Holland. They feared that the unrestricted cultivation and shipment to Holland of these products would glut the market and enable many traders in Europe to dispense with the services of the Dutch middlemen. Some rich and ambitious merchants, however, welcomed the opportunity of a direct First Hand trade with Java. Rotterdam feared that the benefit of a new company might go mainly to Amsterdam. The Amsterdam Chamber of Commerce in 1814 hinted a desire for a new company, though admitting that the suggestion might be untimely.

The products of the East Indies must be regarded as public property. It is not a case, as it would be in the West Indies, of asking for privileged transportation to the detriment of private owners, but purely a question whether free navigation and trade in the East Indies is desirable for the motherland. The East India Company, for example, brought only a limited quantity of spices in order to keep prices high, and sold them at fixed periods. It is to be feared that if spices are imported by private

---

[1] M. L. van Deventer, *Het Nederlandsch gezag*, p. 201.

persons, the imports will exceed the demand.... We hear that the Rotterdam Chamber of Commerce has asked for a free trade with Java. It would be interesting to know their reasons.[1]

The king's support for the abortive Tea Company of 1815 suggests that he sympathized with the wish of many Dutchmen for a new East India Company to recapture the Java trade for the Netherlands. However, he was committed to the policy of Van Hogendorp, especially in the East Indies, and was entirely willing to allow time for that policy to mature before trying experiments more in accordance with his own ideas. He was careful to select as Commissioners to take over the Dutch East Indies men who honestly believed in the official liberalism, and who were unimpeded by any previous experience from forming an impartial opinion as to the best way of reconciling liberal principles with Dutch interests. Their decision in the main was to continue Raffles' policies, though they boasted that their faith in the land-rent system was based on arguments advanced for it by Dutchmen before the British conquest of Java and was held in spite of the chaotic results of its bad administration under Raffles.[2]

After talks with the king and his ministers at Brussels in 1817, Raffles admitted that they 'seemed to mean well', but feared that they had 'too great a hankering after profit, and immediate profit, for any liberal system to thrive under them'. In the first years, however, the Government of the Indies sincerely followed inside Java the advice of Muntinghe, who had been Raffles' chief collaborator in reform: to abandon the old 'mercantile' system of the Company, whereby the native chiefs were left great power over their people but were bound by contract to deliver certain produce to the Dutch; and to adopt instead the 'new system of taxes', whereby the government was to interest itself in the common people, to undertake direct administration, to deprive the native chiefs of most of their power, to leave the cultivators free to sell their products in open trade, and to draw off part of the expected increase in wealth by land-rents. Van der Capellen, the first Governor-General, was aware that this policy might incur the dangerous hostility of the native aristocracy, but he persisted, and boasted that unlike Raffles he did not allow the reforms to remain merely on paper but enforced them systematically and without respect for persons. Even Raffles declared himself in 1820 to be satisfied with the internal administration of Van der Capellen. Falck, who was

[1] *Post. Doc.* II, 5; B. C. E. Zwart, *De Kamer van Koophandel en Fabrieken te Amsterdam*, pp. 55–6.

[2] *2de kamer*, 1825–6, B 346; A. R. Falck, *Gedenkschriften*, p. 452; B. H. M. Vlekke, *Nusantara, A History of the East India Archipelago* (Cambridge, Mass., 1944), p. 254.

Colonial Minister at the Hague during most of Van der Capellen's government, wrote in his memoirs:

> The Colonial Council, the Council of State, and all who deserved a hearing, were at that time agreed that the Javan, having tasted the sweets of reform, could not be ruled again by the system of the Company without insuperable difficulty, and that to make the attempt would be as good as to throw away the colony.

No doubt, he added, the men who made Java profitable by means of forced labour after 1830 deserved well of their country, but they should remember that those who were in charge during his own ministry were not less capable, only more attentive to prudence and justice.[1]

In admitting foreign trade and shipping to Java, the Dutch authorities were guided, however, by considerations of expediency rather than by liberal convictions. In a talk with Raffles in 1817, the king was frank about this.

> While he admitted all the advantages likely to arise from cultivation, and assured me that the system introduced under my administration should be continued, he maintained that it was essential to confine the trade and to make such regulations as would secure it and its profits exclusively to the mother country.[2]

Such regulations were not possible at first. Dutch merchants had little knowledge of trade in the East and no connexions, for the fall of the Company had destroyed the only Dutch commercial organization there. During the Napoleonic wars, the work of supplying Java with European goods and of carrying away her products had been taken over by American, and after 1811, by British, merchants; and their services remained indispensable. The Americans were especially welcome to the colonial authorities, for they brought specie to buy Javan produce. The British had in recent years discovered that manufactured goods, and particularly cottons, could profitably be imported to Java for native consumption. They thus incurred the wrath of Van Alphen, on the ground that the profits of these imports enabled them to bear losses on their return cargoes, and so to pay high prices for Javan produce, which made the trade unprofitable for Dutch merchants and also encouraged excessive cultivation in Java.

---

[1] Lady S. Raffles, *Memoir of the Life of Sir Thom. Stamford Raffles* (London, 1830), pp. 289, 446; A. R. Falck, *Gedenkschriften*, p. 275; P. H. van der Kemp, 'Palembang en Banka in 1816–21', in *B.K.I.* (1900); Art. 105 and 107 of the Regeerings-reglement of 22 Dec. 1818, printed in *Het koloniaal monopolie-stelsel*, by D. C. Steijn Parvé (Zalt Bommel, 1851).

[2] Lady S. Raffles, *Memoir*, p. 289.

During the British occupation, immense pains were taken to retail all kinds of manufactures throughout the whole interior. Everywhere the needs and tastes of the Javans were studied....Incomplete systems of free cultivation, based on freedom of trade, were introduced at a time when only one nation was trading there, and that nation was the occupying power...a power immense in production and insatiable for its market....I know that among all the paradoxes of modern times, false theories are held that production should be stimulated by all means, even the most irregular, including extravagant government measures to encourage production by a large consumption; but such dreams of a disordered imagination are inapplicable to the old nations of Europe, and much more so to a colonial state in its agricultural infancy. Such a state needs wise and moderate measures, even in the interest of its increasing production, in order to restrain all excesses, to prevent loss of circulating capital, and to protect such a state from shocks that it could not support.[1]

Until Dutch trade became more active, however, the government of the Indies had every reason to desire good relations with the enterprising British firms established at Batavia.

Despite the reforms which Raffles had introduced in most of the districts under direct European rule, a main source of revenue in Java was still the coffee grown by forced labour in Preanger and in certain other areas. It was to the interest of the colonial government that this coffee should be sold by public auction, in order that British and American competition might force up the price. This was in accord with the instructions and with the professed liberalism of the home government; but not with its requirement that Netherland trade and shipping should be encouraged. The Dutch merchants who sent ships to Java did not find it an encouraging experience to bid for their return cargoes against foreigners. The colonial government compromised. It felt compelled by its financial needs to begin public auctions in February 1817, but it also continued to hold back supplies for the convenience of Dutch merchants. Further, in order to ensure that the Netherland markets were quickly supplied, it sent coffee home on government account as return cargo for the ships that brought troops and public stores. The shipowners, it seemed, were reluctant to risk their own capital in this way.

These arrangements caused much discontent at Amsterdam in the summer of 1817. If the Java trade was to be free, and yet the home government was to receive occasional and unpredictable remittances in coffee, market conditions would be very uncertain. Those merchants who, with official encouragement, were trading actively with Batavia, were

---

[1] *2de kamer*, 1825–6, A, Van Alphen, 23 Feb. 1826.

naturally indignant. The arrival of American ships with Javan coffee, encouraged by the admission without duty in the Netherlands of all produce legally exported from Java, caused a more general indignation, though not perhaps among the merchants who bought or handled the American cargoes. It was disappointing to find the Americans repeating in peace the successes they had won as neutrals during the wars. The king disliked it, but was advised that only when more Netherland ships were available for the East would it be possible to judge whether new fiscal measures were necessary to secure the trade for them against American intrusion. Meanwhile, the government employed Dutch merchants and shipowners to supply it with stores and freightage for the Indies, and tried to tempt them into trade on their own account. The government paid them in the Netherlands with letters of credit, which the colonial government was instructed to accept in payment for produce at the public sales or by private arrangement. This made it unnecessary to send produce home on government account, a practice which, Falck informed Van der Capellen in 1818, was undesirable as a matter of economic principle.[1]

The colonial authorities were naturally more friendly to foreign trade than the home government, and their tariff for Java, enacted in 1818, gave no grounds for complaint to the watchful British interests concerned. All imports, including those from the Netherlands, were to pay the same duty; 12% *ad valorem* if carried in foreign ships from foreign ports, 9% in foreign ships from Netherland ports, and 6% in Netherland ships. Thus no preference was given to Netherland industry as such, but some was given to Netherland shipping, and some, for the sake of the old staple market, to Netherland ports for goods of any origin. The export duties were the same as the import duties. All goods exported in foreign ships paid 12%, but 3% could be reclaimed on arrival in the Netherlands from funds remitted by the colonial government. It was considered in Batavia that these duties gave reasonable advantages to the motherland, which could not be increased without infringing the general policy of free trade adopted by the Kingdom of the Netherlands. In case the British government made any comment, the information was sent home that British imports would pay only 2% more than during the British occupation of Java.[2]

---

[1] M. L. van Deventer, *Het Nederlandsch gezag*, pp. 200, 206, 210, 248; W. M. F. Mansvelt, *Geschiedenis van de Ned. Handelmaatschappij*, I, 43; P. H. van der Kemp, 'Consignaties voor 1830', in *B.K.I.* (1913).

[2] A. R. Falck, *Gedenkschriften*, p. 476; *Post. Doc.* II, 201; *Parl. Papers*, 1821, VII, 17; P. J. Elout van Soeterwoude, *Bijdragen tot de geschiedenis der onderhandelingen met Engeland 1820–1824* (The Hague, 1865), Bijlage I; P. H. van der Kemp, 'De stichting van Singapore', in *B.K.I.* (1902).

Liberalism at Batavia stimulated the demand at home for the exclusion of foreigners from the Java trade. There were complaints that too much consideration was being shown for the revenues of the colonial government and for the interests of the natives. Van Alphen said:

Our forefathers made the colonies useful to the motherland, excluded foreign commercial and political influence, and monopolised the trade; but they opened the motherland to the beneficial streams of general commerce. We, in 1816, closed the motherland and laid the colonies open. Posterity will judge whether we were wiser than our ancestors.[1]

In 1822, both Dutch and Belgian members of the States General urged that Javan produce should be exempted from Netherland import duty only when carried in Netherland ships. The government replied that it was anxious to increase the privileges of the national flag as soon as enough Netherland ships were available for the trade, but that at present any discouragement of foreign shipping would be disastrous both for the prosperity of Java and for the Second Hand in the Netherlands. Nevertheless, the government finally gave way. Van der Capellen, however, was instructed to increase the Javan duty on coffee exported in foreign ships, so that when they brought it to the Netherlands they might receive a greater rebate. Only Van Hogendorp and a few other doctrinaire free-traders opposed these changes as a step back to the old colonial system.[2]

Dutch shipbuilders demanded that in accordance with the example of the motherland in 1819, and with the ultimate intention expressed by the home government in 1815, foreign-built ships should be refused registration in the colonies. Owing, however, to the failure of Dutch merchants to interest themselves in the country trade of the Archipelago, the colonial government did not do so. Even in 1832, the country vessels registered at Batavia were still 'for the most part owned, officered and commanded by British subjects'. In 1821, foreign-built ships registered in the eastern colonies were excluded from preferences given in the Netherlands to national ships.[3]

These arrangements brought little benefit to Dutch merchants. British and American competition kept up the price of coffee in Java even when the post-war boom was over and prices in Europe were falling, and in the early 1820's the Dutch found the trade wholly unprofitable. They

---

[1] *2de kamer*, 1825–6, A 347 (Van Alphen).
[2] A.R.A., Goldberg 214 (1); G. K. van Hogendorp, *Bijdragen*, VI, 364; *Post. Doc.* II, 71–2; P. A. A. van Mechelen, *Zeevaart en zeehandel van Rotterdam 1813–30* (Rotterdam, 1929), p. 174; B. C. E. Zwart, *De Kamer van Koophandel en Fabrieken te Amsterdam*, p. 90.
[3] J. van Ouwerkerk de Vries, *Verhandeling*; *Knuttel* 24811 (Anon. 1819).

wondered how the Americans could find profit in it. Perhaps they cheated in some way with the specie they bought, or traded on over-easy bank credit. The American financial crisis of 1819 seemed to confirm the latter conjecture, but American activity did not cease, though imports of Javan coffee to the United States diminished:[1]

1816	0·4 m.lb.	1819	3·5 m.lb.
1817	1·8	1821	0·3
1818	2·9	1822	1·7

A prize-essayist in Holland in 1827 blamed the Dutch authorities and merchants for slowness in perceiving the importance of English cotton goods as a new factor in eastern commerce, and suggested that Dutchmen in the East kept silence because they benefited as partners or otherwise from the trade of the British houses at Batavia. Actually, it was well known to all whom it concerned that British shipping at Batavia profited by an outward cargo of cotton goods for the Indies or of convicts for Australia, but it is true that Dutchmen long failed to understand the character of a trade which prospered by an increasing turn-over and a declining rate of profit. They noted that the prices of the cotton goods were continually falling, and supposed, not without some justification, that this was a sign of over-trading and of cut-throat competition which must soon lead to a collapse. Muntinghe, for instance, suggested in 1822 that the success of British cotton goods in Java might be due to a temporary fall in British wages caused by the Continental System and by post-war difficulties, and to export-subsidies by which the British government was attempting to keep the factories working. He therefore advised that the Netherlands should be cautious, and not imitate British methods until the ultimate results could be seen.[2]

In the winter of 1823–4, the king instructed Muntinghe to conduct an inquiry among merchants in the Netherlands as to the state of the Java trade. All who engaged in it agreed that their ventures were unprofitable. Netherland ships could earn a profit in the East only by taking out troops and public stores. The merchants complained bitterly of false economy in this matter; a truly liberal government, they said, would ration out its contracts and pay generously, not take advantage by a system of tenders of competition among the merchants.

Muntinghe criticized the merchants for lack of enterprise. They complained that British firms had well-established connexions at Batavia,

---

[1] *American State Papers*, 1832, Commerce and Navigation, vols. I and II.

[2] J. van Ouwerkerk de Vries, *Verhandeling*, pp. 128–43; *Post. Doc.* II, 67–8; G. W. Earl, *The Eastern Seas* (London, 1837), p. 23.

Calcutta and Madras, and that British merchants everywhere had a certain national solidarity; yet only one or two Dutch firms had set up regular agencies at Batavia. Most Dutch super-cargoes were therefore at the mercy of immediate local circumstances. They took whatever produce they could obtain at Batavia and returned quickly. They did not visit Samarang or Surabaya, and refused freights offered by the colonial government within the Archipelago. It was now the British and American sailors who had intimate experience of those seas; the Dutch merchant sailors were ignorant and timid.

The trade, Muntinghe reported, was kept going at government expense for the benefit of a few great houses. The government's terms varied according to whether the ministries concerned tried to obey the king's wishes for retrenchment or for the encouragement of trade; but seemed in any case insufficient to make voyages profitable in existing circumstances. Muntinghe supposed therefore that some further, illegitimate, advantage was obtained, at the expense of the government or of the troops on board, but that it would be contrary to public interest to prevent this until the trade could be established on a more satisfactory footing. The merchants argued that although their trade was admittedly carried on at government expense, it was the colonial government that paid; and that this was only right, because its revenues benefited from the British trade which was the root of the evil. Dutch merchants said that old-established houses did not defraud the government, but only the upstarts of Antwerp, to whom the government was anyway overgenerous for political reasons.

Muntinghe advised against the continuance of an unduly liberal commercial system in the East. Liberalism, he said, assumed that individuals can judge economic opportunities better than any government and that all government intervention leads to a wasteful use of capital. The eastern trade was an exception, for the Netherland government could judge opportunities there much better than private merchants in the motherland. Only government intervention could preserve the trade from foreigners, or direct into it surplus Dutch capital at present invested in foreign securities. A new Company was needed, of purely commercial character and without any monopoly. It should be encouraged by government contracts and by special facilities for obtaining not only government produce but also the produce of free labour in the interior of the districts where land-rents had been introduced.[1]

---

[1] P. J. Elout van Soeterwoude, *Bijdragen 1820–4*, Bijlage III; *Parl. Papers*, 1821, VII, 230; A.R.A., Staatssec., 6518 (Muntinghe to de Meij, 18 March 1824); J. van Ouwerkerk de Vries, *Verhandeling*, pp. 154–6.

(b) The development of mercantilist policies—1824–30

Positive government action was necessary if a colonial market was to be created for Belgian industry. The Belgians at first professed indifference to the colonial advantages offered to them among the 'compensations' of the union;[1] they complained that only the West Indian possessions, with their familiar market for Belgian linens, were really valuable, and that the best of them had been 'stolen' by Britain. It was in response to petitions from the Dutch woollen manufacturers and makers of gold and silver braid that the king in 1819 issued a decree to amend the Javan tariff of 1818 by exempting Netherland products from import duty in Java. By then, however, the argument about 'compensations' had lost its novelty and Belgian newspapers and deputies were beginning to complain that Java was not being made useful to Belgium. Industrialists noted the potential market there for cotton goods and other manufactures; but asserted that in their post-war distress they had no capital for experimental consignments and that Dutch merchants showed no desire to help. Tangible assistance was wanted from the government, not mere exhortation.[2]

These strictures were unjust, for in 1818 the government procured from Batavia samples of cotton goods for Belgian manufacturers to imitate, and in 1819 sent out a first consignment of such imitations, which, however, did not answer.

Dutch merchants had no wish to export Belgian goods to Java, but they wished that British imports there could be discouraged. They were therefore not opposed to protection in Java for Belgian industry, and hoped that in time the Belgians might accept it as compensation for free trade at home. The idea was acceptable to Falck, whose main purpose in practical politics was the success of the union. In 1818, he was much impressed by an essay submitted to him by a Belgian adventurer named Wappers Melis, who had formerly been employed by the English East India Company in India. The suggestion was that the colonies could enjoy a 'just freedom' for the expansion of their trade and cultivation within a competitive national system, from which foreigners should be excluded. In particular, foreign iron, lead, glass, hardware, and cotton and woollen goods should be excluded, for the benefit of Belgium. Falck soothed his liberal conscience by the hope that this protection could be withdrawn when Belgian industry became stronger; though Wappers Melis held that free trade would always give Britain an undue advantage, since Belgian manu-

---

[1] See above, p. 96.
[2] *L'Observateur* (1819), XVII, 19–26; R. Demoulin, *Guillaume Ier*, pp. 147–8.

facturers had less capital and a smaller home market. The proposed policy would be most inconvenient for the Batavia government, so Falck did not ask its advice but sent Wappers Melis out as a high grade official to see what could be done.[1]

Dutch officials in the East, many of whom had been isolated from the motherland during the wars, showed little enthusiasm for measures to assist merchants in Holland by impeding foreign trade which was advantageous from the colonial point of view; they became hostile when it was suggested that they should put themselves about for the sake of 'bankrupt Belgian factories'. Wappers Melis reported that they regarded Falck and the king 'almost as enemies'. According to Muntinghe, the failure of the Belgian cottons in 1819 was due to the dispatch of the wrong samples from Batavia. Certainly, experiments after the arrival of Wappers Melis were much more successful. In general, the colonial government began to show more concern for the interests of the motherland and less for its own finances, which in the early 1820's appeared for a time to be healthy, despite their dangerous dependence on the price of coffee.[2]

Van der Capellen accepted Wappers Melis as one charged with a royal mandate, and soon appointed him Director-General of Customs, remarking that he supposed vigorous action must be expected. The first result was a stricter enforcement of the existing tariff against the British. The efforts of British merchants and manufacturers to improve their marketing organization and cut out unnecessary middlemen had made trade increasingly competitive and had led to the presentation of misleading invoices for the valuation of goods for import duty. In 1821, Wappers Melis obtained authority to set aside suspect invoices, even when certified by a Dutch consul, and also to treat ships registered at Batavia as foreign if they brought cargoes from a foreign port in Europe or America.[3]

Van der Capellen feared that any serious measure against British imports would lead to a fall in the price of coffee. In obedience to the king, and in order to avoid a direct order from home, he was willing to make the sacrifice, but first he wished to be sure that Belgian industry and Dutch commerce were ready for their opportunity and would keep up the trade of Batavia. When the success of experimental Belgian cotton

[1] P. H. van der Kemp, 'Wappers Melis', in *Indische Gids* (1908), pp. 1601–2; A. R. Falck, *Gedenkschriften*, pp. 469–70, 499; J. A. P. G. Boot, *De Twentsche katoennijverheid*, p. 326.

[2] *Post. Doc.* II, 54–70.

[3] D. C. Steijn Parvé, *Het koloniaal monopoliestelsel*, II, 29; *Staatsblad van Ned.-Indië* (1821), no. 40; P. H. van der Kemp, 'De geschiedenis van het ontstaan der Ned.-Ind. lijnwaden-verordening van 1824', in *B.K.I.* 1908; A. R. Falck, *Ambtsbrieven*, p. 74; *Parl. Papers*, 1821, VII, 128; A. Hoynck van Papendrecht, *A. van Hoboken en Co.* p. 134.

goods in Javan markets at last convinced him that the time was ripe, he let Wappers Melis have his way. Early in 1824, an import duty of 25% was suddenly imposed on European and American cotton and woollen goods, and of 35% if they were imported, indirectly, from ports east of the Cape. Van der Capellen expected that this would prove prohibitive, and asked the home government for action to stimulate Belgian exports to fill the gap.

It was in April 1824 that the king created the Netherland Trading Company, the embodiment of many of his long meditated ideas. It was to revive Netherland trade in many parts of the world, and in particular it was to lead the way in 'nationalizing' the Java trade. Its contracts with the colonial government and with natives were, however, to 'concern only the buying, selling, delivery and encouragement of goods and products' and to 'include no tendency towards monopoly, or the exclusion of the free trade of Netherlanders or of foreigners, or towards forced cultivation or forced deliveries'. It was to hold public auctions of colonial produce in the Netherlands 'in such a way as to draw the general trade as much as possible to this kingdom'. Actually, official statistics in 1824 showed that already nearly four-fifths in value of the exports of Batavia came to Netherlands ports; the Company, however, was intended to remedy the fact that most of this produce came on foreign account in foreign ships, and that it was not paid for with Netherland manufactures for Java.

In secret instructions to the officers of the Company, the king was more explicit.

The Netherland Trading Company would bring great advantage to itself and to the commerce of the Netherlands, if it endeavoured to buy up all the coffee available in Java, since by doing so it would deprive foreigners of the opportunity of using this product as a means of remitting the price obtained for goods imported to Java and sold there at a great profit. The result would probably be that the consequent difficulties would diminish the advantages of the foreigners, and so also their desire to come to market at Batavia. This could be a very useful means of making that market important for the Netherlands.

The Company was also to buy up existing stocks of coffee in the markets of Europe, and to hold them back in order to improve prices and to enable the Netherland staple market quickly to gain a commanding position in this trade; the Company's large capital would always enable it to hold stocks until prices were favourable and until the beans were dry enough to give the best flavour. The Company was to be banker to the colonial government and to farm the opium monopoly for it, and so to free it of the need for loans from English houses; for the king feared that such loans

would have the unfortunate result that the produce to be sold to meet the interest and the yearly repayments of capital would in a great part flow to foreign merchants to the great prejudice of Netherland trade, shipping and industry...and whatever the reason may be, experience shows that the Government of the Indies makes no use of Netherlanders in any of its more important transactions, but places them so to speak in the hands of these foreigners, whose great capital, it cannot be denied, enables them to help when others feel unable to do so.

In general, the Company was to

end the strange state of affairs which has lasted for some years and in consequence of which the colonies are maintained at the expense of the motherland but are useful only to foreigners....The Company seems to have the duty and also the requisite strength to bring to an end all detrimental foreign competition and to bring the government of the Netherland Indies back again into a proper relationship with the motherland.

Thus, without any formal revival of Dutch monopoly to which the British government might object, British merchants and manufacturers were to be deprived of the fruits of the free trade to Batavia.[1]

Owing to lack of information about the king's intentions, the new Javan duties were badly timed; for during 1824, private traders in the Netherlands were discouraged from the Java trade by doubts about the new Company, through which, it seemed clear, all the government's favours would in future be dispensed. Thus until the Company was ready in 1825 to make a serious start, there was little active Netherland trade with the East. This brought bitter complaints from Van der Capellen, who, as he had foretold, was embarrassed by a fall in coffee prices, and, it seemed at first, in vain. However, in the long run, the duties accorded well with the king's policy. Under their protection, the Company, though unable to fulfil the king's more fanciful hopes, succeeded in winning from the British a considerable trade for Belgian cotton goods, in which private merchants later began to participate.[2]

The new Javan duties were introduced at about the time of the signing of the Anglo-Dutch treaty of 1824. This treaty was negotiated by Falck

[1] A.R.A., Nat. Nijv. en Kol., 6 Oct. 1824; *2de kamer*, 1825–6, B 346 and B 360–3; W. M. F. Mansvelt, *Geschiedenis van de Ned. Handelmaatschappij*, ch. ii.
[2] E. Verviers, *De Nederlandsche handelspolitiek*, p. 292.

in ignorance of the impending change in the course of Netherland commercial policy in the East. Clauses were inserted to satisfy the free-trade interest in Britain, though Falck boasted in reports to his government that they were ambiguous enough not to impede future measures for the protection of Netherland trade and industry. The British plenipotentiaries, however, in a public declaration expressed gratitude for 'the readiness with which the Netherland Plenipotentiaries have entered into stipulations calculated to promote the most perfect freedom of trade between the subjects of the two Crowns, and their respective dependencies in that part of the world'. The formal reply of the Dutch plenipotentiaries naturally contained no confirmation of this interpretation, but it did not disavow the principle of 'perfect freedom of trade' in the East.[1]

Value of cotton imports to Java and Madura (millions of florins)

	Foreign	Netherland
1825	1·5	0·2
1826	1·0	1·3
1827	2·0	0·8
1828	1·9	3·0
1829	1·6	3·5

When news of the new Javan duties reached Europe, Falck advised the king that it would be unwise to maintain them in their full vigour, in view of the liberal spirit of the treaty. The king, however, was not pleased with the treaty. He believed that better terms could have been obtained if his plenipotentiaries had informed themselves better about the situation in the East. He supported Van der Capellen on this issue, and arranged for the publication in the Netherlands of a memorandum by Wappers Melis in defence of the new duties. A reference to the English 'squealing like hungry pigs' against the duties was, however, omitted from the published version.[2]

British merchants feared that the new duties would be prohibitive, and that within a few years 'the manufactures of Flanders will supplant us'. Yet their imports continued even after the fulfilment of previous orders. Wappers Melis explained that the British were trading at a loss in order to keep up their connexions, in the hope of successful British diplomatic action against the duties. Dutchmen at Batavia who were hostile to the new policy believed that the duties were failing in their purpose because

---

[1] E. G. Lagemans, *Recueil des traités et conventions conclus par le Royaume des Pays-Bas depuis 1813* (The Hague, 1858), no. 103; *Post. Doc.* II, 318–19.

[2] *Post. Doc.* II, 186–92; P. H. van der Kemp, in *B.K.I.* (1902).

impossible to enforce. A Dutchman wrote home in the summer of 1825:

If our shipping and the Netherland Trading Company must stand or fall by these duties, I shall go straight into mourning, for Thornton and Co. have so organised their smuggling in the Archipelago that more manufactures have entered from England this year already than in the whole of last year.

Officials who were well qualified to judge believed that Wappers Melis grossly overestimated the extent to which smuggling could be prevented by the inadequately equipped customs service. The success of Belgian cotton goods, they supposed, was due less to the Javan duties than to the efforts of the Netherland Trading Company in helping Belgian manufacturers to produce the right goods at the right price. It was believed too that the duties were leniently levied on legal British imports. Wappers Melis and other high customs officers were seen to be on more friendly terms with the British merchants than was likely otherwise. Goods were now valued for duty by a monthly price list drawn up by the authorities after hearing two Netherland and two British merchants. The authorities were said to be mindful of the relation between cotton imports and coffee prices and to be influenced by British threats to withdraw from the trade. However, an investigation of the official price lists by the Netherland Trading Company in 1826 showed them to be reasonably accurate.

Thus, British cotton goods were still able to compete against Belgian in Java. British merchants complained, however, that it was at an enhanced price which 'has had the effect of perpetuating several native manufactures in the remoter parts of these countries, and of narrowing the consumption of European manufactures throughout them all'. No doubt this was true. The Belgians could not compete against native manufacture in the coarser grades, and imports from Continental India continued. In 1828, the king gave instructions that as soon as these fabrics could be effectively imitated in Belgium the Javan import duty on cotton goods made east of the Cape should be much increased. He was dissuaded from a further increase in duty against British cottons by advice that it would merely cause more smuggling.[1]

Commercial opinion in Holland welcomed the Javan duties of 1824, but the Netherland Trading Company was not entirely popular. The king, having subscribed much of its capital and personally guaranteed an annual 5% dividend on the remainder, treated it as an instrument of royal

---

[1] A.R.A., Roëll 158—letters from J. van Ouwerkerk de Vries; *Post. Doc.* II, 98–105, 140, 155, 168, 177–85, 192, 196–7; D. C. Steijn Parvé, *Het koloniaal monopoliestelsel*, II, 30.

policy rather than as a commercial enterprise, and established its head-quarters at the Hague, to the annoyance of Amsterdam. The Company often disregarded commercial traditions, in the autocratic spirit of its master. Nevertheless, it won approval by providing cargoes for Dutch shipowners. By developing Belgian exports to Java, it also created an opportunity for private Dutch merchants to send cargoes on their own account; and the king welcomed such activity, even though it reduced the profits of his own Company. Sailings from the Netherlands to the East increased in all from fifty-one in 1823 to seventy-one in 1828. A Dutch newspaper later boasted that the Company had 'prevented the commerce of our Indian possessions from falling into the hands of the English and Americans'.[1]

The Belgian revolution of 1830 showed how well the king's policy suited Dutch interests, for no change was made when Belgian industry no longer had to be considered. With the support of the Chambers of Commerce of Rotterdam and Amsterdam, the import duties on foreign cotton goods remained undiminished in Java, although they were reduced to a very low level in the Netherlands. In the hope of providing outward cargo for Dutch ships in the new circumstances, the Javan import duty on foreign cotton goods coming in Dutch ships from the motherland was reduced in 1831 to $12\frac{1}{2}\%$, the lowest figure permissible, under the Dutch interpretation of the treaty of 1824, if the duty for British ships remained at 25%. As it proved that this concession encouraged re-exports from Belgium, with whom he was at war, the king cancelled it in the following year. Instead, he sought to provide outward cargoes by creating a Dutch cotton industry, financed and guided by the Netherland Trading Company, with protection not in the Dutch but in the Javan market. In due course, he succeeded.[2]

The success of the Company depended on the cultivation of export crops in Java. The aim could no longer be a restricted production, for

His Majesty judges that our interest by no means requires that the price of coffee should remain high, since that would encourage its cultivation in other countries. This is already being attempted in Bengal, on the Malay peninsula, and elsewhere outside our possessions. The temporary advantage of high prices thus has a bad effect in the long run. The king considers it most important that Java should produce the greatest possible amount of

[1] A.R.A., Roëll 158; A.R.A., G. K. van Hogendorp 44, 5 (3); *Post. Doc.* II, 99 and 186–96; J. van Ouwerkerk de Vries, *Verhandeling*, pp. 133–43; J. A. Drieling, *Bijdragen*, p. 57; G. W. Earl, *The Eastern Seas*, p. 33; P. H. van der Kemp, in *Indische Gids* (1908).

[2] *Post. Doc.* II, 203; J. van Ouwerkerk de Vries, *Verhandeling*, pp. 77–8.

coffee for the market, since Java can produce coffee at lower cost than most if not all other lands.

Here Van der Capellen's policy was unsuccessful. He wished to extend the land-rent system for the benefit of the small cultivator, and therefore set his face against capitalist plantations. The small cultivators, however, showed no wish to cultivate export crops, and efforts on their behalf were followed by a costly colonial war. This was not satisfactory to the king, so the policy was changed.[1]

Value of cotton imports to Java and Madura[2] *(in millions of florins)*

	Foreign	Netherland
1830	1·5	2·4
1831	1·5	1·4*
1832–4 (av.)	3·0	—
1835	2·6	1·5
1838	4·1	5·8

* Mainly re-exports from Belgium.

The Dutch Commissioners had already noted in 1817 that under Raffles' arrangements the land-rent system did not in practice assure to the peasant the fruits of his labours in the cultivation of such crops as coffee. Most of the benefit, they believed, went to moneylenders and middlemen, or to native chiefs and European officials who forced the peasant to sell at disadvantageous prices. Van der Capellen attempted to remedy this by strict administration and by regulation of the Chinese and other moneylenders and traders. Warehouses might be set up only by special licence, for 'the establishment of warehouses by Europeans and others outside the effective supervision of the district authorities often tends to deprive the native of the free disposal of his produce'. Credit contracts were regulated, and were to be valid only if registered at the office of the Dutch Resident of the district. Chinese and Arabs were forbidden to make advance payments on the crops. The government warehouses were to buy all crops offered to them at fixed prices, and to make advances to the cultivators on fixed terms.

This policy failed to protect the cultivator. It was impossible, at least for a long time, to determine each peasant's rent and to collect it individually, as Raffles had intended. The rent had to be fixed by villages and the village headman had to be made responsible for its payment. In fact,

[1] D. C. Steijn Parvé, *Het koloniaal monopoliestelsel*, I, 160–70.
[2] E. Verviers, *De Nederlandsche handelspolitiek*, p. 292.

native institutions were little changed. The cultivator had no confidence that he would be allowed by his superiors to retain more of his produce than was needed for the subsistence of his family. He wanted, therefore, to grow rice, not coffee; and coffee cultivation remained as much as ever a matter of forced labour. However, the higher native chiefs had now less power and less incentive to promote production: the quantity and quality of coffee grown under the land-rent system were therefore inferior to that grown by the old methods in Preanger.[1]

Van der Capellen's successor judged that it had been a mistake to seek to protect the freedom of labour by regulations instead of by the creation of a free market. The Javans could be protected from their oppressors by the admittance of European merchants, who would bring healthy competition to the interior of the country. European planters would create a competitive labour market, so that the Javans could leave their villages to earn individual wages. The cultivation and manufacture of cotton would then soon diminish; for the Javans would prefer to sell their labour when it was not needed in the paddy fields, and to buy imported cotton goods, to the advantage of Belgian industry. European landowners would also establish peasant settlers on the waste lands which might be granted to them; for in many villages there existed a class of poor, who had not the spirit or the means to reclaim waste land, which was plentiful in most districts. European landlords would accumulate capital from their rents and invest in improvements, instead of consuming their whole revenue like the Javan upper class. A competitive market for land, and perhaps competitive rents, would follow, and would force Javan landholders and cultivators to imitate European efficiency or to surrender their holdings. The government could hasten the process by making its land-rent a true, competitive rent instead of simply a tax.[2]

The policy of admitting European enterprise was adopted in 1826. It accorded better than Van der Capellen's policy with the ideas of liberals in the motherland, and with the original intentions of the Commissioners. It was supported by Belgian industrialists: 'for by civilising the natives we shall create new needs among them for the products of our industry, and so at last we shall really take possession of our colonies'. All were agreed that the European capital to be admitted to Java must not be used for industrial establishments, other than those necessary to prepare Javan produce for the trade and industry of the motherland.

The new policy could not produce the speedy results which the king

---

[1] D. C. Steijn Parvé, *Het koloniaal monopoliestelsel*, I, 37; II, 27, 44, 49, 85.

[2] *Ibid.* II, 41, 50, 55, 120–3; T. S. Raffles, *The History of Java* (London, 1817), I, 161, 207.

required; especially in view of the war against Dipa Negara, which made Java less attractive for European investment from 1825 to 1830. Also, it was well understood that, in order to have significant results, the Europeans to be admitted could not be all Netherlanders. Yet every British plantation would diminish the chances of success for the king's policy of 'nationalizing' the Java trade, and accordingly he insisted on restricting British immigration by requiring foreigners to become naturalized before acquiring property in Java. The extension of free cultivation in any form would diminish the importance of the government crops, so that the policy of 1826 might threaten the interests of the Netherland Trading Company. In the end, the king made another personal intervention. In 1830, Raffles' reforms were abandoned, and reliance was placed on the extension and intensification of forced labour for the production of export crops.[1]

Van den Bosch, who devised and realized the 'Culture System' of 1830, believed that European plantations were unlikely to produce crops cheaply enough to compete in European markets against the West Indies, which were nearer, and his policy was to restrict European enterprise in Java to a few experimental areas. For lack of capital and energy, peasant cultivation of export crops seemed to him unlikely to be more successful than had been the cultivation of sugar by freed slaves in San Domingo. Forced labour therefore seemed indispensable. He argued that even in Europe most labour was really forced, for few men would voluntarily work beyond the extent necessary for bare subsistence. Apart from a few who strove to save in order to better themselves, Europeans of the working class produced a surplus beyond their bare needs only because that was the condition on which the owners of capital gave them employment. Their whole surplus earnings had therefore to be taken from them, and the only real difference between the European and West Indian systems was that the West Indian slave usually enjoyed a larger proportion of the product of his labour than did the free worker of Europe, who was much more efficient and industrious. Civilization must always be based on forced labour. The Javan was likely to be happier under the traditional kind of compulsion which experience proved to be most suitable for him, than under a system imitated from the European example.[2]

It is notable that there had been little public demand in the Netherlands for such a policy. Even so conservative a Dutchman as Van Alphen had asked only for government supervision of Javan agriculture, not for

[1] A.R.A., Staatssec. 6518—memo, by Le Cocq, 17 May 1827; D. C. Steijn Parvé, *Het koloniaal monopoliestelsel*, II, 250.

[2] D. C. Steijn Parvé, *Het koloniaal monopoliestelsel*, II, 306-20.

abandonment of the principle of free cultivation. Indeed, he had proposed that the cultivators' land-rents should be fixed in the manner of the Permanent Settlement in Bengal; for he well knew that, otherwise, zealous officials would always seek to raise more revenue and thus would probably deprive the cultivators as effectively as had their native chiefs of the fruits of any special efforts and improvements.[1]

[1] *2de kamer*, 1825–6, A, Van Alphen, 23 Feb. 1826.

Chapter XIII

THE FAILURE OF DUTCH-BELGIAN UNION

(a) The success of the fiscal union

The government had reason to be satisfied with the legislation of 1821-2, for it quieted the commercial party without upsetting the Dutch-Belgian fiscal union. Dutch hankerings for a Dual Monarchy that would leave them free to follow their traditional policies, became purely sentimental. As later events proved, fiscal separation was likely to benefit Holland's trade only if it could be accompanied by a new closure of the Scheldt; that would be impossible if the separation were amicably arranged, and the outcome of any violent separation must depend not on the wishes of the Dutch but on the decisions of the great powers. The Dutch therefore accepted the government's attitude that fiscal union was an unalterable fact imposed by the Powers. The concessions of 1821-2 were clearly the utmost that could be obtained in a united kingdom under William I, and the leaders of the commercial party accepted them 'in a spirit of compromise', hoping that animosity between Dutch and Belgians on the fiscal question would now subside.[1]

In 1830, Van Hogendorp still supposed that fiscal incompatibility was the main danger to Dutch-Belgian union, because the Dutch desired free trade, and the Belgians a system of prohibitions.[2] This was not realistic. The old Dutch harmony of interests was now dead, and the commercial leaders spoke only for a minority of the Dutch nation. In 1825, even the Chamber of Commerce at Middelburg ceased to support traditional free trade. It had abandoned hope that commerce could revive in the minor Dutch ports, and attached more importance to its interests as the market town of an agricultural area. It asked for the protection of small-scale enterprise producing goods for a local market against the irresistible flood from the English factories, which it denounced in the manner of the Belgian protectionists:

In the years 1810-13, when English manufactures could not be exported, the English government spent millions of pounds in relieving the manufacturers of their goods, solely in order to keep the common people quiet. These goods were afterwards offered in lotteries, on the condition that they should be exported. The prizes were considerable. Anyone who

[1] *2de kamer*, 1825-6, A 347 (Van Alphen).
[2] *Knuttel* 25938 (Van Hogendorp, 1830).

drew a prize, probably worth thousands of pounds, sent the goods to other countries and had them sold at any price, for everything was profit to him. This did much harm on the Continent, and no one could understand how English goods could be made so cheaply, since often the price would not even pay for the raw material. Our own productions have made great progress for many years, but are not yet fit to face such competition without fear.[1]

Dutch agriculture remained on the whole protectionist. This was proved in the 1830's. Immediately after the Belgian Revolution, the grain duties were reduced to the 1822 level, in order to encourage imports during the war and to reward the commercial party for their loyalty. In 1835, after agitation by agricultural interests, a sliding scale of protective import duties was introduced, in spite of petitions, in the familiar language of the commercial party, from Amsterdam and Rotterdam.[2]

The system of 1821 proved broadly satisfactory to the Belgians. Their iron, coal, and cotton and woollen goods continued to enjoy valuable protection in the Dutch market, and acquired it in the Dutch colonies too in the latter cases. These interests could not desire fiscal separation, unless perhaps it could be followed by union with France; and when it became clear that the king's policies were bringing them real prosperity, their requests for still higher protection lost their anti-Dutch flavour. The cotton industry in 1829 used nearly twice as many spindles as in 1810 and its weaving had trebled. It was believed that over 200,000 persons now lived by the industry.[3] The industry had no reason to feel that it was being victimized by Dutch commercial influences. In 1828, the king personally insisted that the government should accede to petitions for still higher import duties on cotton cloth, because the development of the power-loom had reduced the weight of English cloth. The new duties were:

	In (florins)	Out (florins)	Transit (florins)
Cottons, white, per 100 kg.	85·0	0·35	3·50
Cottons, dyed or printed	100·0	0·35	3·50

Commercial opposition to the measure was not strenuous, and came from Belgium as well as from Holland. Merchants of Brussels, for instance, petitioned that English technical progress by cheapening the goods in

[1] *Post. Doc.* I, 236–7.   [2] *Ged.* X (1), 381–2.
[3] F.-X. van Houtte, *L'Évolution de l'industrie textile en Belgique et dans le monde de 1800 à 1939* (Louvain, 1949), p. 130; J. A. van Houtte, *Esquisse*, p. 171; C. White, *The Belgic Revolution of 1830* (London, 1835), II. 411.

relation to their weight was really making the existing duties more severe and smuggling more widespread. It was said, however, that foreign agents were to blame for this free-trade agitation in Belgium.[1] Belgian agricultural interests were not entirely satisfied with the grain duties of 1825, but they were hostile to the government in any case on religious grounds and were dangerous only when they had support from the towns, which regarded the duties of 1825 as sufficiently protective. Some bitterness was caused by the fact that the Dutch distilleries continued to use Baltic rye and competed successfully against Belgian rural distilleries.[2] However, there were now few major fiscal issues which could be presented as a direct conflict of interest between Holland and Belgium, and few economic grievances about which Belgian opinion was sufficiently united for an appeal to national feeling to be possible. Accordingly, after 1822 the politicians could find little fun in economic matters and other symbols were chosen for national excitement.

The flour excise, however, continued to be a Belgian national grievance, though the Dutch agricultural provinces struggled against it too. Its abolition in 1829, and its replacement by a coffee excise in 1830, were hailed as Belgian victories. The Dutch commercial party now made little effort to defend the flour excise. Its leaders still asserted that the tax was a good one in principle, but argued that it had been spoiled by previous concessions and converted into a direct tax in most districts, instead of being a beautifully imperceptible levy on the whole population. The commercial party conceded that since the tax could not be properly enforced, it had better be abolished, in order that the government might regain the good will of the Belgians and of the Dutch agricultural provinces. Van Hogendorp agreed. He said that he had always considered a just taxation of the poor to be possible only in the prosperity which he expected to follow from free trade. As things were, the inferior working class should not be made to pay their proper share, but should bear no burdens beyond the existing duties on salt, gin and beer. He wished, however, for some new excise to replace that on meat as a means of taxing the superior working class.[3]

In reintroducing the coffee excise in 1830, the government justly argued that the former objections could no longer apply, since the bonding system had now been made acceptable to Dutch commerce. This was shown by the fact that most imported coffee was now bonded as long as

[1] *2de kamer*, 1827–8, A66 and B615; R. Demoulin, *Guillaume Ier*, p. 127.
[2] *2de kamer*, 1827–8, A (Van den Hove, 27 May); J. A. van Houtte, *Esquisse*, pp. 197–8.
[3] *2de kamer*, 1827–8, B37 and 1828–30, A144–5; G. K. van Hogendorp, *Lettres sur la prospérité*, pp. 117, 158.

it remained in the ports, although it was liable only to a moderate import duty. The fact that the Netherland Trading Company was now the main importer also made arrangements easier.[1] The commercial opposition was perfunctory, and came from Antwerp as much as from Amsterdam. Dutch deputies explained that more would have been heard from Amsterdam and Rotterdam had they not been reluctant to make use of the right of petition, which had recently been so much abused by Belgian agitators. In view of the deteriorating political situation in Belgium, the Dutch did not wish to embarrass the government, even though the Belgians were boasting that the coffee excise was only the first of the taxes on commercial goods they hoped to secure.[2]

The fact that Dutch-Belgian quarrels were now not economic was shown by the debates on the second decennial budget in 1829. Belgian opposition was based entirely on political grievances, especially in regard to language and education. The government was gradually redressing these grievances, but the Belgians always found new ones to feed their passions. The Dutch deputies forbore to seek fiscal concessions in return for their support of the budget, explaining that its rejection would benefit only the Jesuits and those Belgians who at the behest of their directors of conscience were trying to plunge the Netherlands into medieval darkness. Since the Belgian deputies were not revolutionaries, their votes were less intransigent than their language, and the budget finally passed almost unanimously.[3]

The yearly amendments to the tariff roused echoes of the old controversies. The successful exhibition of Dutch and Belgian products at Haarlem in 1825 proved to protectionists that home industry could supply all needs and deserved a monopoly of the home market; and to free-traders that the industries had outgrown the need for protection, or indeed that only over-protected ones like ironmaking remained 'infants'. One Dutch deputy boasted that the progress of the Belgian cotton industry was due not to the tariff but to the stimulating competition of smuggled imports; and added that the Belgians should be grateful for 'the irresistible impulse of the Netherlander to be free and to trade freely, whether by means of legal or of smuggling trade'. When the import duty on cotton cloths was increased, Dutch deputies asserted that Hamburg merchants had piled up stocks of English piece-goods in readiness for the increased incentive for smuggling them into the Netherlands.[4]

[1] *2de kamer*, 1829–30, B 809.
[2] *2de kamer*, 1829–30, A 29, A 417 and A 473.
[3] *2de kamer*, 1829–30.
[4] *2de kamer*, 1825–6, A 174 and A 347–55; *2de kamer*, 1827–8, A, debate of 27 March 1828.

The success of the Dutch cotton industry in the 1820's was certainly due to smuggling. The domestic weavers of Twente needed the cheap English cotton yarns in order that their bombazines and the pure cotton cloths they were now making might compete in the home market. Thus the duties that protected Belgian cotton spinning involved the sacrificing of an infant Dutch industry, though Dutch free-traders, apart from Van Hogendorp, showed little interest in the fact. However, Twente was fortunately near the frontier, so English yarn was sent across it from the ports under the transit system and immediately smuggled back. Thus Almelo instead of Amsterdam became the central market for cotton yarn in the Dutch provinces, and when it was needed for the pauper industries of Holland it was obtained from there. The facts were well known in commercial circles and came to the attention of the government in 1829, but no action was taken.[1]

The implications of most of the tariff amendments after 1822 were too complicated and insignificant for the attempt to make them a subject for Dutch-Belgian disputes to be successful. When the import duty on tulle was raised from 6 to 10%, the opposition came from Belgian merchants who put out English tulle for finishing and exported to France mixed consignments of English and Belgian work. They complained that the new duty would cause English tulle to be smuggled directly into France instead of through the Netherlands. Small increases in the import duties on refined borax and sawn timber brought disputes between Dutch merchants and Dutch commercial industries; the merchants urged that subsidies should be given from the Fund instead of the new duties, and asserted as usual that the small Dutch entrepreneurs concerned did not want protection, although they signed petitions for it. When the export duty on butter was reduced as compensation for an increase in the salt excise, the leaders of Dutch commercial opinion protested that this would increase costs in their cities, since a little butter was one of the few luxuries of the workmen; it was unfair to enrich at their expense the already prosperous dairy farmers.[2]

Since Dutch merchants realized after 1822 that a more liberal tariff was unlikely, they became more interested in the benefits obtainable by bonding, and more co-operative towards the authorities in the matter. In introducing the new grain duties in 1825, the government explained that it could not make them higher without forcing the whole re-export trade into bond, which would be troublesome both to the merchants and to the

---

[1] A.R.A., Nat. Nijv. en Kol., 1 May 1829, no. 6G; J. A. P. G. Boot, *De Twentsche katoennijverheid*, ch. i.

[2] *2de kamer*, 1827-8, A196, B6 and 1829-30, A295-9.

authorities responsible for ensuring that bonding did not lead to fraud. It hoped that merchants would prefer to pay the new import duties rather than use the transit system. Amsterdam merchants decided otherwise, and demanded that fictitious bonding should be permitted in order that the whole general trade in grains might be conducted *in transito*. The Governor of North Holland, with the support of the provincial States, put pressure on the government, pointing out the inconvenience of ordinary bonding arrangements for so bulky an article. The government conceded the point in 1826. Its decision was received gratefully by the merchants and appeared to mark the beginning of a real recovery in the corn trade.[1] Growing opposition to the Corn Laws in England and a temporary opening of the English ports in 1825 encouraged optimism. Falck wrote from London:

I hope that sooner or later we shall be able to dispose of considerable quantities of corn on the English market; and thus, from the quarter from which one would least have expected it, will come a de facto refutation of the arguments we have so often heard in recent years that our corn trade can no longer be important or profitable.

For such trade, however, Rotterdam was better placed than Amsterdam.[2]

The Dutch merchants also became willing to co-operate with the government in arranging and financing general 'entrepôt' docks. A law of 1828 facilitated this, and granted the incentive of exemption from transit duty of goods re-exported from 'entrepôt' by sea. The preamble explained that London had benefited from her 'entrepôt' dock in spite of the prohibitive character of the ordinary English tariff.

How much more may not the Netherlands expect, which seem chosen by nature to be the centre of Europe's general commerce? It is to be expected, for instance, that Americans will be attracted if they can find here along with articles of our own production which they require other merchandise at reasonable prices which otherwise they would have to search for and load at other ports. This example applies also to the trade between north and south Europe, of which the Netherlands are the centre. The proposed measure will also facilitate the preparation in good confidence of certain foreign and especially northern products for the completion of cargoes for the colonies, as happens in England. And since increased imports imply increased exports, and the greatest demand comes

---

[1] A.R.A., Nat. Nijv. en Kol. 2 April 1827, no. 15; A.R.A., Van Hogendorp 44 (5b); *2de kamer*, 1825–6, B269–76; B. C. E. Zwart, *De Kamer van Koophandel en Fabrieken te Amsterdam*, p. 213; J. C. Westermann, *Gedenkboek*, I, 179–81.

[2] A.R.A., Roëll 118; *Parl. Papers*, 1826–7, no. 333, p. 149.

where there is the greatest choice and the largest supply, this measure will also feed the special transit trade for which our location has a double worth.

The government had already in 1825 attempted to encourage the traditional Dutch carrying trade between northern and southern Europe by exempting from duty goods directly transhipped in Netherland ports, but this had naturally proved to be of little use.[1] The new entrepôt docks, however, were useful and popular, and proved the most effective step yet taken towards William IV's aim of separating the general trade from the home market, an aim which the more conservative free-traders still declared to be impossible. The use of dock warrants slowly made the 'entrepôt' more convenient than fictitious bonding for grain, and it was said that even under a tariff drawn up in the 'spirit of 1821' the new arrangements would be useful. The Americans now began to take Swedish iron from Amsterdam. Amsterdam merchants, led by the Chamber of Commerce and the dock committee, began to agitate for duty-free exportation from the 'entrepôt' by land and river as well as by sea. The government was sympathetic, but unable to devise adequate administrative safeguards against fraud. The merchants replied that in any case there could hardly be more fraud than already occurred. The proposal necessarily provoked opposition from the smaller ports, which could not maintain an entrepôt dock, and from inland market towns; and Rotterdam feared that it might assist Amsterdam too much in developing her river trade.[2]

By thus demanding free transit under bond, even though only as a privilege for the 'entrepôt' docks, the Amsterdam merchants had reversed their former attitude. Having themselves taken to trading in bond, they naturally desired that the transit duties should be low or non-existent, and had shown that when real advantages were to be gained by abandoning old prejudices they were able to learn from experience rather quickly. It was only in conditions of stagnation that they clung to obsolete ways. Already in 1822 they had not opposed the considerable reductions in transit duty rather suddenly proposed by the government, though in view of their controversy with Belgian protectionists they had then been unwilling to admit that they had changed their minds on this point. In 1825, the merchants asked for and obtained a reduction in the transit duty on spirits, despite protests from the distillers; and in 1829 they obtained the admission of raw salt to the 'entrepôt' for free re-export by sea, against the wishes of the refiners. In 1826-7, commercial opinion still

[1] *2de kamer*, 1827-8, A286-9 and B641.
[2] A.R.A., Nat. Nijv. en Kol., 1 May 1829, no. 6G; *Knuttel* 25853 (R. Beerenbroek, 1829); *2de kamer*, 1827-8, A650; J. C. Westermann, *Gedenkboek*, I, 187-9.

opposed any general freeing of traffic on the Rhine from duties other than the river dues authorized by the Treaty of Vienna; but in 1829 it was willing to agree.[1]

The trade conducted through the 'entrepôt' docks was successful partly because its conditions encouraged elimination of the normal channels of the Dutch general market. Bonding had always been said to be especially detrimental to the Second Hand, whose functions were perhaps incompatible with efficient commercial organization in most trades in the nineteenth century. By accepting the transit and bonding systems, the commercial party was probably sacrificing the immediate interests of the Second Hand. The Second Hand could not easily make its voice heard. The Amsterdam Chamber of Commerce, despite its reorganization in 1815, remained predominantly a First Hand body, in harmony again after 1821 with the leaders of the commercial party; and it fully approved of the 'entrepôt' dock, declaring in 1828: 'The entrepôt dock is like a machine, by which trade may be conducted with greater speed and efficiency; and the introduction of a new machine, however beneficial for the community, always hurts individual interests.' The dock, and the harbour improvements of the time, diminished the need for lighting and porterage and so did not help to solve Amsterdam's problem of unemployment.[2]

Amsterdam's change of opinion about transit brought her wishes in regard to commercial policy very much into line with those of Antwerp. In 1825, the Chamber of Commerce at Antwerp asked for duty-free transit, and at the same time condemned Belgian protectionism in language similar to that of the Dutch commercial party.

> Few of our factories would be the worse for foreign competition, and those which can only be maintained by prohibitive duties bring forth no good fruits, since the nation has to be taxed on their behalf and forced to pay more for their products than would be needed for foreign imports.... A duty of from 4 to 8% is enough encouragement for national industry, being sufficient to counteract the effect on our factories of any chance fall in foreign prices.[3]

(b) The system of William I

Having settled the fiscal controversy in 1821–2, the king was free gradually to shape a positive economic policy. His principle was to interfere only when the need seemed obvious, and then to act boldly by trial and error, abandoning failure and following up success. By 1830, he had in hand

[1] *2de kamer*, 1825–6, B384 and 1829–30, B11; T. P. van der Kooy, *Hollands stapelmarkt*, pp. 119–21.

[2] J. C. Westermann, *Gedenkboek*, I, 198–9.   [3] *Post. Doc.* I, 275–8.

a definite and successful policy. The Belgian and Dutch provinces were to be brought into economic unity, together with the colonies; and Dutch commerce was to find a new purpose as one of the links in this system of exchange. In each part of this structure, the king found it necessary to create special institutions to stimulate and educate private enterprise.[1] Capital and credit were pumped into Belgian industry by means of the Société Générale, the Fund of 1821 and the personal investments of the king. Since successive Governors failed to stimulate adequately either native or European enterprise in Java, the discipline of the Culture System was introduced. Since Dutch merchants showed little energy in fulfilling their part of the bargain of 1815–16 by providing commercial credit and seeking out foreign and colonial markets for Belgian industry, the Netherland Trading Company was created to set them an example and if necessary to do the work for them.

The king's secret instructions to the Netherland Trading Company's directors show what he regarded as the proper role for Dutch commerce in the nineteenth century. The main purpose of the Company was to make available to Netherland industry the unlimited potential demand of millions of natives in the Netherland East Indies. Any goods needed in the colonies which the Netherlands could not produce were to be obtained from the sphere of Netherland commerce, but this was to be secondary

and would even deserve no encouragement were it not that a vent must be found for our imported colonial produce and that it seems this object cannot better be attained than by importing the products of these foreign countries and thus creating in them the desire and the need to draw their own supplies from the same market.

He foresaw in 1824 that the Javan trade might not be profitable for some years and urged the Company to seek its profit meanwhile by exporting Netherland products to America, South and Central especially, and to the Levant. As far as possible, it was to seek raw materials in exchange. Re-export business was to be secondary. The Company was to export all the national goods it could, especially linens, even if profits were very low and occasional losses were incurred. This, he believed, would not be contrary to the intentions of the shareholders, since either they were interested personally in one of the branches of the national economy which would gain by the prosperity stimulated by the Company or else they were mere rentiers and must be content with their guaranteed 5%. The Company was to finance, by commercial credits or by taking shares in partnerships

[1] Z. W. Sneller, *Economische en sociale denkbeelden in Nederland in de aanvang der 19de eeuw* (Haarlem, 1922).

and joint-stock companies, all kinds of enterprise; including insurance, and fishing off Newfoundland to supply the plantations of the Netherland West Indies. It was to collect useful information and make it available to business men at home through the Chambers of Commerce and Industry:

The idea on which this is based is to bring all branches of enterprise into unity as it were, with the Company at the centre in permanent contact with the Chambers of Commerce and Industry and the Commissions of Agriculture, in order that all may help each other by advice and deed in the general interest.

The Company was to be a main link between government and people in economic matters. 'Subject like all institutions in a well ordered state to the supervision of the government and to the laws', it was to receive special attention and assistance from the government: 'but the Company should remember that it has no exclusive right to favours and that therefore it is by efficiency that it must assure itself the privilege of being entrusted with government business'. Among the consequences of this activity was to be a renewal of the Dutch general market. 'It seems within the power of the Netherland Trading Company to make the Netherlands once more the stapling place for a not inconsiderable part of world trade, to which this kingdom has a claim by virtue of its location.' For: 'The large capital of the Company gives the opportunity to make use of foreign enterprise and to gain advantages by making the Netherlands the stapling place to which the foreigner brings his products either for consumption here or for re-export overseas or elsewhere.' The main advantages which the king saw in such trade were the employment it might offer for Netherland shipping and the wider choice of raw materials it would offer for Netherland industry. He also hoped that it would increase the export of Netherland goods, especially in mixed consignments. He saw special advantage in trade with the 'commercial hinterland', which he defined as the area served by the Rhine, Maas and Ems, and more hesitantly that served by the Weser, Elbe and Eider. Apart from northern France, this area did not belong to colonial powers, and every effort must be made to attract its oceanic trade to Netherland ports and to establish permanent trade connexions. The government might even have to grant specially easy access to the Netherland market for the products of this area, provided that it could be done without encouraging the smuggling in of goods from other countries. The countries further to the north and north-east were not in the Netherlands' trading area in any special sense, and though trade with them was desirable no special efforts or sacrifices were required, for no doubt there would always be enough of it to provide the Netherlands with such necessary Baltic goods as could not nowadays be obtained equally well from elsewhere.

The king believed that obsolete trade practices did more than anything else to prevent Dutch commerce from fulfilling the role allotted to it. 'Regulations would be of no use in this matter, for we have already seen an association of commercial houses attempt and fail to achieve reform.' The Netherland Trading Company was to set an example and to exercise discipline by dealing for preference with progressive firms. If it succeeded, even those who lost their traditional perquisites would be better off,

for they will find the change to their advantage if the Netherlands again become the stapling place for a good part of the general trade. The high profits they now seek to obtain from a few transactions are evidence that their trade is in decline, and indeed precisely as a result of the high profits it must ultimately be wholly lost. The remedy is mainly in the merchants' own hands. Low duties are not always enough to encourage trade, and sacrifices made by the state are useless for the general good if the costs and burdens which trade lays on itself are not reduced or removed simultaneously.[1]

The costs of the Dutch general market had always been kept up by imperfect competition among the merchants. In the eighteenth century they had been able to keep the prices of many commodities stable over long periods.[2] In the nineteenth century, prices could not be prevented from fluctuating in accordance with international movements, but Dutch merchants continued by mutual consent to respect many traditional practices long after Amsterdam had ceased to have any monopoly of general commerce. The 'spirit of the Placaat of 1725' was only one means by which concealed profits were levied from foreign correspondents. Complicated weights and measures, warehouse charges, and tares all served the same purpose. The merchants had a sentimental affection for old customs, and the Second Hand traders, who had most to lose, especially strove to preserve them.[3] During the controversies of 1816–22, Dutch merchants often asserted that revival of the general market was only possible if it could be organized in the classic manner. This was naturally the view of those who held, like the head of a famous firm in 1825 that 'in time of trouble the post of honour is in the rear'.[4] It could not satisfy

---

[1] A.R.A., Nat. Nijv. en Kol., 6 Oct. 1824.
[2] N. W. Posthumus, *Nederlandse prijgeschiedenis*, I, pp. lxxi, lxxvii.
[3] T. P. van der Kooy, *Hollands stapelmarkt*, pp. 45–6, 95–7; P. A. A. van Mechelen, *Zeevaart en zeehandel van Rotterdam*, pp. 89–91; M. G. de Boer, *Leven en bedrijf van G. M. Roentgen.* pp. 8, 46.
[4] Quoted by R. Demoulin, *Guillaume Ier*, ch. v.

energetic men who were not content merely to wait for the old trade to turn up again. One Amsterdam merchant argued in 1820 that the Second Hand ought no longer to be considered.

The former Second Hand hardly exists now, except in tobacco and tea: that is to say, wholesale houses which bought goods arriving by sea, sorted and re-packed them, and sold them again in smaller parcels. The name 'Second Hand' is now given not only to the small remnant of this class; but also to those who buy here in small quantities and often, to the injury of the general market, order small quantities from abroad; and to commission agents, and retailers.

Conservative merchants hoped for a revival of the Second Hand, and believed that it still helped to attract foreign consignments by employing a worth-while amount of capital in speculative buying.[1]

Energetic merchants had some success in reforming trading conditions at Rotterdam, but not at Amsterdam.[2] However, the First Hand at Amsterdam became increasingly impatient of the practices of the Second Hand. In 1815 the old Chamber of Commerce complained to the burgomasters that the official assessors of tobacco were exaggerating the damage suffered by imported tobacco on the voyage, in order to justify deductions in price for the benefit of the Second Hand, which were likely to drive American consignments to Hamburg and Bremen. The burgomasters rebuked the Chamber for its tenderness to foreign interests. In 1823, a number of Amsterdam merchants requested the Chamber of Commerce to investigate the trade practices of the Second Hand. In due course, the Chamber published a tariff for tares and similar deductions at a reduced rate. The Second Hand refused to comply. The Second Hand merchants, sugar refiners and tobacco manufacturers complained that the Chamber had listened only to evidence from the First Hand. The vigour of their protest took the Chamber by surprise, and its tariff had to be withdrawn.[3] In 1824, a progressive Amsterdam sugar-refining firm, which was later the first to adopt steam, tried to simplify marketing procedure by offering to distribute its product to all who would buy in small or large quantities. The brokers and regular tradesmen thereupon assaulted the sugar refiners as a body in the Bourse, and the offer had to be withdrawn.[4] The Nether-

---

[1] J. C. Westermann, 'Bescheiden betreffende den Amsterdamschen handel in de eerste helft der 19de eeuw', in *Econ. Hist. Jaarboek* (1936).

[2] P. A. A. van Mechelen, *op. cit.* pp. 37–64; A. Hoynck van Papendrecht, *A. van Hoboken en Co.* pp. 104–7.

[3] J. C. Westermann, *Gedenkboek*, I, 114–15, 171–3; A.R.A., Falck, B85, no. 199.

[4] C. Boissevain, *Onze voortrekkers*, p. 278; J. J. Reesse, *De suikerhandel van Amsterdam*, pp. 16, 81.

land Trading Company was not much more successful in its efforts to reduce the charges levied on trade by middlemen who, it was said, were struggling to maintain a social status beyond that proper to their economic functions and possible only in former days of Dutch monopoly.[1] The Company was importuned by Second Hand merchants and brokers who wished it to sell Javan produce only in large amounts, and by retailers and provincial tradesmen who wanted small quantities.[2] It attempted to pursue a liberal policy and to discipline the Second Hand, but after a time it found it advisable to abide in the main by the existing customs. The Amsterdam Chamber of Commerce, which had urged the Company on, was again surprised by the amount of opposition aroused.[3]

The Netherland Trading Company was not successful in its efforts to find foreign markets for national products. In South America, Belgian and Dutch cloth could not well compete against British, nor Belgian linens against direct imports from Germany, nor Belgian lace against cheap English tulle, nor Dutch cheese against the inferior product of the United States. The British consul in Peru concluded:[4]

The Netherland Society will thus find that a commerce restricted to its own products and those of Germany will not answer to any extent in these countries, and that numerous obstacles will oppose its importing successfully a proportion of goods from England and France.

The king insisted on unprofitable export experiments. In 1825, for instance, he persuaded the Company to relieve a corn glut in the Louvain district by sending a cargo to Brazil, which heated and had to be thrown overboard.[5] The attempt to export nails, cloth and other manufactured goods to Egypt in exchange for raw cotton was abandoned owing to the activity of Greek privateers.[6] The export of Leiden camlets to Canton in exchange for tea brought serious losses, but the king insisted that it should continue none the less, thus complying with the often repeated demand of the Leiden Chamber of Commerce for compulsory exports to Canton.[7]

The comparative success of its Javan trade soon led the Company to concentrate its efforts there. From 1829 it abandoned its Mediterranean

---

[1] A.R.A., Nat Nijv. en Kol., 2 April 1827, no. 15.

[2] A.R.A., Staatssec. 6518.

[3] W. M. F. Mansvelt, *Geschiedenis van de Nederlandsche Handelmaatschappij*, I, 167–78, 215–22, 256; J. C. Westermann, *Gedenkboek*, I, 200–1.

[4] *British Consular Reports on the Trade and Politics of Latin America*, Camden Soc., 3rd ser. (1940), LXIII, 135–7.

[5] A. J. L. van den Bogaerde de Ter-Brugge, *Essai*, II, 89.

[6] W. M. F. Mansvelt, *Geschiedenis van de Nederlandsche Handelmaatschappij*, I, 138–9.

[7] W. M. F. Mansvelt, *op. cit.* I, 177; W. L. D. van den Brink, *Bijdrage*, pp. 106–17.

activities, apart from arrangements to receive Turkish opium through another firm. In 1828 it abandoned trade in the Americas, and the king created a West Indian Company to renew the struggle there. The new Company was not very successful, but by 1830 Belgian industry had felt some benefit from its activity.

The Netherland Trading Company evoked more enthusiasm in Belgium than in Holland. A Belgian deputy said in 1826:[1]

All nations have turned their eyes towards industry, the sure and inexhaustible source of wealth; and towards foreign trade, which can give immense extension to industry. We alone seemed determined to remain in a lethargy that might have been mortal, but from which royal words called us. Our wise monarch believed that the time had come to forge new links between the two parts of the kingdom by employing the capital, ships and trade of the one to export the products of the other and to make them known in distant lands. He therefore founded the Netherland Trading Company. It is agreed that our industry has already felt the benefit of this great institution....A new source of prosperity is offered to us in our own colonies....It is to be hoped that the promises that have been made to us will be kept; namely that in future the colonies will be administered no longer in the interests of American, English or European commerce, but of our own.

The main opposition to the king's Javan policy came from a few die-hards of the Dutch commercial party. They expressed doubts as to whether his efforts were worthwhile, for greedy foreign eyes were fixed on Java, which would be lost in any new maritime war, and in any case it seemed to them unlikely that Java, alone among colonies, would remain unmoved by the new spirit of independence abroad in the world. They feared that great expense might be needed to maintain Dutch colonial power in the East, especially if the monopolistic tendencies of the Dutch Trading Company provoked a spirit of revolt among natives now familiar with the advantages of a free market. They therefore opposed guarantees by the Netherlands of loans contracted by the Indian government, and demanded that it should rely only on colonial revenues in suppressing Javan disaffection.[2] Such views were mainly an expression of bad temper towards the Netherland government. Van Hogendorp, however, condemned the whole system of William I on doctrinal grounds. The government, he said, had seen what was necessary in 1821; and had tried to return to free trade, in order to undo the damage it had caused by adopting the system of 1816 in a moment of panic at the Belgian industrial crisis. The

---

[1] *2de kamer*, 1825–6, A322; W. M. F. Mansvelt, *op. cit.* I, 174–8.
[2] *2de kamer*, 1825–6, A195, A212, A314 and B346–52, B368, B581.

government had not had the courage of its convictions, and was now trying to restore prosperity, not by free trade, but by privileges and monopoly, as in the case of the Netherland Trading Company. Its remedies were artificial, not natural.[1] Most Dutch merchants, however, came to admit that the king's policies deserved some credit for the modest revival in their trade after 1825.

In the long run, the road-, canal- and harbour-works instituted by the king, and criticized as extravagant by many cautious merchants—'as though we possessed a gold mine'[2]—were of great importance in equipping Dutch commerce to take advantage of future opportunities. The greatest opportunity came with the more rapid development, in the second half of the nineteenth century, of that transit trade which both the king and the merchants had for long disliked and opposed, being disturbed by the notion of a fleet of special steamers plying directly between London and Mainz or Frankfurt.[3]

The king could do little to remedy urban poverty in Holland. New industrial enterprises were subsidized, but proved abortive. Distress reached its maximum only in the 1840's.[4] All that the government achieved in the 1820's was the establishment of agricultural colonies in the eastern provinces for the deserving poor and of disciplinary institutions for the undeserving. Both were unpopular, and the government met a good deal of resistance in its attempt to force municipal authorities and charities to supply inmates.[5]

(c) The Belgian Revolution

A British observer thus described Belgian conditions as they had been on the eve of the revolution:[6]

The collieries of Hainault and the lower Meuse were in a state of full activity, with a constant demand from Holland and France. The armourers of Liége, and the clothiers of Verviers, were no less busily employed with extensive orders for the Levant, Germany and South America. The mines and forges of Luxemburg, the cutleries of Namur, the silk weavers of Tournai and Brussels, the paper manufactories of the upper Meuse, the refineries and cotton mills of Ghent, the linen trade of Courtrai and St Nicholas, were all at work. Each succeeding day witnessed the erection

[1] *Ged.* IX (2), 867–8.
[2] A.R.A., Van Hogendorp, 44, 5 (i), 3.   [3] *Ged.* VIII (1), 320.
[4] I. J. Brugmans, *De arbeidende klasse*, p. 152.
[5] *Ged.* IX (2), 896; F. Allan, *Geschiedenis en beschrijving van Haarlem* (Haarlem, 1888), p. 165.
[6] C. White, *The Belgic Revolution of 1830* (London, 1835), I, 89–90.

of buildings destined for manufacturing purposes, or was marked by the formation of new associations, for the exploitation of various novel sources of industry, either above or below the ground.

He considered much of this prosperity to be artificial, since over-production·was first stimulated by the Fund and then relieved by purchases by the Netherland Trading Company which were philanthropic rather than profitable.

The great vice of the system of the 'million of industry' was, that at at least one third of the manufacturers were thereby encouraged to push their produce beyond the demand or even the possibility of immediate consumption; and as the government generally intervened and purchased the excess, this led to a further glut in the market. Admitting, however, that the extreme anxiety of government to force produce, so as to bring it into competition with that of England, gave rise to many evils, and that it was highly impolitic to impose heavy prohibitive duties on commerce, in order wherewithal to subsidize manufactures,[1] still the system was productive of some benefits; for an extraordinary spirit of industry and speculative emulation was aroused throughout the country. A mass of capital that would otherwise have lain dormant was lavishly employed.... Employment was given to a large portion of the population, the demand for fuel was augmented, and the value of collieries and forests increased; a question of immense importance to Luxemburg and Liége, whose principal wealth is derived from the sale of wood, coal and mineral products. It is generally admitted, by practical men, that the southern provinces had reason to be satisfied with the measures of the king, as regarded the general industry of the kingdom.

The grievances that served as pretexts for the revolution were indeed not economic. Van Hogendorp was of opinion that 'the resentment of the Hollanders against the Belgians on the single point of the abandonment of free-trade is more profound and just than the resentment of the Belgians on all their grievances together can be against the Hollanders'.[2]

It has been suggested that William I's policy contributed to the Belgian Revolution by its very success; that the prosperity of Belgium made her more confident of her national destiny and less willing to remain a junior partner to the stagnant Dutch.[3] However, the groups that most gained by Dutch-Belgian union were Orangist. The merchants of Antwerp were naturally opposed to a revolution that for a time, as was expected, inter-

---

[1] The Fund of 1821, being designed as compensation for low import duties, was charged against customs revenue. The Dutch merchants liked to describe it as a levy on commerce for the benefit of industry.

[2] *Knuttel* 25938.

[3] R. Demoulin, *Guillaume Ier*, p. 12.

rupted their access to the sea; to the great temporary advantage of Dutch commerce.[1] Among the industrialists, the cotton-masters were most keenly Orangist, the coal and iron interests rather less so, and the woollen interests were comparatively moderate in their loyalty. Some Walloon industrialists hoped that the revolution would lead to reunion with France, but few wished for a separate national existence. The reasons they gave for their attitude were wholly economic; and were justified by events, for a severe industrial crisis, similar to that after the fall of Napoleon, followed the revolution.[2] The Belgian government tried to alleviate it by imitating many of the policies of William I.[3]

William I, however, did not succeed in giving his kingdom any real economic cohesion. The northern and southern provinces never formed a single national market, and their currencies remained separate for all ordinary purposes. The Dutch showed little interest in private investment in Belgium. In fact, the countries developed separately within the framework created by William I. Amsterdam merchants developed trading relations with Antwerp, as a more convenient port than their own for the south-west, similar to those they already had with Rotterdam. Otherwise, the Netherland Trading Company provided almost the only example of economic activity in which there was real co-operation between Dutch and Belgians.

Belgian Orangism proved remarkably ineffectual. As an English observer wrote after the revolution:[4]

Were Belgium now restored to the same commercial advantages that it enjoyed during the union, there would be no Orangism. For, in fact, Orangism is a mere commercial question; a question of interest, totally distinct from policy, patriotism or personal sympathy. It is in this that it essentially differs both from the Carlism of France and Spain, and the Miguelism of Portugal. In these countries, there is a degree of self-abnegation and chivalrous devotion in the conduct of the legitimists that ennobles their cause... but in Belgium scarcely a single instance can be advanced of an Orangist having made a single *voluntary* sacrifice, or having courted the slightest danger or risk, in support of the avowed object of his affections.

The main revolutionary element in 1830 in Belgium was the miscellaneous urban middle class, and especially the lawyers and other professional men. Moderate Belgians had for some time been advising the

---

[1] *Ged.* x (1), 289–90.
[2] *Ged.* x (4), 391–5.
[3] J. A. van Houtte, *Esquisse*, p. 177.
[4] C. White, *The Belgic Revolution*, ii, 99.

government of the dangerous discontent of educated young men for whom there were no longer such attractive opportunities as under Napoleon; the professions, they said, were overstocked, and the government would be well advised to make available as many appointments as possible, in the Indies perhaps, or under the Netherland Trading Company.[1] The presence of Dutch officials in Belgium was specially irritating to this class.

William I's policies provided increasing industrial employment for the increasing Belgian population, but hastened the growth of an urban proletariat exposed to the consequences of trade fluctuations and to all the disturbing experiences of industrial progress. The economic and emotional repercussions of the French revolution made Netherland officials in August 1830 aware of a serious danger of working-class unrest in Belgium. The Société Générale and the Netherland Trading Company proved most useful in keeping up the level of employment in the early stage of the crisis, but this did not prevent a wave of workers' demonstrations and machine-breaking from spreading across Belgium from northern France, and on to Aachen. This movement was not national in character, and the workers took up slogans without much discrimination: 'Vive la liberté' or 'Vive Napoléon'. Many of the machine-breakers seem not to have been the persons who worked on them, and the loyalty of Cockerill's men at Seraing prevented attacks on his works there. The machine-breakers were willing to agree, when it was pointed out to them, that Belgian industry could not compete against British without machines, but that did not cause them to desist.[2] Some Englishmen, indeed, hoped for considerable advantages from the Belgian disturbances:[3]

We should be able to derive great commercial advantages both for our colonial and native produce, and the more so as from the irrevocable separation from Holland, Ghent and St Nicholas must sink into comparative ruin, whilst our colonies would probably monopolise the Antwerp market.... It would likewise be no difficult matter to obtain for ourselves an advantageous commercial treaty, which might open a still greater field for our manufactures, for it is positive that the separation will be the death-blow to the *haut-commerce* and leading industry of this country.

The Belgian middle classes had no difficulty in controlling the outbreaks of machine-breaking and sheer plunder. The revolutionary organizations

[1] A.R.A., Staatssec. 6518.
[2] C. White, *The Belgic Revolution*, I, 191, 235 and 265; *Ged.* x (4), 77–87, 52.
[3] *Ged.* x (1), 95.

used the working-class movement to intimidate the Orangists. The workers of Antwerp were encouraged to demonstrate outside the Bourse against Orangist merchants, and the property of industrialists who were too active in their Orangism was made a special target for attack. Later, when it became clear that the revolution had brought unemployment, the Orangists managed to organize a few workers' demonstrations in their own cause.[1]

[1] *Ged.* x (4), 317, 439.

Table XVII.   *Netherland tariffs and trade 1819–27* [1]

	CUSTOMS DUTIES					FOREIGN TRADE					
	Tariff of 1819		Tariff of 1822			(Av. 1824–7)			Imports (av. 1825–6) (incl. trans.)		
	In	Out	In	Out	Trans.	In	Out	Trans.	Amsterdam	Rotterdam	Antwerp
INDUSTRIAL GOODS (METAL)											
	% ad valorem					Value in £000's:					
Clockwork	10	2	6	½	1	12	1	1	—	—	—
Copper, coin	—	—	6	—	—	2	10	—	—	—	—
Copper, work of	10	—	6	½	1	18	2	3	1	4	1
Cutlery	12	—	6	½	1	2	3	12	1	1	—
Fire-arms	10	—	6	½	1	1	82	7	—	—	1
Gold and silver, work of	10	—	6	½	1	15	6	2	1	1	3
Machinery	—	15	6[2]	½	1	10	19	3	3	2	2
Small-ware	8	—	6	½	1	90	24	20	2	4	3
Steel, work of	8	—	6	½	1	4	2	12	1	2	2
White-iron, work of	12	—	6	½	1	9	2	—	1	2	—
	Florins per 100 kg.:					In £000's:		In 000's kg.:			
Copper, unwrought	0·30	81·0	0·60	0·60	0·60	86	17	196	649	291	314
Copper wrought	1·52	0·35	6·0	0·40	1·50	69	4	86	173	457	27
Iron, pig	0·05	1·01	0·25	1·0	0·20	10	21	58	13	68	52
Iron, bar	4·05	0·05	4·25	0·05	0·20	61	13	1,056	1,342	1,480	480
Iron, cast, work of	6·07	0·10	6·30	0·10	0·20	3	9	449	54	123	20
Iron, wrought, work of	10·12	0·10	10·35	0·10	0·60	15	14	363	57	292	24
Iron, nails	6·07	0·10	6·30	0·10	0·60	1	35	6	—	1	3
Lead	1·01	0·10	1·35	0·10	0·80	90	8	15	1,791	1,012	1,025
Steel	—	—	0·40	0·20	0·40	28	10	182	1	21	25
Tin	0·81	1·21	1·50	0·50	1·20	30	20	89	65	173	85
Tin, work of	10·12	0·35	10·0	0·35	0·80	3	2	—	—	5	12
White-iron	6·07	0·20	6·30	0·20	1·60	11	1	150	6	26	1
Zinc	1·21	0·40	2·0	0·25	1·0	4	31	75	55	5	142
INDUSTRIAL GOODS (TEXTILES)											
	% ad valorem					Value in £000's:					
Bed-tick	12	—	6	½	1	1	17	—	—	—	—
Braid	10	—	6	½	1	10	4	1	—	—	—
Carpets	10	—	10	½	1	6	7	—	1	2	—
Clothes, new	10	—	10	½	1	4	18	2	—	2	—
Drapers' goods	8	—	6	½	1	560	64	12	63	65	56
Gauze and marley	3	—	3	¼	1	39	17	1	2	3	1
Lace	10	—	6	—	1	40	30	6	—	—	—
Linens, unbleached	2	—	1	—	½	252	530	6	45	3	2
Linens, bleached	4	—									
Linens, dyed, etc.	4	—	3	—	1	19	1	—	5	—	—
Linens, damask	5	—	3	—	1	14	21	—	—	—	—
Linens, cambric	5	—	2	—	½	9	—	6	1	6	—
Linen yarn, raw	—	3	½	3	1	50	34	17	27	—	—
Linen yarn for weaving	1	1	1	1	1	7	4	17	—	—	—

[1] J. A. Drieling, *Bijdragen*; *Staatsblad*.   [2] Might be remitted by royal licence.

Table XVII (cont.)

	CUSTOMS DUTIES					FOREIGN TRADE					
	Tariff of 1819		Tariff of 1822			(Av. 1824–7)			Imports (av. 1825–6) (incl. trans.)		
	In	Out	In	Out	Trans.	In	Out	Trans.	Am-sterdam	Rotter-dam	Ant-werp
INDUSTRIAL GOODS (TEXTILES, cont.)											
	% ad valorem					Value in £ooo's:					
Linen yarn (sewing thread)	12	—	6	½	1	7	19	—	—	—	—
Millinery	10	—	10	½	1	28	4	11	—	—	4
Nankinettes	10	—	10	½	1	24	2	—	5	1	1
Ribbons	6	—	6	½	1	46	3	17	—	—	—
Socks, etc.	10	—	10	½	1	35	4	2	1	2	1
Socks, etc. Iceland and Scottish (for seamen)	3	—	3	½	1	18	—	—	5	1	—
	Florins per 100 kg.:					In £ooo's:			In ooo's kg:		
Cotton yarn, raw	40·48	0·35	40·0	1·0	2·0	—	11	1,962	9	1,206	19
Cotton yarn, twist	48·57	0·35	50·0	0·50	2·50	54	4	28	7	46	7
Cotton, raw	0·81	1·52	0·80	1·50	1·50	410	90	1,568	1,100	1,900	2,300
Cottons, cloth white	60·72	0·35	60·0	0·35	3·0	88	32	35	11	95	64
Cottons, printed	70·84	0·35	70·0	0·35	3·50	253	50	24	13	150	66
Silk, raw	0·35	10·12	2·0	10·0	3·0	16	1	11	2	4	8
Silk, thrown	20·0	10·0	20·0	10·0	4·0	5	—	—	—	—	—
Silk, sewing thread	40·0	10·0	40·0	10·0	4·0	13	1	1	—	—	—
Turkish thread, raw	2·02	4·05	2·0	4·0	2·0	11	2	—	33	14	—
Turkish thread, dyed, etc.	12·14	2·02	12·0	2·0	2·50	1	8	—	—	—	—
	% ad valorem					Value in £ooo's:					
Silks	6	—	6	½	1	93	8	25	1	2	2
	% ad valorem		Florins per 100 kg.:			In £ooo's:			In ooo's kg.:		
Woollen cloth	8	—	40·0–150·0	—	5·0	129	266	33	4	4	1
Woollen yarn, raw	3	3	6·0	1·0	1·75	14	2	2	1	33	—
Woollen, yarn, twist	4	1	8·0	0·50	2·0	12	5	2	—	7	2
	% ad valorem		Florins per roll:			In £ooo's:			Rolls:		
Sail-cloth	2	—	0·50	—	0·25	5	5	140	1000	90	370
INDUSTRIAL GOODS (MISCELLANEOUS)											
	% ad valorem					Value in £ooo's:					
Bones,[3] boiled	—	8	½	6	1	—	13	—	—	—	—
Furniture	10	—	6	½	1	7	13	1	1	1	—
Glass	4–12	—	4–6	½	1	29	13	2	5	2	—
Hats	15	—	10	½	1	8	8	3	1	3	—
Paper	15	—	15	½	1	2	33	2	—	—	—
Pottery, common earthenware	15	—	6	½	1	8	2	1	—	—	—
Rabbit skins	—	4[4]	1	6	1	51	3	2	2	1	2

[3] Unboiled bones prohibited for export and transit under both tariffs.
[4] 12 % if exported by land (or river).

Table XVII (*cont.*)

| | CUSTOMS DUTIES | | | | | FOREIGN TRADE | | | | | |
| | Tariff of 1819 | | Tariff of 1822 | | | (Av. 1824–7) | | | Imports (av. 1825–6) (incl. trans.) | | |
	In	Out	In	Out	Trans.	In	Out	Trans.	Amsterdam	Rotterdam	Antwerp
INDUSTRIAL GOODS (MISCELLANEOUS, *cont.*)											
	% ad valorem		Florins per 100 kg.:			In £000's:			In 000's kg.:		
Books, un-bound	3	2	15·0	5·0	10·0	34	6	4	1	2	1
Books, bound	5	2	20·0	3·0	10·0	11	20	8	2	3	1
Porcelain, white	10	—	10·0	0·50	1·0	40	11	4	7	1	—
Pottery, fine	12	—	6·0	0·30	0·60	78	6	59	227	556	81
Rabbit hair	1	12	8·0	48·0	2·0	4	5	10	—	—	—
Smalts	1	—	0·60	0·30	0·60	71	9	11	381	5	35
	Florins per 100 kg.:										
Coal	0·69	—	0·70	0·01	0·30	4	308	275	150	770	—
Glue	4·05	—	4·0	0·20	1·50	2	7	—	1	8	1
Gunpowder	16·19	1·01	16·0	1·0	2·0	1	2	—	—	—	—
Oakum	0·10	2·02	0·10	2·0	0·10	5	11	—	—	—	—
Saltpetre, raw	1·01	4·05	1·0	0·50	1·0	6	1	205	—	117	180
Saltpetre, refined	1·01	4·05	1·50	0·20	1·50	4	1	52	—	116	73
Turnsole	3·04	0·35	3·0	0·25	1·80	—	19	—	3	—	1
White lead	4·05	0·10	4·0	0·10	1·20	—	42	1	1	—	4
	Florins per barrel:					In £000's:			Barrels (in 000's):		
Beer,	(Excise,[5] only)		6·0	0·50	1·50	—	7	—	—	—	—
Spirits, in barrels	(Excise,[5] only)		1·0	1·50	1·50	67	113	2	3	4	3
AGRICULTURAL GOODS											
	% ad valorem					Value in £000's:					
Bulbs	—	—	¼	¼	¼	—	9	—	—	—	—
Flax, un-heckled	—	4	¼	4	1	1	490	—	—	—	—
Flax, heckled	5	—	5	½	1	—	26	—	—	—	—
Hides, salt or fresh	—	5[6]	1	6	1	2	80	1	—	—	1
Tan-bark, raw	—	1½	¼	1½	¼	15	110	98	—	—	—
Tan-bark, milled	6	1½	6	½	2	—	5	—	—	—	—
Wool	—	2[7]	—	1[7]	1	268	133	1	8	—	10
	Florins per quarter:					In £000's:			Quarters (in 000's):		
Barley	0·34	0·04	0·45	0·04	0·25	97	20	10	20	17	—
Beans	0·55	0·05	0·60	0·06	0·24	5	31	1	2	—	—
Buckwheat	0·85	0·05	0·90	0·06	0·24	10	19	—	5	—	—
Oats	0·20	0·04	0·25	0·03	0·10	14	120	1	12	—	2
Rye	0·45	0·04	0·50	0·05	0·16	151	6	14	38	12	—
Seed, rape etc., for oil	0·15	1·00[8]	0·20	1·0	0·60	216	50	—	79	4	2
Seed, clover	0·10	0·60	0·10	0·60	0·30	71	113	—	—	—	—
Wheat	0·65	0·08	0·75	0·06	0·25	205	48	—	52	2	—
	Florins per 100 kg.:					In £000's:			In 000's kg.:		
Butter	3·04	3·04	3·0	1·50	1·50	3	610	1	1	—	—
Cheese	4·05	0·67	5·0	0·50	1·50	5	521	11	—	—	2
Hops	—	—	0·60	0·30	0·30	—	21	1	—	2	2
Madder, powder	6·02	1·01	6·0	1·0	2·0	3	180	16	—	—	11
	% ad val.:		Florins per 100 kg.:			In £000's:			In 000's kg.:		
Chicory, roots	1	1	0·05	0·05	0·05	—	3	—	—	—	—
Chicory pre-pared	15	—	1·20	0·10	0·60	—	—	—	—	—	—

[5] The excise on foreign beer and spirits was higher than on home produced.
[6] 15 % if exported across the land frontier.
[7] 1819—Export duty for foreign wool in original bales, 1 %. 1822—Power reserved for the king to prohibit exports at any time across any sections of the land frontier.
[8] 1·50 florins if exported across the land frontier.

Table XVII (cont.)

	CUSTOMS DUTIES					FOREIGN TRADE					
	Tariff of 1819		Tariff of 1822			(Av. 1824–7)			Imports (av. 1825–6) (incl. trans.)		
	In	Out	In	Out	Trans.	In	Out	Trans.	Amsterdam	Rotterdam	Antwerp
AGRICULTURAL GOODS (cont.)											
	Florins per head:					In £000's:		In 000's:			
Cattle	20·0	1·50	20·0	1·0	1·50	—	126	—	—	—	—
Horses	6·0	3·50	6·0	3·0	2·0	19	133	1	—	—	—
Pigs	1·50	0·50	1·50	0·30	0·50	—	152	—	—	—	—
	Florins per 100 kg.:					In £000's:		In 000's kg.:			
Oil-cakes	0·10	1·01[9]	0·10	1·0[9]	0·50	36	41	—	18	—	—
	Florins per barrel:					In £000's:		Barrels (in 000's):			
Seed-oil	5·80	0·13	5·80	0·20	0·80	1	38	1	2	—	—
			Florins per barrel:			In £000's:		Barrels (in 000's):			
Wine, in barrels	(Excise,[10] only)		0·10	1·0	1·0	347	6	22	60	40	62
			Florins per 100 bottles:			In £000's:		Bottles (in 000's):			
Wine, in bottles	(Excise[10] only)		5·0	0·50	1·50	10	4	28	—	—	87
COMMERCIAL GOODS											
	% ad valorem					Value in £000's:					
Cork, raw	3	2	1	½	1	3	—	—	1	—	—
Corks, cut	20		10	½	1	7	—	—	—	1	1
Drugs	3	2	1	½	1	19	11	1	6	3	4
Herring, Dutch	—	—	—	—	—	—	47	—	—	—	—
Spices	3[11]	2	3[11]	½	1	29	31	1	13	19	2
	Florins per 100 kg.:					In £000's:		In 000's kg.:			
Ashes, pot- and pearl-	0·51	0·51	0·80	0·40	0·50	262	10	188	1,224	527	3,508
Borax, raw	4·05	0·10	1·0	3·0	1·0	1	—	—	—	9	—
Borax, refined	8·10	0·10	6·0	0·20	2·0	—	2	—	3	—	—
Cables and rigging	10·12	0·61[12]	10·0	0·20[12]	1·50	—	6	6	2	1	6
Cochenille	9·74	3·04	10·0	3·00	3·00	12	5	1	1	—	3
Cocoa	3·04	0·30	1·50	0·30	0·30	37	4	12	45	5	146
Cod	0·10	0·25	0·30	0·15	0·15	91	18	10	906	491	43
Coffee	1·0[11]	0·20	2·0[13]	0·50	1·0	2,067	538	2,178	7,500	6,450	16,000
Hemp, unheckled	0·51	0·67	0·65	0·65	0·50	78	1	11	1,253	251	139
Hemp, heckled	2·70	0·51	3·0	0·50	1·0	—	1	—	—	—	—
Hides, prepared	14·17[14]	0·20	15·0	0·30	1·50	8	113	52	3	3	—
Indigo	4·01	4·05	4·0	2·0	2·50	183	54	138	7	86	208
Pepper	6·07	4·05	1·50	0·50	1·0	71	10	251	44	220	715
Raisins	0·40	0·30	0·40	0·20	0·40	50	6	50	630	800	326
Rice	0·25	0·25	0·30	0·20	0·30	130	25	10	1,300	1,250	2,700
Salt, raw, in foreign ships	2·02	—[16]	2·0	Prohibited[15]		1	—	—	—	350	—
Salt, raw in Netherland ships	—	—[16]	—	Prohibited[15]		74	—	—	800	4,300	22,500
Salt, refined	2·02	—[16]	16·0	—[16]	Prohibited	—	9	—	3	—	—

9 Duty for maritime exports via Hellevoetsluis might be reduced by royal licence to 0·40 florins.
10 At a much higher rate than for home-grown.
11 Exempt if imported directly from Batavia. Import of 'foreign' cloves prohibited in 1819.
12 Export prohibited if old and unserviceable.
13 Exempt if imported directly from Batavia in a Netherland ship.
14 24·29 florins if imported across the land frontier.
15 Royal Licences might be granted at a duty of 0·05 florins per 100 kg. for export by sea only[16].
16 Excise drawback granted, as for other excise goods, with discrimination against foreign refined.

Table XVII (*cont.*)

| | CUSTOMS DUTIES | | | | | FOREIGN TRADE | | | | | |
| | Tariff of 1819 | | Tariff of 1822 | | | (Av. 1824–7) | | | Imports (av. 1825–6) (incl. trans.) | | |
	In	Out	In	Out	Trans.	In	Out	Trans.	Amsterdam	Rotterdam	Antwerp
COMMERCIAL GOODS (*cont.*)											
	Florins per 100 kg.:					In £000's:		In millions of kg.:			
Sugar, raw	0·60	1·50	1·20[17]	1·50	1·50	1,037	2	1	10	4	11
								In 000's kg.:			
Sugar, refined	20·0	0·20	36·0	0·20	2·00	—	439	200	23	87	30
Tar	0·11	0·03	0·05	0·02	0·05	19	3	9	1,260	240	321
Tea	16·19[18]–32·38	0·35	18·0[18]–34·0	0·35	Prohibited	311	17	—	746	335	344
Tuf, raw	0·02	0·24	0·04	0·20	0·50	14	—	—	—	—	—
Tuf, milled	0·81	0·08	0·80	0·05	0·10	5	3	308	1	—	—
	% ad valorem		Florins per 100 kg.:			In £000's:		In 000's kg.:			
Dyewoods[19]	1	2	0·10–2·0	0·10–2·0	0·10–2·0	70	27	170	874	1,090	2,806
Hides, dried[20]	1	1	1·0	1·0	1·0	182	15	1,560	196	226	4,600
Tobacco, American and West Indian, in leaf	2	2	1·10–2·50	0·30–2·00	0·65–2·0	337	78	102	2,661	3,242	52
Tobacco, home, and other European	2	—	0·65	0·50	0·20	3	36	57	25	34	5
Tobacco, prepared	3–8	0–1	0·80–12·0	0·20	0·40–4·0	14	222	100	207	309	35
	Florins per ship's ton:					In £000's:		In 000's tons:			
Timber, complete cargoes, unsawn, from Norway etc.	0·25	—	0·25	—	—	260	—	—	69	6	54
	% ad valorem					Value in £000's:					
Timber, other unsawn, including raft huts	3	—	2½	1	1	121	19	5	—	1	—
Timber, planks and beams	2	½	6	½	1	18	28	—	2	1	—
	Florins per barrel:					In £000's:		Barrels (in 000's):			
Train oil, foreign	1·37	0·23	1·0	0·25	1·0	37	20	—	8	3	1
Train oil, Dutch	—	0·23	—	0·25	—	—	18	—	—	—	—

[17] Duty reduced to 0·50 florins if imported in Netherland ship.
[18] Tea imported in Netherland ships: 1819—5·06–10·12 florins; 1822—7·0–12·0 florins.
[19] Milled dyewoods were prohibited for import and transit in both tariffs.
[20] Dried Netherland hides were treated as 'salt or fresh' for export duty.

Annual average value of TOTAL IMPORTS 1824–7   £11½ m.
Annual average value of TOTAL EXPORTS 1824–7   £8 m.
N.B. The tariff of 1819 was a revised version of that of 1816.

Table XVIII

Ships entering ports in the Netherlands in 1829

A.R.A. Staatssec. 6516.

	NETHERLAND SHIPS				BRITISH SHIPS			
	With cargo		In ballast		With cargo		In ballast	
	No. of ships	Total tons	No. of ships	Total tons	No. of ships	Total tons	No. of ships	Total tons
Arrived from								
Mecklenburg (Lübeck, etc.)	173	18,447	68	1,949	2	244	—	—
Hanover	150	4,941	21	616	—	—	—	—
Denmark	94	5,433	—	—	—	—	—	—
Prussia	459	34,728	—	—	9	962	1	35
Russia	249	30,427	—	—	28	4,067	—	—
Sweden and Norway	358	31,103	6	221	1	125	1	67
United Kingdom	669	62,062	109	6,737	757	82,533	408	28,481
France	166	15,917	27	1,372	6	825	1	8
Portugal	50	4,901	5	176	2	235	—	—
Spain	24	2,536	1	41	10	1,131	—	—
Italy	16	1,787	—	—	6	1,053	—	—.
Levant, Egypt and Barbary Coast	25	3,673	—	—	3	463	—	—·
Cape of Good Hope and East Indies	58	20,593	—	—	19	7,446	—	—
China	3	1,561	—	—	—	—	—	—
Ports of South American Governments (Pacific)	2	322	—	—	—	—	—	—
Ports of South American Governments (Atlantic)	21	4,248	1	600	33	5,625	—	—
Curacao	2	439	—	—	—	—	—	—
Brazil	14	2,628	—	—	58	10,725	—	—
Berbice and Demerara	12	3,330	—	—	—	—	—	—
Surinam	60	15,902	—	—	—	—	—	—
Mexico	1	159	—	—	—	—	—	—
North America	16	2,560	—	—	18	4,273	—	—
Greenland and Davis Straits	2	614	—	—	—	—	—	—
Undeclared	7	594	4	167	2	151	1	7
TOTAL	2,631	268,905	242	11,879	954	119,858	412	28,598

Table XVIII (*cont.*)

	UNITED STATES SHIPS				FRENCH SHIPS			
	With cargo		In ballast		With cargo		In ballast	
	No. of ships	Total tons	No. of ships	Total tons	No. of ships	Total tons	No. of ships	Total tons
Arrived from								
Mecklenburg (Lübeck, etc.)	—	—	—	—	—	—	—	—
Hanover	—	—	—	—	—	—	—	—
Denmark	—	—	—	—	—	—	—	—
Prussia	—	—	—	—	1	31	—	—
Russia	—	—	—	—	—	—	—	—
Sweden and Norway	—	—	—	—	—	—	—	—
United Kingdom	1	123	—	—	14	487	16	1,232
France	—	—	—	—	42	3,200	26	1,119
Portugal	—	—	—	—	—	—	—	—
Spain	1	281	—	—	—	—	—	—
Italy	2	508	—	—	—	—	—	—
Levant, Egypt and Barbary Coast	—	—	—	—	—	—	—	—
Cape of Good Hope and East Indies	6	2,286	—	—	—	—	—	—
China	1	310	—	—	—	—	—	—
Ports of South American Governments (Pacific)	—	—	—	—	—	—	—	—
Ports of South American Governments (Atlantic)	32	8,088	—	—	4	1,203	—	—
Curacao	—	—	—	—	—	—	—	—
Brazil	—	—	—	—	1	162	—	—
Berbice and Demerara	—	—	—	—	—	—	—	—
Surinam	—	—	—	—	—	—	—	—
Mexico	—	—	—	—	—	—	—	—
North America	174	46,077	—	—	1	193	—	—
Greenland and Davis Straits	—	—	—	—	—	—	—	—
Undeclared	—	—	1	252	—	—	—	—
TOTAL	217	57,673	1	252	63	5,276	42	2,351

Table XVIII (*cont.*)

	Russian Ships		Swedish Ships		Norwegian Ships		Danish Ships			
	With cargo		With cargo		With cargo		With cargo		In ballast	
	No. of ships	Total tons	No. of ships	Total tons	No. of ships	Total tons	No. of ships	Total tons	No. of ships	Total tons
Arrived from										
Mecklenburg (Lübeck, etc.)	—	—	—	—	—	—	96	3,193	—	—
Hanover	—	—	—	—	—	—	10	429	1	27
Denmark	—	—	2	184	1	50	169	7,391	1	30
Prussia	2	234	5	732	7	952	34	1,804	—	—
Russia	49	9,577	27	4,928	55	11,727	25	3,355	—	—
Sweden and Norway	3	457	37	3,984	363	74,345	7	657	—	—
United Kingdom	—	—	—	—	1	86	—	—	—	—
France	—	—	6	935	7	975	4	663	—	—
Portugal	—	—	—	—	—	—	1	125	—	—
Spain	—	—	2	402	2	75	2	245	—	—
Italy	—	—	7	942	3	419	4	431	—	—
Levant, Egypt and Barbary Coast	—	—	4	894	2	320	1	169	—	—
Cape of Good Hope and East Indies	1	350	—	—	—	—	—	—	—	—
China	—	—	—	—	—	—	—	—	—	—
Ports of South American Governments (Pacific)	—	—	—	—	—	—	1	160	—	—
Ports of South American Governments (Atlantic)	—	—	—	—	—	—	3	705	—	—
Curacao	—	—	—	—	—	—	—	—	—	—
Brazil	—	—	1	259	—	—	1	200	—	—
Berbice and Demerara	—	—	—	—	—	—	—	—	—	—
Surinam	—	—	—	—	—	—	—	—	—	—
Mexico	—	—	—	—	—	—	—	—	—	—
North America	—	—	8	1,462	1	120	1	181	—	—
Greenland and Davis Straits	—	—	—	—	—	—	—	—	—	—
Undeclared	—	—	—	—	—	—	—	—	—	—
Total	55	10,618	99	14,722	442	89,069	359	19,708	2	57

Table XVIII (*cont.*)

	Prussian Ships		Hanoverian Ships				Mecklenburg Ships		Oldenburg Ships	
	With cargo		With cargo		In ballast		With cargo		With cargo	
	No. of ships	Total tons	No. of ships	Total tons	No. of ships	Total tons	No. of ships	Total tons	No. of ships	Total tons
Arrived from										
Mecklenburg (Lübeck, etc.)	—	—	85	3,285	—	—	4	604	54	1,895
Hanover	—	—	292	9,111	1	24	—	—	94	3,159
Denmark	1	152	22	1,025	—	—	1	79	11	364
Prussia	130	19,191	87	7,876	—	—	11	1,805	7	427
Russia	78	13,535	86	11,074	—	—	136	22,370	—	—
Sweden and Norway	1	147	33	3,422	—	—	1	141	1	79
United Kingdom	—	—	2	124	1	41	1	121	—	—
France	16	2,940	32	3,083	—	—	—	—	3	384
Portugal	—	—	—	—	—	—	—	—	—	—
Spain	—	—	—	—	—	—	—	—	—	—
Italy	—	—	3	419	—	—	—	—	—	—
Levant, Egypt and Barbary Coast	—	—	—	—	—	—	—	—	—	—
Cape of Good Hope and East Indies	—	—	—	—	—	—	—	—	—	—
China	—	—	—	—	—	—	—	—	—	—
Ports of South American Governments (Pacific)	—	—	—	—	—	—	—	—	—	—
Ports of South American Governments (Atlantic)	—	—	—	—	—	—	—	—	—	—
Curacao	—	—	1	64	—	—	—	—	—	—
Brazil	1	250	—	—	—	—	—	—	—	—
Berbice and Demerara	—	—	—	—	—	—	—	—	—	—
Surinam	—	—	—	—	—	—	—	—	—	—
Mexico	—	—	—	—	—	—	—	—	—	—
North America	—	—	—	—	—	—	—	—	—	—
Greenland and Davis Straits	—	—	—	—	—	—	—	—	—	—
Undeclared	—	—	—	—	—	—	—	—	—	—
Total	227	36,215	643	39,483	2	65	154	25,120	170	6,308

Table XVIII (*cont.*)

	Lübeck Ships		Bremen Ships		Hamburg Ships		Rostock Ships		Austrian Ships	
	With cargo		With cargo		With cargo		With cargo		With cargo	
	No. of ships	Total tons	No. of ships	Total tons	No. of ships	Total tons	No. of ships	Total tons	No. of ships	Total tons
Arrived from										
Mecklenburg (Lübeck, etc.)	—	—	1	120	12	457	—	—	—	—
Hanover	—	—	—	—	5	190	—	—	—	—
Denmark	—	—	—	—	6	247	—	—	—	—
Prussia	1	114	1	203	3	153	—	—	—	—
Russia	5	858	5	822	9	1,212	1	190	—	—
Sweden and Norway	—	—	—	—	3	168	—	—	—	—
United Kingdom	—	—	—	—	—	—	—	—	—	—
France	1	150	5	894	5	554	—	—	—	—
Portugal	—	—	—	—	1	70	—	—	—	—
Spain	—	—	—	—	—	—	—	—	—	—
Italy	—	—	—	—	—	—	—	—	1	367
Levant, Egypt and Barbary Coast	—	—	—	—	—	—	—	—	1	348
Cape of Good Hope and East Indies	—	—	—	—	—	—	—	—	—	—
China	—	—	—	—	—	—	—	—	—	—
Ports of South American Governments (Pacific)	—	—	—	—	—	—	—	—	—	—
Ports of South American Governments (Atlantic)	—	—	—	—	2	480	—	—	—	—
Curacao	—	—	—	—	—	—	—	—	—	—
Brazil	—	—	—	—	1	250	—	—	—	—
Berbice and Demerara	—	—	—	—	—	—	—	—	—	—
Surinam	—	—	—	—	—	—	—	—	—	—
Mexico	—	—	—	—	—	—	—	—	—	—
North America	—	—	—	—	—	—	—	—	—	—
Greenland and Davis Straits	—	—	—	—	—	—	—	—	—	—
Undeclared	—	—	—	—	—	—	—	—	—	—
TOTAL	7	1,122	12	2,039	47	3,781	1	190	2	715

Table XVIII (*cont.*)

| | EAST FRISIAN SHIPS | | EMDEN SHIPS | | NEAPOLITAN SHIPS | | SPANISH SHIPS | | | |
| | With cargo | | With cargo | | With cargo | | With cargo | | In ballast | |
	No. of ships	Total tons	No. of ships	Total tons	No. of ships	Total tons	No. of ships	Total tons	No. of ships	Total tons
Arrived from										
Mecklenburg (Lübeck, etc.)	2	75	—	—	—	—	—	—	—	—
Hanover	—	—	2	74	—	—	—	—	—	—
Denmark	—	—	—	—	—	—	—	—	—	—
Prussia	1	36	—	—	—	—	—	—	—	—
Russia	—	—	—	—	—	—	—	—	—	—
Sweden and Norway	—	—	—	—	—	—	—	—	—	—
United Kingdom	—	—	—	—	—	—	—	—	2	107
France	—	—	—	—	—	—	—	—	—	—
Portugal	—	—	—	—	—	—	—	—	—	—
Spain	—	—	—	—	—	—	2	109	—	—
Italy	—	—	—	—	3	680	—	—	—	—
Levant, Egypt and Barbary Coast	—	—	—	—	4	843	—	—	—	—
Cape of Good Hope and East Indies	—	—	—	—	—	—	—	—	—	—
China	—	—	—	—	—	—	—	—	—	—
Ports of South American Governments (Pacific)	—	—	—	—	—	—	—	—	—	—
Ports of South American Governments (Atlantic)	—	—	—	—	—	—	—	—	—	—
Curacao	—	—	—	—	—	—	—	—	—	—
Brazil	—	—	—	—	—	—	—	—	—	—
Berbice and Demerara	—	—	—	—	—	—	—	—	—	—
Surinam	—	—	—	—	—	—	—	—	—	—
Mexico	—	—	—	—	—	—	—	—	—	—
North America	—	—	—	—	—	—	—	—	—	—
Greenland and Davis Straits	—	—	—	—	—	—	—	—	—	—
Undeclared	—	—	—	—	—	—	—	—	—	—
TOTAL	3	111	2	74	7	1,523	2	109	2	107

Table XVIII (*cont.*)

| | Ships of Buenos Aires | | Total | | | |
| | With cargo | | With cargo | | In ballast | |
	No. of ships	Total tons	No. of ships	Total tons	No. of ships	Total tons
Arrived from						
Mecklenburg (Lübeck, etc.)	—	—	429	28,320	68	1,949
Hanover	—	—	553	17,904	23	667
Denmark	—	—	307	14,925	1	30
Prussia	—	—	758	69,248	1	35
Russia	—	—	753	114,142	—	—
Sweden and Norway	—	—	808	114,628	7	288
United Kingdom	—	—	1,445	145,536	536	36,598
France	—	—	293	30,520	54	2,499
Portugal	—	—	54	5,331	5	176
Spain	—	—	43	4,779	1	41
Italy	—	—	45	6,606	—	—
Levant, Egypt and Barbary Coast	—	—	40	6,710	—	—
Cape of Good Hope and East Indies	—	—	84	30,675	—	—
China	—	—	4	1,871	—	—
Ports of South American Governments (Pacific)	—	—	3	482	—	—
Ports of South American Governments (Atlantic)	1	164	96	20,513	1	600
Curacao	—	—	3	503	—	—
Brazil	—	—	77	14,474	—	—
Berbice and Demerara	—	—	12	3,330	—	—
Surinam	—	—	60	15,902	—	—
Mexico	—	—	1	159	—	—
North America	—	—	219	54,866	—	—
Greenland and Davis Straits	—	—	2	614	—	—
Undeclared	—	—	9	745	6	426
Total	1	164	6,098	702,783	703	43,309

Table XIX

Ships leaving ports in the Netherlands in 1829

A.R.A. Staatssec. 6516.

Destination	NETHERLAND SHIPS				BRITISH SHIPS			
	With cargo		In ballast		With cargo		In ballast	
	No. of ships	Total tons	No. of ships	Total tons	No. of ships	Total tons	No. of ships	Total· tons
Mecklenburg (Lübeck, etc.)	210	19,063	11	395	2	187	—	—
Hanover	71	2,315	88	3,005	—	—	—	—
Denmark	19	1,359	8	657	—	—	—	—
Prussia	49	3,718	149	12,944	—	—	7	1,933
Russia	77	9,170	87	11,560	2	427	14	3,289
Sweden and Norway	84	7,783	190	16,221	4	119	1	383
United Kingdom	714	58,922	119	15,176	1,186	115,143	69	12,637
France	206	16,715	21	2,440	4	70	3	319
Portugal	43	3,207	5	676	2	11	1	311
Spain	38	3,345	5	577	1	85	5	858
Italy	10	1,332	—	—	1	113	—	—
Levant, Egypt and Barbary Coast	4	583	1	103	—	—	—	—
Canaries, Azores and Cape Verde Islands	1	333	—	—	—	—	—	—
Coast of Guinea	1	87	—	—	—	—	—	—
Cape of Good Hope and East Indies	62	22,838	1	298	2	475	—	—
China	—	—	—	—	—	—	—	—
Ports of South American Governments (Pacific)	3	302	—	—	—	—	—	—
Ports of South American Governments (Atlantic)	19	4,515	—	—	4	519	4	877
Curacao	2	273	—	—	—	—	—	—
Brazil	14	2,199	1	139	1	240	2	582
Berbice and Demerara	8	2,591	—	—	1	142	—	—
Surinam	66	16,513	1	359	—	—	—	—
Mexico	—	—	—	—	—	—	—	—
North America	10	1,522	1	378	3	482	3	1,465
Greenland and Davis Straits	—	—	2	625	—	—	—	—
Undeclared	6	628	499	38,956	1	18	8	993
TOTAL	1,717	179,313	1,189	104,501	1,214	118,031	117	23,647

Table XIX (cont.)

	UNITED STATES SHIPS				FRENCH SHIPS			
	With cargo		In ballast		With cargo		In ballast	
	No. of ships	Total tons	No. of ships	Total tons	No. of ships	Total tons	No. of ships	Total tons
Destination								
Mecklenburg (Lübeck, etc.)	—	—	—	—	—	—	—	—
Hanover	—	—	—	—	—	—	—	—
Denmark	—	—	—	—	—	—	—	—
Prussia	1	226	1	179	—	—	—	—
Russia	1	285	2	384	—	—	—	—
Sweden and Norway	4	1,068	16	4,535	5	69	—	—
United Kingdom	4	1,058	17	5,738	16	540	—	—
France	1	331	1	188	77	5,748	6	417
Portugal	5	1,473	28	7,524	—	—	—	—
Spain	2	430	12	2,599	1	22	—	—
Italy	—	—	—	—	—	—	—	—
Levant, Egypt and Barbary Coast	—	—	—	—	—	—	—	—
Canaries, Azores and Cape Verde Islands	—	—	1	122	—	—	—	—
Coast of Guinea	—	—	—	—	—	—	—	—
Cape of Good Hope and East Indies	—	—	—	—	—	—	—	—
China	1	342	—	—	—	—	—	—
Ports of South American Governments (Pacific)	—	—	—	—	—	—	—	—
Ports of South American Governments (Atlantic)	6	1,324	5	1,332	—	—	—	—
Curacao	—	—	—	—	—	—	—	—
Brazil	—	—	—	—	—	—	—	—
Berbice and Demerara	—	—	—	—	—	—	—	—
Surinam	—	—	—	—	—	—	—	—
Mexico	—	—	—	—	—	—	—	—
North America	59	14,688	43	11,729	2	348	—	—
Greenland and Davis Straits	—	—	—	—	—	—	—	—
Undeclared	—	—	4	811	—	—	2	118
TOTAL	84	21,225	130	33,146	101	6,727	8	535

Table XIX (*cont.*)

	RUSSIAN SHIPS				SWEDISH SHIPS			
	With cargo		In ballast		With cargo		In ballast	
	No. of ships	Total tons	No. of ships	Total tons	No. of ships	Total tons	No. of ships	Total tons
Destination								
Mecklenburg (Lübeck, etc.)	—	—	—	—	2	234	—	—
Hanover	—	—	—	—	—	—	—	—
Denmark	3	290	—	—	—	—	1	103
Prussia	1	245	6	1,180	4	718	7	1,194
Russia	21	3,988	14	2,998	2	367	4	630
Sweden and Norway	2	291	—	—	19	2,291	12	2,145
United Kingdom	1	324	3	699	—	—	—	—
France	1	111	—	—	3	266	3	407
Portugal	1	224	1	247	2	313	11	1,999
Spain	—	—	—	—	3	481	1	131
Italy	—	—	—	—	—	—	—	—
Levant, Egypt and Barbary Coast	—	—	—	—	—	—	—	—
Canaries, Azores and Cape Verde Islands	—	—	—	—	—	—	—	—
Coast of Guinea	—	—	—	—	—	—	—	—
Cape of Good Hope and East Indies	—	—	—	—	—	—	—	—
China	—	—	—	—	—	—	—	—
Ports of South American Governments (Pacific)	—	—	—	—	—	—	—	—
Ports of South American Governments (Atlantic)	—	—	—	—	—	—	—	—
Curacao	—	—	—	—	—	—	—	—
Brazil	—	—	—	—	—	—	—	—
Berbice and Demerara	—	—	—	—	—	—	—	—
Surinam	—	—	—	—	—	—	—	—
Mexico	—	—	—	—	—	—	—	—
North America	—	—	—	—	—	—	—	—
Greenland and Davis Straits	—	—	—	—	—	—	—	—
Undeclared	—	—	2	606	—	—	9	1,349
TOTAL	30	5,473	26	5,730	35	4,670	48	7,958

Table XIX (cont.)

	NORWEGIAN SHIPS				DANISH SHIPS			
	With cargo		In ballast		With cargo		In ballast	
	No. of ships	Total tons	No. of ships	Total tons	No. of ships	Total tons	No. of ships	Total tons
Destination								
Mecklenburg (Lübeck, etc.)	3	371	1	52	131	4,705	3	378
Hanover	—	—	—	—	3	82	—	—
Denmark	1	85	2	423	96	4,646	33	2,542
Prussia	1	57	6	2,421	10	404	9	1,257
Russia	6	1,389	10	3,096	3	328	2	285
Sweden and Norway	298	56,906	89	20,855	3	242	4	520
United Kingdom	3	287	1	94	12	506	5	377
France	—	—	1	161	10	503	—	—
Portugal	1	239	9	1,440	2	272	2	577
Spain	—	—	—	—	—	—	1	171
Italy	1	259	1	155	—	—	—	—
Levant, Egypt and Barbary Coast	—	—	—	—	—	—	—	—
Canaries, Azores and Cape Verde Islands	—	—	—	—	—	—	—	—
Coast of Guinea	—	—	—	—	—	—	—	—
Cape of Good Hope and East Indies	—	—	—	—	—	—	—	—
China	—	—	—	—	—	—	—	—
Ports of South American Governments (Pacific)	—	—	—	—	—	—	—	—
Ports of South American Governments (Atlantic)	—	—	—	—	—	—	—	—
Curacao	—	—	—	—	—	—	—	—
Brazil	—	—	—	—	—	—	—	—
Berbice and Demerara	—	—	—	—	—	—	—	—
Surinam	—	—	—	—	—	—	—	—
Mexico	—	—	—	—	—	—	—	—
North America	—	—	—	—	1	181	—	—
Greenland and Davis Straits	—	—	—	—	—	—	—	—
Undeclared	1	502	6	1,480	—	—	12	1,093
TOTAL	315	60,095	126	30,177	271	11,869	71	7,210

Table XIX (*cont.*)

Destination	PRUSSIAN SHIPS				HANOVERIAN SHIPS			
	With cargo		In ballast		With cargo		In ballast	
	No. of ships	Total tons	No. of ships	Total tons	No. of ships	Total tons	No. of ships	Total tons
Mecklenburg (Lübeck, etc.)	2	217	—	—	96	3,659	3	219
Hanover	—	—	—	—	101	3,584	157	4,673
Denmark	2	333	—	—	5	175	1	44
Prussia	51	8,013	72	11,114	10	905	40	4,975
Russia	17	2,627	10	1,997	8	774	10	1,402
Sweden and Norway	1	141	1	152	5	363	16	1,505
United Kingdom	3	363	1	159	13	594	—	—
France	2	175	—	—	17	1,008	4	352
Portugal	—	—	—	—	—	—	2	254
Spain	—	—	—	—	1	59	—	—
Italy	—	—	—	—	—	—	—	—
Levant, Egypt and Barbary Coast	—	—	—	—	1	136	—	—
Canaries, Azores and Cape Verde Islands	—	—	—	—	—	—	—	—
Coast of Guinea	—	—	—	—	—	—	—	—
Cape of Good Hope and East Indies	—	—	—	—	—	—	—	—
China	—	—	—	—	—	—	—	—
Ports of South American Governments (Pacific)	—	—	—	—	—	—	—	—
Ports of South American Governments (Atlantic)	—	—	—	—	—	—	—	—
Curaçao	—	—	—	—	2	128	—	—
Brazil	—	—	—	—	—	—	—	—
Berbice and Demarara	—	—	—	—	—	—	—	—
Surinam	—	—	—	—	—	—	—	—
Mexico	—	—	—	—	1	59	—	—
North America	—	—	—	—	—	—	—	—
Greenland and Davis Straits	—	—	—	—	—	—	—	—
Undeclared	4	719	59	9,637	—	—	120	10,919
TOTAL	82	12,588	143	23,059	260	11,444	353	24,343

Table XIX (*cont.*)

	MECKLENBURG SHIPS				OLDENBURG SHIPS			
	With cargo		In ballast		With cargo		In ballast	
	No. of ships	Total tons	No. of ships	Total tons	No. of ships	Total tons	No. of ships	Total tons
Destination								
Mecklenburg (Lübeck, etc.)	7	967	10	1,545	55	1,987	15	562
Hanover	—	—	—	—	6	197	48	1,581
Denmark	1	136	5	724	3	104	2	158
Prussia	3	516	79	13,025	—	—	2	274
Russia	1	157	6	806	—	—	—	—
Sweden and Norway	—	—	2	318	—	—	—	—
United Kingdom	—	—	5	867	—	—	—	—
France	—	—	—	—	2	305	—	—
Portugal	—	—	—	—	—	—	—	—
Spain	—	—	—	—	—	—	—	—
Italy	—	—	—	—	—	—	—	—
Levant, Egypt and Barbary Coast	—	—	—	—	—	—	—	—
Canaries, Azores and Cape Verde Islands	—	—	—	—	—	—	—	—
Coast of Guinea	—	—	—	—	—	—	—	—
Cape of Good Hope and East Indies	—	—	—	—	—	—	—	—
China	—	—	—	—	—	—	—	—
Ports of South American Governments (Pacific)	—	—	—	—	—	—	—	—
Ports of South American Governments (Atlantic)	—	—	—	—	—	—	—	—
Curacao	—	—	—	—	—	—	—	—
Brazil	—	—	—	—	—	—	—	—
Berbice and Demerara	—	—	—	—	—	—	—	—
Surinam	—	—	—	—	—	—	—	—
Mexico	—	—	—	—	—	—	—	—
North America	—	—	—	—	—	—	—	—
Greenland and Davis Straits	—	—	—	—	—	—	—	—
Undeclared	—	—	15	2,448	—	—	27	984
TOTAL	12	1,776	122	19,733	66	2,593	94	3,559

Table XIX (*cont.*)

	LÜBECK SHIPS				BREMEN SHIPS			
	With cargo		In ballast		With cargo		In ballast	
	No. of ships	Total tons	No. of ships	Total tons	No. of ships	Total tons	No. of ships	Total tons
Destination								
Mecklenburg (Lübeck, etc.)	1	117	—	—	—	—	2	176
Hanover	—	—	—	—	—	—	—	—
Denmark	—	—	—	—	—	—	—	—
Prussia	—	—	2	381	—	—	1	203
Russia	1	179	—	—	—	—	3	493
Sweden and Norway	—	—	—	—	—	—	—	—
United Kingdom	—	—	—	—	—	—	—	—
France	1	231	1	194	1	199	—	—
Portugal	—	—	—	—	—	—	—	—
Spain	—	—	—	—	—	—	—	—
Italy	—	—	—	—	—	—	—	—
Levant, Egypt and Barbary Coast	—	—	—	—	—	—	—	—
Canaries, Azores and Cape Verde Islands	—	—	—	—	—	—	—	—
Coast of Guinea	—	—	—	—	—	—	—	—
Cape of Good Hope and East Indies	—	—	—	—	—	—	—	—
China	—	—	—	—	—	—	—	—
Ports of South American Governments (Pacific)	—	—	—	—	—	—	—	—
Ports of South American Governments (Atlantic)	—	—	—	—	—	—	—	—
Curacao	—	—	—	—	—	—	—	—
Brazil	—	—	—	—	—	—	—	—
Berbice and Demerara	—	—	—	—	—	—	—	—
Surinam	—	—	—	—	—	—	—	—
Mexico	—	—	—	—	—	—	—	—
North America	—	—	—	—	—	—	—	—
Greenland and Davis Straits	—	—	—	—	—	—	—	—
Undeclared	—	—	2	396	—	—	1	203
TOTAL	3	527	5	971	1	199	7	1,075

Table XIX (*cont.*)

	HAMBURG SHIPS				ROSTOCK SHIPS			
	With cargo		In ballast		With cargo		In ballast	
	No. of ships	Total tons	No. of ships	Total tons	No. of ships	Total tons	No. of ships	Total tons
Destination								
Mecklenburg (Lübeck, etc.)	17	1,274	—	—	2	609	1	176
Hanover	1	37	—	—	—	—	—	—
Denmark	—	—	1	59	—	—	—	—
Prussia	—	—	—	—	—	—	1	159
Russia	2	146	—	—	—	—	—	—
Sweden and Norway	1	56	2	112	—	—	—	—
United Kingdom	—	—	—	—	—	—	—	—
France	2	126	2	291	—	—	—	—
Portugal	—	—	—	—	—	—	—	—
Spain	—	—	—	—	—	—	—	—
Italy	—	—	—	—	—	—	—	—
Levant, Egypt and Barbary Coast	—	—	—	—	—	—	—	—
Canaries, Azores and Cape Verde Islands	—	—	1	234	—	—	—	—
Coast of Guinea	—	—	—	—	—	—	—	—
Cape of Good Hope and East Indies	—	—	—	—	—	—	—	—
China	—	—	—	—	—	—	—	—
Ports of South American Governments (Pacific)	—	—	—	—	—	—	—	—
Ports of South American Governments (Atlantic)	1	361	—	—	—	—	—	—
Curacao	—	—	—	—	—	—	—	—
Brazil	—	—	—	—	—	—	—	—
Berbice and Demerara	—	—	—	—	—	—	—	—
Surinam	—	—	—	—	—	—	—	—
Mexico	—	—	—	—	—	—	—	—
North America	—	—	—	—	—	—	—	—
Greenland and Davis Straits	—	—	—	—	—	—	—	—
Undeclared	—	—	3	288	—	—	—	—
TOTAL	24	2,000	9	984	2	609	2	335

Table XIX (*cont.*)

| | AUSTRIAN SHIPS | | SARDINIAN SHIPS | | EMDEN SHIPS | | NEAPOLITAN SHIPS | | | |
| | In ballast | | In ballast | | In ballast | | With cargo | | In ballast | |
	No. of ships	Total tons	No. of ships	Total tons	No. of ships	Total tons	No. of ships	Total tons	No. of ships	Total tons
Destination										
Mecklenburg (Lübeck, etc.)	—	—	—	—	—	—	—	—	—	—
Hanover	—	—	—	—	1	36	—	—	—	—
Denmark	—	—	—	—	—	—	—	—	—	—
Prussia	—	—	—	—	—	—	—	—	—	—
Russia	—	—	—	—	—	—	—	—	—	—
Sweden and Norway	1	367	—	—	—	—	—	—	2	251
United Kingdom	—	—	—	—	—	—	—	—	—	—
France	—	—	1	145	—	—	—	—	—	—
Portugal	—	—	—	—	—	—	1	148	1	128
Spain	—	—	—	—	—	—	—	—	—	—
Italy	—	—	—	—	—	—	1	190	6	661
Levant, Egypt and Barbary Coast	—	—	—	—	—	—	—	—	—	—
Canaries, Azores and Cape Verde Islands	—	—	—	—	—	—	—	—	—	—
Coast of Guinea	—	—	—	—	—	—	—	—	—	—
Cape of Good Hope and East Indies	—	—	—	—	—	—	—	—	—	—
China	—	—	—	—	—	—	—	—	—	—
Ports of South American Governments (Pacific)	—	—	—	—	—	—	—	—	—	—
Ports of South American Governments (Atlantic)	—	—	—	—	—	—	—	—	—	—
Curacao	—	—	—	—	—	—	—	—	—	—
Brazil	—	—	—	—	—	—	—	—	—	—
Berbice and Demerara	—	—	—	—	—	—	—	—	—	—
Surinam	—	—	—	—	—	—	—	—	—	—
Mexico	—	—	—	—	—	—	—	—	—	—
North America	—	—	—	—	—	—	—	—	—	—
Greenland and Davis Straits	—	—	—	—	—	—	—	—	—	—
Undeclared	—	—	—	—	—	—	—	—	—	—
TOTAL	1	367	1	145	1	36	2	338	9	1,040

Table XIX (*cont.*)

| | Spanish Ships | | Brunswick Ships | | Ships of Buenos Aires | | | |
| | With cargo | | In ballast | | With cargo | | In ballast | |
	No. of ships	Total tons	No. of ships	Total tons	No. of ships	Total tons	No. of ships	Total tons
Destination								
Mecklenburg (Lübeck, etc.)	—	—	—	—	—	—	—	—
Hanover	—	—	—	—	—	—	—	—
Denmark	—	—	—	—	—	—	—	—
Prussia	—	—	—	—	—	—	—	—
Russia	—	—	—	—	—	—	—	—
Sweden and Norway	—	—	—	—	—	—	—	—
United Kingdom	—	—	1	179	—	—	1	82
France	—	—	—	—	—	—	—	—
Portugal	—	—	—	—	—	—	—	—
Spain	4	219	—	—	—	—	—	—
Italy	—	—	—	—	—	—	—	—
Levant, Egypt and Barbary Coast	—	—	—	—	—	—	—	—
Canaries, Azores and Cape Verde Islands	—	—	—	—	—	—	—	—
Coast of Guinea	—	—	—	—	—	—	—	—
Cape of Good Hope and East Indies	—	—	—	—	—	—	—	—
China	—	—	—	—	—	—	—	—
Ports of South American Governments (Pacific)	—	—	—	—	1	89	—	—
Ports of South American Governments (Atlantic)	—	—	—	—	—	—	—	—
Curacao	—	—	—	—	—	—	—	—
Brazil	—	—	—	—	—	—	—	—
Berbice and Demerara	—	—	—	—	—	—	—	—
Surinam	—	—	—	—	—	—	—	—
Mexico	—	—	—	—	—	—	—	—
North America	—	—	—	—	—	—	—	—
Greenland and Davis Straits	—	—	—	—	—	—	—	—
Undeclared	—	—	—	—	—	—	—	—
Total	4	219	1	179	1	89	1	82

Table XIX *(cont.)*

	TOTAL			
	With cargo		In ballast	
	No. of ships	Total tons	No. of ships	Total tons
Destination				
Mecklenburg (Lübeck, etc.)	528	33,390	46	3,503
Hanover	182	6,215	294	9,295
Denmark	130	7,128	53	4,710
Prussia	130	14,802	382	51,239
Russia	141	19,837	162	26,940
Sweden and Norway	426	69,329	336	47,364
United Kingdom	1,952	177,737	222	36,008
France	327	25,788	43	4,914
Portugal	57	5,887	60	13,156
Spain	50	4,641	24	4,336
Italy	13	1,899	7	816
Levant, Egypt and Barbary Coast	5	719	1	103
Canaries, Azores and Cape Verde Islands	1	333	2	361
Coast of Guinea	1	87	—	—
Cape of Good Hope and East Indies	64	23,313	1	298
China	1	342	—	—
Ports of South American Governments (Pacific)	3	302	—	—
Ports of South American Governments (Atlantic)	31	6,808	9	2,209
Curacao	4	401	—	—
Brazil	15	2,439	3	721
Berbice and Demerara	9	2,733	—	—
Surinam	66	16,513	1	351
Mexico	1	59	—	—
North America	75	17,221	47	13,572
Greenland and Davis Straits	—	—	2	625
Undeclared	12	1,867	769	70,281
TOTAL	4,224	439,785	2,464	290,802

INDEX

Printed in the United States
By Bookmasters